Studies of Fossilization
in Second Language Acquisition

SECOND LANGUAGE ACQUISITION
Series Editor: Professor David Singleton, *Trinity College, Dublin, Ireland*

This new series will bring together titles dealing with a variety of aspects of language acquisition and processing in situations where a language or languages other than the native language is involved. Second language will thus be interpreted in its broadest possible sense. The volumes included in the series will all in their different ways offer, on the one hand, exposition and discussion of empirical findings and, on the other, some degree of theoretical reflection. In this latter connection, no particular theoretical stance will be privileged in the series; nor will any relevant perspective – sociolinguistic, psycholinguistic, neurolinguistic, etc. – be deemed out of place. The intended readership of the series will be final-year undergraduates working on second language acquisition projects, postgraduate students involved in second language acquisition research, and researchers and teachers in general whose interests include a second language acquisition component.

Other Books in the Series
Portraits of the L2 User
    Vivian Cook (ed.)
Learning to Request in a Second Language: A Study of Child Interlanguage Pragmatics
    Machiko Achiba
Effects of Second Language on the First
    Vivian Cook (ed.)
Age and the Acquisition of English as a Foreign Language
    María del Pilar García Mayo and Maria Luisa García Lecumberri (eds)
Fossilization in Adult Second Language Acquisition
    ZhaoHong Han
Silence in Second Language Learning: A Psychoanalytic Reading
    Colette A. Granger
Age, Accent and Experience in Second Language Acquisition
    Alene Moyer
Studying Speaking to Inform Second Language Learning
    Diana Boxer and Andrew D. Cohen (eds)
Language Acquisition: The Age Factor (2nd edn)
    David Singleton and Lisa Ryan
Focus on French as a Foreign Language: Multidisciplinary Approaches
    Jean-Marc Dewaele (ed.)
Second Language Writing Systems
    Vivian Cook and Benedetta Bassetti (eds)
Third Language Learners: Pragmatic Production and Awareness
    Maria Pilar Safont Jordà
Artificial Intelligence in Second Language Learning: Raising Error Awareness
    Marina Dodigovic

For more details of these or any other of our publications, please contact:
Multilingual Matters, Frankfurt Lodge, Clevedon Hall,
Victoria Road, Clevedon, BS21 7HH, England
http://www.multilingual-matters.com

SECOND LANGUAGE ACQUISITION 14
Series Editor: David Singleton, *Trinity College, Dublin, Ireland*

Studies of Fossilization in Second Language Acquisition

Edited by
ZhaoHong Han and Terence Odlin

MULTILINGUAL MATTERS LTD
Clevedon • Buffalo • Toronto

Library of Congress Cataloging in Publication Data
Studies of Fossilization in Second Language Acquisition
Edited by ZhaoHong Han and Terence Odlin.
Second Language Acquisition: 14
Includes bibliographical references and index.
1. Second language acquisition. 2. Fossilization (Linguistics). I. Han, Zhaohong.
II. Odlin, Terence. III. Second Language Acquisition (Clevedon, England): 14.
P118.2.S88 2005
418–dc22   2005014687

British Library Cataloguing in Publication Data
A catalogue entry for this book is available from the British Library.

ISBN 1-85359-836-4 / EAN 978-1-85359-836-4 (hbk)
ISBN 1-85359-835-6 / EAN 978-1-85359-835-7 (pbk)

Multilingual Matters Ltd
UK: Frankfurt Lodge, Clevedon Hall, Victoria Road, Clevedon BS21 7HH.
USA: UTP, 2250 Military Road, Tonawanda, NY 14150, USA.
Canada: UTP, 5201 Dufferin Street, North York, Ontario M3H 5T8, Canada.

Typeset by Techset Ltd.
Printed and bound in Great Britain by MPG Books Ltd.

Contents

Acknowledgments

We would like to thank all the contributors to this volume for the thoughts and attention they invested in their chapters. The present volume would not have been possible without the intellectual inspiration we gained from Professor Larry Selinker, who coined the term *fossilization* and who was the first to draw the wide attention to the phenomenon as a core issue for SLA research. Numerous controversies have arisen since his original formulations, but much in these debates has helped lay the ground work for the research reported and discussed here.

Our thanks also go to Jung Eun Year for her bibliographic assistance, and to Marjukka Grover, Ken Hall, and their colleagues in Multilingual Matters for their support and efficiency.

Contributors

Rosa Alonso Alonso
Universidade de Santiago de Compostela

David Birdsong
University of Texas at Austin

ZhaoHong Han
Teachers College, Columbia University

Usha Lakshmanan
Southern Illinois University at Carbondale

Donna Lardiere
Georgetown University

Diane Larsen-Freeman
University of Michigan

Brian MacWhinney
Carnegie Mellon University

Constancio Nakuma
Clemson University

Terence Odlin
Ohio State University

Larry Selinker
New York University

Elaine Tarone
University of Minnesota

Cristina Alonso-Vázquez
Universidad Castilla y la Mancha

Chapter 1
Introduction

ZHAOHONG HAN and TERENCE ODLIN

A quote from Ellis (1993) provides an apt point of departure for this opening chapter. Ellis notes:

> [T]he end point of L2 acquisition – if the learners, their motivation, tutors and conversation partners, environment, and instrumental factors, etc., are all optimal – is to be as proficient in L2 as in L1. So proficient, so accurate, so fluent, so automatic, so implicit, that there is rarely recourse to explicit, conscious thought about the medium of the message. (Ellis, 1993: 315)

The above statement evokes at least two questions for us. The first is whether all learners wish to become as proficient in their L2 as in their L1, and the second whether they can be when the 'if' condition is met. This book is motivated by the second question, namely, whether or not learners are *able* to reach nativelikeness in their L2 as in their L1.

Thirty years of research has generated mixed responses to the question, from which two polarized positions can be gleaned. On the one hand, there are researchers who have long claimed that it is not possible for adult L2 learners to speak or perform like native-speakers (Gregg, 1996; Long, 1990). On the other hand, there are researchers who argue that nativelikeness is attainable by a meaningful size of L2 population (see e.g. Birdsong, 1999, 2004). The latter position appears to have gained increasing acceptance in recent years, as seen in the increased estimates about successful learners. For example, while earlier second language acquisition (SLA) research gave very low estimates – Selinker (1972) suggests 5%, Scovel (1988) estimates one in 1000 learners, and Long (1990, 1993) no learners at all, more recent research has yielded a much higher range, from 15% to 60% (see, e.g. Birdsong, 1999, 2004; Montrul & Slabakova, 2003; White, 2003).

What do we make of the gaps? The early, conservative estimates (e.g. below 5%) came from theorists and are largely extrapolated from the literature, reinforced by personal observations, whereas the more recent and optimistic assessments (e.g. over 15%) are based on empirical research results. Does this mean, then, that at least 15% of L2 learners will normally reach the end point depicted by Ellis above? The answer is clearly negative if we look closer at the design of the empirical studies that have generated those figures, where factors such as the nature of the population sampled could obviously affect any estimate. Furthermore, these studies largely involved use of a limited number of interpretation and production tasks. Thus, the conservative and the optimistic estimates are not really comparable. Nonetheless, both are revealing in that an estimate of 5% at the highest captures, albeit impressionistically, the likelihood that the vast majority of L2 learners fail to reach native-speaker competence. Optimistic estimates, such as over 15%, on the other hand, come from relatively successful performances of learners on limited measures. This seemingly contradictory picture is explained in Han (2004a) in a review of scores of theoretical and empirical studies from the last three decades.

Han argues for the need to represent L2 ultimate attainment at three levels: (a) a cross-learner level, (b) an inter-learner level, and (c) an intra-learner level. At the cross-learner level, L2 ultimate attainment shows that few, if any, are able to gain a command of the target language that is comparable to that of a native speaker of that language. At the inter-learner level, however, a great range of variation exists in that some are highly successful while others are not at all (Bley-Vroman, 1989; Lightbown, 2000). Then at the intra-learner level, an individual learner exhibits differential success on different aspects of the target language (Bialystok, 1978; Han, 2004a; Lardiere, this volume: chap. 3; Sharwood Smith, 1991). Success here means attainment of native-speaker competence (White, 2003). The notion of native-speaker competence is, of course, problematic in some respects and will be discussed further on (Cook, 1999; Davies, 2003; Han, 2004b).

The ultimate attainment of L2 acquisition, if there is such a thing, thus shows two facets: success and failure. This is different from that of first language acquisition where uniform success is observed for children reaching the age of five. On the ability of L2 learners to ultimately converge on native-speaker competence, White (2003) comments that 'native-like performance is the exception rather than the rule' (p. 263). The lack of full success among second language learners raises a fundamental question: why is it that 'most child L1 or L2 learning is successful, afterall, whereas most adolescent and adult L1 or L2 learning ends in at least partial failure even when motivation, intelligence, and opportunity are not at issue and despite the availability of (presumably advantageous) classroom instruction' (Long & Robinson, 1998: 19). Even with the more optimistic estimates of success (i.e. over 15%), the difference between L1 and L2 acquisition is striking (Schachter, 1988).

As early as 1972, Selinker provided the first explanation for the above generic observation, contending that adult second language acquisition is driven by a mechanism known as the latent psychological structure. This mechanism is made up of five processes: (a) transfer, (b) overgeneralization, (c) learning strategies, (d) communication strategies, and (e) transfer of training. The five processes underlying the latent psychological structure would account, Selinker argued, for learning as well as non-learning. In regard to the latter, Selinker introduced the construct of *fossilization* to characterize a type of non-learning that represents a permanent state of mind and behavior, noting:

> Fossilizable linguistic phenomena are linguistic items, rules, and subsystems which speakers of a particular L1 tend to keep in their IL relative to a particular TL, no matter what the age of the learner or amount of explanation and instruction he receives in the TL ... Fossilizable structures tend to remain as potential performance, re-emerging in the productive performance of an IL even when seemingly eradicated. (Selinker, 1972: 215)

Although it does not define fossilization, the above conceptualization does provide a loose framework from which some inferences can be made regarding properties of the construct. Briefly, fossilization appears to have five properties (Selinker & Han, 2001). First, it pertains to IL features that deviate from the TL norms. Second, it can be found in every linguistic domain (e.g. phonology, syntax, morphology). Third, it exhibits persistence and resistance. Fourth, it can occur with both adult and child learners. Fifth, it often takes the form of backsliding.

In spite of the lack of a straightforward definition, the notion of fossilization nevertheless struck an immediate chord among second language researchers (and teachers). Since its postulation, it has been employed, widely and almost indiscriminately, to either describe or explain lack of learning in L2 learners. As Long (2003) aptly points out, the literature has seen a conflated use of fossilization as *explanans* and as *explanandum*, exploiting more of the latter than of the former.

Is Fossilization the *Explanans* or the *Explanandum*?

Many researchers have, following Selinker (1972), conceived a causal relationship between fossilization and ultimate attainment. Lightbown (2000), for example, remarks that 'For most adult learners, acquisition stop – "fossilizes" – before the learner has achieved native-like mastery of the target language' (p. 179). Hence, in her view, fossilization means a cessation which entails a lack of success in L2 attainment (Towell & Hawkins, 1994). Interesting to note also is that often the same researchers would then attempt to explain what causes fossilization. For instance, Lightbown (2000) speculates:

> [Fossilization] happens when the learner has satisfied the need for communication and/or integration in the target language community, but this is a complicated area, and the reasons for fossilization are very difficult to determine with any certainty. Recently, there has been some evidence that the interlanguage systems which tend to fossilize are those which are based on the three-way convergence of some general – possibly universal – patterns in language and some rule or rules of the target language and the native language. (Lightbown, 2000: 179)

While aware of the complications, Lightbown offers here two types of cause of fossilization: one involving psychological and social factors, and the other involving the construction of interlanguages. These types of cause are not the only explanations that researchers have advanced, however.

The survey of the L2 literature by Han (2004a) identifies well over 40 factors that putatively manufacture fossilization, and these factors cluster into environmental, cognitive, neuro-biological, and socio-affective explanations. Apparently, the level of interest in fossilization has been high, suggesting a widespread belief in its prevalence in L2 acquisition. However, one major problem evident in the literature is that researchers have not been uniform in their employment of the term. Among the variables referred to in characterizations of fossilization are low proficiency, typical errors, and ultimate attainment (for more, see Han, 2003; 2004a).

It is also clear that many have simply used the term as a handy metaphor for describing any lack of progress in L2 learning, regardless of its character – a 'catch-all' term, as Birdsong (2003) aptly deemed it. As a catch-all, its varying use in the research literature certainly diverges from the initial, though not rigorous, postulation by Selinker (1972; for review, see Han, 2004a: chap. 2). The problems engendered by varying uses are compounded by a relative, though not total, lack of empirical studies. Not only has there been a continuous paucity of longitudinal evidence, but the existing non-longitudinal evidence is also suspect, due to various conceptual and methodological shortcomings (for review, see Han, 2004a: chap. 6; Long, 2003).

We should also note a problem that is difficult to avoid: using the verb *fossilize* risks some ambiguity, and the noun *fossilization* entails a similar risk. On the one hand, *fossilize* can denote a process, yet on the other it can also denote a resulting state. Many other verbs in English have the same potential for ambiguity: e.g. *The ice melted* (the ice may have been in the process of melting or it may have completely changed to a liquid state). In any case, the problem of conflating the *explanans* (i.e. the process) and the *explanandum* (the resulting state) is hard to avoid when English is the metalanguage used to discuss the theoretical issues.

What is the Empirical Basis for Fossilization?

Evidence for fossilization has so far been of two types: anecdotal and empirical. Neither, however, abounds in the literature. An example of anecdotal evidence can be found in VanBuren (2001) who wrote of a friend of his from Scandinavia. This person had resided in Britain for 42 years and yet kept saying 'The man which I saw ...'; 'He said it when I first met him 41 years ago, and last month he was still saying it' (p. 457). Similar anecdotes appear in Krashen (1981), Bates and MacWhinney (1981), and MacWhinney (2001). All of them seem to have one thing in common, namely, long-term stabilization of a deviant interlanguage feature in spite of continuous exposure to the target language.

While the anecdotal evidence is largely based on informal, personal observations, empirical research on fossilization uses a variety of methodologies to find evidence of non-progression of learning. In brief, there have been five major approaches to researching fossilization: (a) the longitudinal approach, (b) the corrective feedback approach, (c) the advanced learner approach, (d) the length of residence approach, and (e) the typical error approach (Han, 2003, 2004a). All things considered, a longitudinal approach is arguably superior to the rest in that it holds the best promise for obtaining reliable and valid evidence of fossilization. For one thing, a longitudinal approach can simultaneously allow learners to display learning and/or non-learning. This approach thus makes it possible for researchers to detect of any form of lack of learning, and thereby to tease non-learning apart from learning. This has, at least, been the current understanding.

Accordingly, it is therefore not surprising that most of the recent studies have resorted to longitudinal data as an empirical basis for launching claims about fossilization and/or ultimate attainment (see, e.g. Han, 1998; Hawkins, 2000; Jarvis & Pavlenko, 2000; Lardiere, 1998, this volume: chap. 3; Long, 2003; Thep-Acrapong, 1990; White, 2001). By way of illustration, Jarvis and Pavlenko (2000) report on a case study of a 33-year-old woman pseudo-named Aino, a native speaker of Finnish, who had lived in the United States for 10 years consecutively. The researchers established a five-year longitudinal database of Aino's oral and written production data which provided, among other things, evidence of fossilization. In diagnosing fossilization, it is worth noting, two criteria were applied: (a) that the errors were regular, and (b) that they had persisted in the interlanguage for a number of years. By these measurements, Aino's fossilized errors included, but were not limited to, the following:

[1] Tense and Aspect
   She *had called* today to say that she won't be there. (1995, 1996, 1997)

[2] Countability
   I think she's got *fever*. (1995, 1996, 1997)

Two important observations were made on these errors. First, they 'straightforwardly represent influence from L1 Finnish'; and second, 'they alternate with corresponding target-like or correct forms' (p. 5). The former supports Selinker and Lakshmanan's (1992) Multiple Effects Principle in that L1 functions as a privileged and perhaps necessary factor in bringing about fossilization. The latter, on the other hand, appears to support Schachter's (1996) notion of 'fossilized variation' (Han, 2003, 2004a; Selinker & Han, 2001; see, however, Birdsong, 2003; Long, 2003), and/or Sorace's (1996) notion of 'permanent optionality.'
   Unlike longitudinal studies which seek to first *determine* whether fossilization exists and, if it does, subsequently describe it, non-longitudinal ones *assume* that fossilization already exists, and subsequently verify it through one-time tasks. There is a fundamental difference between the two approaches in that the former is *a posteriori* and data-driven – letting the data speak for themselves, so to speak, whereas the latter is *a priori* and presumptive, influenced largely by the researchers' prior conceptions of what fossilization is. Logically, the latter approach may fall short of validity and reliability (for review, see Han, 2004a; for a recent application of the approach, see Romero Trillo, 2002).

To recapitulate, the state of the art of fossilization research, as discussed above, manifests two major weaknesses. The first is that idiosyncratic conceptualizations of the construct still prevail. A second problem is that explanation and description have been 'flip-flopped.' As Selinker and Han (2001) noted, 'what we have here is not the logically prior description before explanation, but worse: explanation without description' (p. 276). Figure 1.1 gives a visual approximation of the scenario.

The top box in Figure 1.1 signifies that fossilization has been widely used as an explanation for a myriad of SLA phenomena; the middle box shows that it has mostly been treated as an object of explanation; and the bottom box shows that it has received, relatively, the least attention as an object of empirical description.

The scenario raises legitimate questions as to whether fossilization is a viable construct or whether it should be abandoned. Long (2003) suggests that SLA researchers may eventually desist from formulating the problem as an issue of fossilization and instead address more specific concerns such as stabilization and ultimate attainment. Much of the suspicion of fossilization, as we see it, stems from a conception that is not quite accurate, which takes fossilization as isomorphic to non-nativelikeness. The construct of fossilization, as initially postulated and later elaborated by Selinker, refers to *a particular type of non-nativelikeness which comes about and persists in spite of optimal learning conditions* (Han, 2004a; Long, 2003; Selinker & Lamendella, 1978, 1979). For example, Selinker and Lamendella (1979) explain that 'the conclusion that a particular learner had indeed fossilized could be drawn only if the cessation of further IL learning persisted in spite

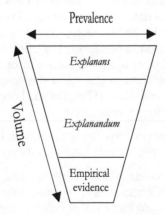

Figure 1.1 Fossilization 'flip-flop'

of the learner's ability, opportunity, and motivation to learn the target language and acculturate into the target society' (p. 373). Thus, identifying fossilization with non-nativelikeness at large, which has been quite a prevalent practice among L2 researchers, is a gross over-simplification. By way of illustration, Birdsong (2003) asserts:

> From its origins in the early 1970's fossilization has been associated with observed non-nativelikeness. Historically, the diagnostics of fossilization have been pegged to the native standard, and indeed the theoretical linchpin of the construct of fossilization is non-nativeness. (Birdsong, 2003: 3)

The conceptual confusion over fossilization, additionally, arises from researchers invoking it to characterize L2 ultimate attainment (as a monolith). White (2003), for instance, claims that 'the ultimate attainment of the L2 speaker might be native-like, near-native or non-native' (p. 249). Similarly yet even more narrowly, Tarone (1994) notes that 'a central characteristic of any interlanguage is that it fossilizes – that is, it ceases to develop at some point short of full identity with the target language' (p. 1715), thereby hinting that fossilization is the state of L2 ultimate attainment (Bley-Vroman, 1989).

Whereas there is little empirical evidence for the (albeit pervasive) monolithic views, study after study has shown that not only do nativelikeness and non-nativelikeness co-exist, but they do so among L2 learners across all levels of proficiency, including those who are allegedly at an end state (see Birdsong, this volume: chap. 9; Han, this volume: chap. 4; Lardiere, 1998, this volume: chap. 3). Additional evidence comes from mixed results that L2 studies of the supposed end state have provided, with some showing that nativelike attainment is possible (e.g. Montrul & Slabakova, 2003; White & Genesee, 1996) and others impossible (Coppieters, 1987; Johnson & Newport, 1989; Sorace, 1993, 2003).

Indeed, compelled by an increasing amount of empirical evidence as above and the well-noted methodological shortcomings associated with studies at large of L2 end state (Han, 2004a; Long, 2003; White, 2003), we would even like to hypothesize that:

> L2 acquisition will never have a global end state; rather, it will have fossilization, namely, permanent local cessation of development.

The hypothesis has three corollaries. First, as long as there is continued exposure to 'robust' (Gregg, 2003), 'representative' (Sorace, 2003), or 'rich and consistent' (MacWhinney, this volume) input, learning will continue, albeit slowly at times (Klein & Perdue, 1993). Second, the individual learner's interlanguage system will, forever, be partly nativelike and partly non-nativelike. To borrow Birdsong's (2003) terms, there is narrow, but not comprehensive, nativelikeness. Third, part of the target language is subject to continuous learning, and part of it not. This is true even of the so-called closed domains such as syntax, morphology, and phonology.

The hypothesis, along with its corollaries, theoretically, renders a number of SLA distinctions obsolete, and these include the distinction that Cook (1999) makes between an L2 *learner* and an L2 *user*, Tarone *et al.*'s (1976) distinction between a *fossilized learner* and a *non-fossilized learner*, and, similarly, a distinction that many have assumed between a *fossilized* and a *non-fossilized* interlanguage or competence (passim the SLA literature). In the view expounded here, every member of the L2 community is both a learner and a user, and in each and every interlanguage, there can be found evidence of acquisition and fossilization.

How Widely Applicable is Fossilization?

Since we are convinced of the need to think of *learners* as also *users* of language in their community (or communities), we see a need to consider how communities differ and what such differences imply for the concept of fossilization. The variations seen across communities make it at least a debatable proposition that the notion of fossilization applies to all situations. Selinker's discussion of Indian English shows how complex the applicability question is. In illustrating fossilization, Selinker cited case of pronunciation that varied from native speaker norms among highly proficient speakers of English in India. Some specialists of Indian English (e.g. Sridhar & Sridhar, 1986) have strongly disagreed with Selinker's apparent assumption that the target language for Indian learners is any form of British or American English. These specialists have, moreover, pointed to research (e.g. Bansal, 1976) suggesting that in pronunciation there is considerable homogeneity among highly proficient users of Indian English, this homogeneity thus indicating a norm, and the norm does not reflect much substrate influence from any single Indian language.

The Indian case is not at all unique. The global reach of English has come about in a wide range of social settings, including many where the notion of 'target language' is more problematic than it is in North American and British universities where so much SLA research is conducted. Other second language settings likewise vary a great deal, as in the case of French in West Africa (e.g. LaFarge, 1985). Still another case of a complex language contact situation, in Spain, is discussed by Odlin *et al.* in Chapter 5 of this volume. Although Castilian varieties of Spanish are the most prestigious, other varieties such as Galician Spanish diverge from Castilian in significant ways including a likely L1 influence from Galiciain (which, like Catalan, is an Iberian Romance language distinct from Spanish). Many citizens of Galicia are now more proficient in Spanish than in Galician, but their variety of Spanish is non-Castilian in significant respects.

Should the historical shift from Galician to Spanish be viewed as a non-attainment of Castilian norms, or should it be seen as the ultimate attainment of some non-Castilian norm? As is the case with Irish English, Galician Spanish reflects a long history of language contact that has led to the creation of a new community of native speakers (cf. Filppula, 1999; Odlin, 1992, 2003; Thomason & Kaufman, 1988). Native speaker communities obviously vary, and the creation of new NS communities as in Galicia and Ireland shows that native speaker competence should not be assumed to be invariant or static (a point to be returned to later in this chapter). The dynamic nature of many language contact situations makes it at least plausible to argue that fossilization is a construct applicable only in social settings where the target language is a variety spoken by a native speaker majority that changes rather slowly. However, it is also possible to argue that even in regions such as India and Galicia there are some members of the community who have fully attained the target (here considered as an indigenized version of a stable contact variety of a language) yet other members who fall short of ultimate attainment and who match the profile of the fossilized learner posited by Selinker.

How Does Cross-Linguistic Influence Affect Fossilization?

As mentioned before, the Multiple Effects Principle posited by Selinker and Lakshmanan (1992) holds that language transfer is a privileged co-factor of fossilization. Facts such as the persistence of a distinctive foreign accent in the pronunciation of highly proficient L2 speakers make the Multiple Effects Principle intuitively appealing. Even so, the problematic status of the notion of the 'target language' in contexts such as India and Galicia complicates any attempt to understand either transfer or fossilization – or their interaction. A similar complexity is evident when cognitive concerns are in the foreground and social considerations in the background. Recent work on transfer and linguistic relativity raises important questions about the problem of global and local fossilization.

Although studies of semantic transfer go back a long way (e.g. Weinreich, 1953), researchers have begun to look closely at a subset of cases that can be called conceptual transfer (e.g. Jarvis, 1998; Pavlenko, 1999), where the semantic (or pragmatic) transfer indicates not only linguistic but also cognitive predispositions and where the cognitive predispositions reflect a shaping influence of the L1 (most typically, although L2 might also be involved, for example, in cases of L3 acquisition). Jarvis and Pavlenko looked at the performance of bilinguals with varying degrees of proficiency in English and interpret some of the L1 influences as conceptual transfer.

Such work on conceptual transfer might have only marginal relevance to the issues of fossilization and ultimate attainment were it not for the results of research that focuses on the second language performance of highly proficient users of the target language (e.g. Carroll *et al.*, 2000; von Stutterheim, 2003). One of the findings of the Carroll study well illustrates the relevance of the research to ultimate attainment. In comparison with native speakers of German, highly proficient users of L2 German use very few 'coadverbials' such as *dazu* and *darin*, some of which have Germanic cognates in English as in *thereto* and *therein*; in comparison with speakers of Spanish, a language that does not have such coadverbials, English speakers used these constructions more, which suggests positive transfer. However, the relative infrequency of coadverbials in L1 English in comparison with L1 German helps to explain why English speakers do not rely on the structure very much in their L2. To use a phrase coined by Slobin (1993) in another context, infrequent co-adverbials in English do not provide a mainline pattern of 'thinking for speaking' in L2 German which is in fact readily available to native speakers of that language. Moreover, Carroll offers other evidence to support their contention that coadverbials are one indicator of a linguistic difference correlated with a cognitive one. Because the studies described here are not longitudinal, the eventual attainment of coadverbials cannot be ruled out. However, Carroll and von Stutterheim have identified an intriguing difference between native speakers of the target language and highly proficient non-native speakers.

The studies of Carroll and von Stutterheim of highly proficient learners thus raise the question of whether the cognitive as well as the linguistic systems of second language learners can ever be identical. The question itself is not new: the German relativist Wilhelm von Humboldt viewed second language acquisition as always incomplete, whereas another famous relativist, Benjamin Lee Whorf, considered it possible to over-come the 'binding power' of the L1 (Odlin, 2005). Whichever position turns out to be correct clearly has crucial implications for the Multiple Effects Principle.

How Real is the End State?

Through most of this chapter we have adopted the conventional assumption that there is an ultimate attainment in L1 acquisition, even if L2 learners rarely or never reach the end state. While some evidence from studies of cross-linguistic influence supports this conventional assumption, other evidence calls it into question. Two skeptics about an L1 end state, Pavlenko and Jarvis (2002), emphasize the fact that knowl-edge of an L2 can affect knowledge of an L1, a fact now getting more attention in SLA research, although studies of language contact have long examined many instances of such transfer (Cook, 2003; Odlin, 1989; Thomason & Kaufman, 1988; Weinreich, 1953).

Yet even while L1 knowledge is itself subject to change, native speaker competence does seem to have a special status in some ways, as seen clearly in the influence of the native language on interlanguage pronun-ciation. A study of multilingualism by Hammarberg (2001) considers the case of a native speaker of English developing her proficiency in Swedish. The learner was also highly proficient in German (and Hammarberg's research indicates that she was sometimes mistaken for a native speaker of that language). In the earlier stages of this individual's acquisition of Swedish, her pronunciation showed more German than English influence. However, as she became more fluent, English features began to affect her pronunciation – despite the learner's desire not to 'sound English.' Hammarberg attributes the shift from German to English influence to the automaticity of neuro-motor patterns (established early in L1 acquisition) as the learner became quite proficient in Swedish. It is conceivable, therefore, that even if an end state is not really character-istic of L1 competence in other domains (as Pavlenko and Jarvis contend), the phonetic settings of L1 do reflect such an end state, with the nature of this state making it virtually impossible the acquisition of completely native-like settings in a new language (Leather & James, 1996). If true, such a surmise also argues strongly for the position argued earlier that fossilization is best thought of in local rather than global terms, i.e. where some but not all parts of the target language are fully attainable.

What is in This Book?

As we pointed out earlier, the current literature on fossilization is long on speculations about causal factors but short on empirical research and analysis. This book tilts the imbalance; of the eight chapters that ensue, four are empirical studies and four analytical in nature. The collection concludes with a commentary by Larsen-Freeman (Chapter 10), which synthesizes the major arguments as presented in the foregoing chapters and further discusses concepts that are at the heart of fossilization research, including non-nativelikeness, stability, cessation of learning, and native speaker.

In Chapter 2, Nakuma connects fossilization with attrition, and challenges the phenomenological basis of both constructs. The main thrust of his argument is that neither is a phenomenon, but both are hypotheses. The chapter concludes with a list of questions, which he considers easy to ask but difficult to answer. In fact, some of these questions with their underlying assumptions are not unpopular among second language researchers and teachers. They, therefore, are worth revisiting, particularly in light of the conceptual issues discussed above and findings from the empirical research presented in this volume and elsewhere.

In Chapter 3, Lardiere reports new findings from her on-going longitudinal study of Patty, an adult native speaker of Chinese who has been living in an English-speaking environment for 23 years. This time, targeting Patty's knowledge of the verb-raising constraint in English via two grammaticality judgment tasks, each administered 18 months apart, Lardiere shows that Patty has stabilized, target-like knowledge of the syntactic feature in question. She accordingly points out that 'fossilization in one domain (inflectional morphology) does not preclude development in another (knowledge of syntactic features and word order)' (p. 41), arguing that 'we certainly cannot speak of fossilization in any global sense' (p. 48).

In Chapter 4, Han examines the viability of the grammaticality judgment (GJ) methodology for investigating fossilization. The study reported was part of an on-going longitudinal investigation and it involved longitudinal cross-comparisons of the GJ and naturalistic production data collected from the same two subjects, Geng and Fong, as were in Han (1998, 2000). Findings showed both synchronic and diachronic consistency between the two types of data, thereby suggesting the reliability of the GJ methodology. Han notices, however, that while largely reinforcing each other, the GJ and the naturalistic production data were nevertheless complementary. Using a native speaker of English to provide longitudinal base-line data, the study also sheds important light on such constructs as indeterminacy and end state.

Chapter 5 reports on an exploratory study of fossilization in third language acquisition. Participants included Galician and Spanish speakers learning English (as well as native speakers of the target language). Using passage correction (Odlin, 1986) as a measure of subjects' English proficiency in general and their knowledge of English present perfect in particular, Odlin, Alonso Alonso, and Alonso-Vázquez provide evidence suggesting that either Galician or Garlician-influenced Spanish of students may influence their noticing in L3-English of semantic and pragmatic conditions accompanying the use of the present perfect tense, a linguistic structure predicted by the researchers and noted by teachers to be of insurmountable difficulty for students due to transfer from what may be a fossilized version of Spanish as used in the language contact setting of Galicia.

In Chapter 6, Lakshmanan examines fossilization in the context of child second language acquisition. She begins by discussing definitions of child L2 acquisition, and goes on to argue in favor of the Sliding Window Hypothesis (Foster-Cohen, 2001), which, in essence, advocates: (a) a non-discrete division of L1 and L2 acquisition, and (b) cross-age examinations of developmental patterns. In line with this hypothesis as well as the Full Transfer/Full Access Model (Schwartz & Sprouse, 1996), Lakshmanan then conducted a reanalysis of L2 attrition and reacquisition patterns in two child native speakers of English acquiring Hindi/Urdu as an L2 (Hansen, 1980, 1983). In the interlanguages of both children, she found consistent evidence of L1-based backsliding.

Chapter 7 by MacWhinney presents a survey of 12 psychological accounts of fossilization, and these are: (1) the lateralization hypothesis (Lenneberg, 1967), (2) the neural commitment hypothesis (Lenneberg, 1967), (3) the parameter-setting hypothesis (Flynn, 1996), (4) the metabolic hypothesis (Pinker, 1994), (5) the reproductive fitness hypothesis (Hurford & Kirby, 1999), (6) the aging hypothesis (Barkow *et al.*, 1992), (7) the fragile rule hypothesis (Birdsong, 2005), (8) the starting small hypothesis (Elman, 1993), (9) the entrenchment hypothesis (Marchman, 1992), (10) the entrenchment and balance hypothesis (MacWhinney, 2005), (11) the social stratification hypothesis, and (12) the compensatory strategies hypothesis. Following a critical evaluation of the first 10 hypotheses, MacWhinney endorses the entrenchment-and-transfer account as 'the best currently available account of AoA (age of arrival) and fossilization effects' (p. 149). He nevertheless points out that this account alone is inadequate in that it falls short of explaining the widely noted inter-learner variance. To explain the latter, MacWhinney proposes the social stratification hypothesis and the compensatory strategies hypothesis.

Chapter 8 by Tarone elaborates on the role of social and socio-psychological factors in creating, as well as counteracting, fossilization. Tarone argues that fossilization is, at least in part, a function of 'a complex web of social and socio-psychological forces that increases in complexity with the increasing age of second language learners' (p. 170). Drawing on Larsen-Freeman's (1997) chaos theory of inter-language, which views interlanguage as the product of balancing forces of stability and creativity, she hypothesizes that language play may potentially destabilize an interlanguage, thus counteracting, and even preventing, fossilization. This hypothesis, she points out, has yet to be subject to longitudinal verification.

In Chapter 9 Birdsong launches a critique of the problematic nature of the term fossilization by focusing on the notion of non-nativelikeness, which he took to be the ontological lynchpin of fossilization. He argues that the notion of non-nativelikeness itself defies a proper characteriz-ation, as is its counterpart, nativelikeness, which thereby renders fossili-zation an imprecise, 'protean, catch-all term' (Birdsong, 2004: 87). Hence, research on fossilization is 'not without peril' (p. 173). In his view, what would both be less perilous and of considerable heuristic value would be to study the upper limits of late L2 learning. Citing recent research on the nativelike attainment by late L2 learners, Birdsong advances the Universal Learnability Hypothesis, which, essentially, states that everything in the L2 is learnable.

What Can We Conclude at This Point?

The field of SLA has seen a long-term interest in seeking an adequate understanding of the L2 end state, and over the last two decades, it has witnessed an increasing awareness that language learning ability is not a single undifferentiated whole (MacWhinney, this volume: chap. 7). Two lines of research, in particular, have contributed to the awareness. The first is the body of research on fossilization which has generated evi-dence that any permanent failure to learn can only be local, not global. The second line is the body of research investigating the upper limits of adult L2 learning, which, similarly, shows that there is narrow, but not comprehensive, nativelikeness. Though the two lines of research differ in their respective orientation – one towards failure and the other success, they nevertheless converge on the understanding that there is neither complete success nor complete failure in L2 acquisition. Research on fossilization, in fact, has revealed that any L2 learner, regardless of their age of onset of learning and level of proficiency, is able to demonstrate some degree of nativelike competence and performance. Hence, if nativelike attainment is the sole measurement of L2 success, then we are compelled to recognize that success and failure occur in all learners at various points in an infinite process of learning, vis-à-vis their acquisition of different aspects of the target language. This amounts to arguing that the L2 end state is neither global nor monolithic, and as such, it can be studied in learners at any stage of the process.

Research on the L2 end state, be it success or failure oriented, should, among other things, *identify* what learners can and cannot do and *differentiate* it from what they do not do, as Birdsong has insightfully pointed out. This mission, however, can never be adequately achieved unless longitudinal research is conducted, utilizing multiple sources of data for internal validation. Establishing a reliable database would not only satisfy a requirement necessitated by any attempt to develop a scientific theory of the L2 end state – and hence the L2 learning capacity, but it should also benefit second language educators when making policy and instructional decisions. The dual importance, therefore, makes this empirical desideratum a priority for future research on the L2 end state.

References

Bansal, R.K. (1976) *The Intelligibility of Indian English*. (ERIC Report ED 177849). Hyderabad: Central Institute of English and Indian Languages.

Barkow, J., Cosmides, L. and Tooby, J. (1992) *The Adapted Mind: Evolutionary Psychology and the Generation of Culture*. New York: Oxford University Press.

Bates, E. and MacWhinney, B. (1981) Second language acquisition from a functionalist perspective: Pragmatics, semantics and perceptual strategies. In H. Winitz (ed.) *Annals of the New York Academy of Sciences Conference on Native and Foreign Language Acquisition* (pp. 190–214). New York: New York Academy of Sciences.

Bialystok, E. (1978) A theoretical model of second language learning. *Language Learning* 28 (1), 69–83.

Birdsong, D. (1999) *Second Language Acquisition and the Critical Period Hypothesis*. Mahwah, NJ: Lawrence Erlbaum Associates.

Birdsong, D. (2003, March) *Why Not Fossilization*. Paper presented at the AAAL (American Association for Applied Linguistics) 2003 International Conference, Arlington, Virginia.

Birdsong, D. (2004) Second language acquisition and ultimate attainment. In A. Davies and C. Elder (eds) *The Handbook of Applied Linguistics* (pp. 82–104). Malden, MA: Blackwell.

Birdsong, D. (2005) Interpreting age effects in second language acquisition. In J.F. Kroll and A.M.B. deGroot (eds) *Handbook of Bilingualism: Psycholinguistic Approaches* (pp. 109–127). New York: Oxford University Press.

Bley-Vroman, R. (1989) What is the logical problem of foreign language learning? In S. Gass and J. Schachter (eds) *Linguistic Perspectives on Second Language Acquisition* (pp. 41–68). Cambridge, UK: Cambridge University Press.

Carroll, M., Murcia-Serra, J., Watorek, M. and Bendiscioli, A. (2000) The relevance of information organization to second language acquisitions studies: The descriptive discourse of advanced adult learners of German. *Studies in Second Language Acquisition* 22, 441–466.

Cook, V.J. (1999) Going beyond the native speaker in language teaching. *TESOL Quarterly* 33 (2), 185–207.

Cook, V.J. (2003) *Effects of the Second Language on the First.* Clevedon: Multilingual Matters.

Coppieters, R. (1987) Competence differences between native and near-native speakers. *Language* 63 (3), 544–573.

Davies, A. (2003) *The Native Speaker: Myth and Reality.* Clevedon: Multilingual Matters.

Davies, A. (2004) The native speaker in applied linguistics. In A. Davies and C. Elder (eds) *The Handbook of Applied Linguistics.* Oxford: Blackwell.

Ellis, N. (1993) Rules and instances in foreign language learning: Interactions of explicit and implicit knowledge. *European Journal of Cognitive Psychology* 5 (3), 289–318.

Elman, J. (1993) Incremental learning, or the importance of starting small. *Cognition* 48, 71–99.

Filppula, M. (1999) *The Grammar of Irish English.* London: Routledge.

Flynn, S. (1996) A parameter-setting approach to second language acquisition. In W.C. Ritchie and T. K. Bhatia (eds) *Handbook of Second Language Acquisition* (pp. 121–158). San Diego: Academic Press.

Foster-Cohen, S. (2001) First language acquisition . . . second language acquisition: What's Hecuba to him or he to Hecuba? *Second Language Research* 17, 329–344.

Gregg, K. (1996) The logical and developmental problems of second language acquisition. In W.C. Ritchie and T.K. Bhatia (eds) *Handbook of Second Language Acquisition* (pp. 50–84). New York: Academic Press.

Gregg, K. (2003) SLA theory: Construction and assessment. In C. Doughty and M. Long (eds) *The Handbook of Second Language Acquisition* (pp. 831–865). Oxford: Blackwell.

Hammarberg, B. (2001) Roles of L1 and L2 in L3 production and acquisition. In J. Cenoz, B. Hufeisen and U. Jessner (eds) *Cross-Linguistic Influence in Third Language Acquisition: Psycholinguistic Perspectives* (pp. 21–41). Clevedon: Multilingual Matters.

Han, Z.-H. (1998) *Fossilization: An Investigation into Advanced L2 Learning of a Typologically Distant Language.* Unpublished PhD dissertation, Birkbeck College, University of London.

Han, Z.-H. (2000) Persistence of the implicit influence of NL: The case of the pseudo-passive. *Applied Linguistics* 21 (1), 78–105.

Han, Z.-H. (2003) Fossilization: From simplicity to complexity. *International Journal of Bilingual Education and Bilingualism*, 6 (2), 95–128.

Han, Z.-H. (2004a) *Fossilization in Adult Second Language Acquisition* (1st edn). Clevedon: Multilingual Matters.

Han, Z.-H. (2004b) To be a native speaker means not to be a non-native speaker. *Second Language Research* 22 (2), 166–187.

Hansen, L. (1980) *Learning and Forgetting a Second Language: the Acquisition, Loss and Reacquisition of Hindi-Urdu Negated Structures by English-Speaking Children.* Unpublished PhD dissertation, University of California, Berkeley.

Hansen, L. (1983) The acquisition and forgetting of Hindi-Urdu negation by English-speaking children. In K. Bailey, M. Long and S. Peck (eds) *Second Language Acquisition Studies* (pp. 93–103). Rowley, Massachusetts: Newbury House.

Hawkins, R. (2000) Persistent selective fossilization in second language acquisition and the optimal design of the language faculty. *Essex Research Reports in Linguistics* 34, 75–90.

Hurford, J. and Kirby, S. (1999) Co-evolution of language size and the criticial period. In D. Birdsong (ed.) *Second Language Acquisition and the Critical Period Hypothesis* (pp. 39–63). Mahwah, NJ: Lawrence Erlbaum Associates.

Jarvis, S (1998) *Conceptual Transfer in the Interlanguage Lexicon*. Bloomington: Indiana University Linguistics Club.

Jarvis, S. and Pavlenko, A. (2000) *Conceptual Restructuring in Language Learning: Is There an End State?* Paper presented at the SLRF 2000, Madison, WI.

Johnson, J. and Newport, E. (1989) Critical period effects in second language learning: The influence of maturational state on the acquisition of English as a second language. *Cognitive Psychology* 21, 60–99.

Klein, W. and Perdue, C. (1993) Utterance structure. In C. Perdue (ed.) *Adult Language Acquisition: Cross-linguistic Perspective* (Vol. II, pp. 3–40). Cambridge: Cambridge University Press.

Krashen, S. (1981) *Second Language Acquisition and Second Language Learning*. Oxford: Pergamon.

Lafarge, S. (1985) *Français Écrit et Parlé en Pays Éwé*. Paris: Société d'Études Linguistiques et Anthropologiques de France.

Lardiere, D. (1998) Dissociating syntax from morphology in a divergent L2 end-state grammar. *Second Language Research* 14 (4), 359–375.

Larsen-Freeman, D. (1997) Chaos/complexity science and second language acquisition. *Applied Linguistics* 19 (2), 141–165.

Leather, J. and James, A. (1996) Second language speech. In W.C. Ritchie and T.K. Bhatia (eds) *Handbook of Second Language Acquisition* (pp. 269–326). San Diego: Academic Press.

Lenneberg, E. (1967) *Biological Foundations of Language*. New York: Wiley.

Lightbown, P. (2000) Classroom SLA research and second language teaching. *Applied Linguistics* 21 (4), 431–462.

Long, M. (1990) Maturational constraints on language development. *Studies in Second Language Acquisition* 12, 251–285.

Long, M. (1993) Second language acquisition as a function of age: Substantive findings and methodological issues. In K. Hyltenstam and A. Viberg (eds) *Progression and Regression in Language* (pp. 196–221). Cambridge: Cambridge University Press.

Long, M. (2003) Stabilization and fossilization in interlanguage development. In C. Doughty and M. Long (eds) *The Handbook of Second Language Acquisition* (pp. 487–536). Oxford: Blackwell.

Long, M. and Robinson, P. (1998) Focus on form. In C. Doughty and J. Williams (eds) *Focus on Form in Classroom Second Language Acquisition* (pp. 16–41). Cambridge, UK: Cambridge University Press.

MacWhinney, B. (2001) The competition model: The input, the context, and the brain. In P. Robinson (ed.) *Cognition and Second Language Instruction* (pp. 69–70). Cambridge: Cambridge University Press.

MacWhinney, B. (2005) A unified model of language acquisition. In J.F. Kroll and A.M.B. deGroot (eds) *Handbook of Bilingualism: Psycholinguistic Approaches* (pp. 49–67). New York: Oxford University Press.

Marchman, V. (1992) Constraint on plasticity in a connectionist model of the English past tense. *Journal of Cognitive Neuroscience* 4, 215–234.

Montrul, S. and Slabakova, R. (2003) Competence, similarities between native and near-native speakers: An investigation of the preterite-imperfect contrast in Spanish. *Studies in Second Language Acquisition* 25 (3), 351–398.

Odlin, T. (1986) Another look at passage correction tests. *TESOL Quarterly* 20, 123–130.

Odlin, T. (1989) Word-order transfer, metalinguistic awareness, and constraints on foreign language learning. In B. VanPatten and J. Lee (eds) *Second Language Acquisition and Foreign Language Learning* (pp. 95–117). Clevedon: Multilingual Matters.

Odlin, T. (1992) *Language Transfer*. Cambridge: Cambridge University Press.

Odlin, T. (2003) Cross-linguistic influence. In C. Doughty and M. Long (eds) *The Handbook of Second Language Acquisition* (pp. 436–486). Oxford: Blackwell.

Odlin, T. (2005) Cross-linguistic influence and conceptual transfer: What are the concepts? *Annual Review of Applied Linguistics* 25, 3–25.

Pavlenko, A. (1999) New approaches to concepts in bilingual memory. *Bilingualism: Language and Cognition* 2, 209–230.

Pavlenko, A. and Jarvis, S. (2002) Bidirectional transfer. *Applied Linguistics* 23, 190–214.

Pinker, S. (1994) *The Language Instinct*. New York: William Morrow.

Romero Trillo, J. (2002) The pragmatic fossilization of discourse markers in non-native speakers of English. *Journal of Pragmatics* 34 (6), 769–784.

Schachter, J. (1988) Testing a proposed universal. In S. Gass and J. Schachter (eds) *Linguistic Perspectives on SLA* (pp. 73–88). New York: Cambridge University Press.

Schachter, J. (1996) Maturation and the issue of universal grammar in second language acquisition. In W.C. Ritchie and T.K. Bhatia (eds) *Handbook of Second Language Acquisition* (pp. 159–194). San Diego: Academic Press.

Schwartz, B. and Sprouse, R. (1996) L2 cognitive states and the full transfer/full access model. *Second Language Research* 12, 40–72.

Scovel, T. (1988) *A Time to Speak: A Psycholinguistic Inquiry into the Critical Period for Human Speech*. New York: Newbury House.

Selinker, L. (1972) Interlanguage. *International Review of Applied Linguistics* 10 (2), 209–231.

Selinker, L. and Lamendella, J. (1978) Two perspectives on fossilization in interlanguage learning. *Interlanguage Studies Bulletin* 3 (2), 143–191.

Selinker, L. and Lamendella, J. (1979) The role of extrinsic feedback in interlanguage fossilization: A discussion of 'rule fossilization: A tentative model'. *Language Learning* 29 (2), 363–375.

Selinker, L. and Han, Z.-H. (2001) Fossilization: Moving the concept into empirical longitudinal study. In C. Elder, A. Brown, E. Grove, K. Hill, N. Iwashita, T. Lumpley, T. McNamara and K. O'Loughlin (eds) *Studies in Language Testing: Experimenting with Uncertainty* (pp. 276–291). Cambridge: Cambridge University Press.

Selinker, L. and Lakshmanan, U. (1992) Language transfer and fossilization: The multiple effects principle. In S. Gass and L. Selinker (eds) *Language Transfer in Language Learning* (pp. 197–216). Amsterdam: John Benjamins.

Sharwood Smith, M. (1991) Speaking to many minds: on the relevance of different types of language information for the L2 learner. *Second Language Research* 7 (2), 118–132.

Slobin, D.I. (1996) From 'thought and language' to 'thinking for speaking'. In J. Gumperz and S. Levinson (eds) *Rethinking Linguistic Relativity* (pp. 70–96). Cambridge: Cambridge University Press.

Sorace, A. (1993) Incomplete vs. divergent representations of unaccusativity in non-native grammars of Italian. *Second Language Research* 9 (1), 22–47.

Sorace, A. (2003) Near-nativeness. In C. Doughty and M. Long (eds) *The Handbook of Second Language Acquisition* (pp. 130–152). Oxford: Blackwell.

Sorace, A. (1996) *Permanent Optionality as Divergence in Non-Native Grammars.* Paper presented at EUROSLA 6, Nijmegen, Holland.

Sridhar, K. and Sridhar, S. (1986) Bridging the paradigm gap: Second language acquisition theory and indigenized varieties of English. *World Englishes* 5, 3–14.

Tarone, E. (1994) Interlanguage. In R.E. Asher (ed.) *The Encyclopedia of Language and Linguistics* (Vol. 4, pp. 1715–1719). Oxford: Pergamon.

Tarone, E., Frauenfelder, U. and Selinker, L. (1976) Systematicity/variability and stability/instability in interlanguage systems. *Language Learning* 4, 93–134.

Thep-Ackrapong, T. (1990) *Fossilization: A Case Study of Practical and Theoretical Parameters.* Unpublished PhD dissertation, Illinois State University, Illinois: USA.

Thomason, S. and Kaufman, T. (1988) *Language Contact, Creolization, and Genetic Linguistics.* Berkeley: University of California Press.

Towell, R. and Hawkins, R. (1994) *Approaches to Second Language Acquisition.* Clevedon: Multilingual Matters.

VanBuren, P. (2001) Brief apologies and thanks. *Second Language Research* 17 (4), 457–462.

von Stutterheim, C. (2003) Linguistic structure and information organization: The case of very advanced learners. *EUROSLA Yearbook* 3, 183–206.

Weinreich, U. (1953) *Languages in Contact.* The Hague: Mouton.

White, L. (2001) *Revisiting Fossilization: The Syntax/Morphology Interface.* Paper presented at Babble, Trieste, Italy.

White, L. (2003) *Second Language Acquisition and Universal Grammar.* Cambridge: Cambridge University Press.

White, L. and Genesee, F. (1996) How native is near-native? The issue of ultimate attainment in adult second language acquisition. *Second Language Research* 12 (3), 233–265.

Chapter 2

Researching Fossilization and Second Language (L2) Attrition: Easy Questions, Difficult Answers

CONSTANCIO K. NAKUMA

Having been represented over the years as observable 'phenomena' that contribute to the perception of some 'deficiency' or 'failure' in L2 learning, fossilization and L2 attrition have derived their interest for second language acquisition (SLA) scholars from their presumed impact on the L2 learner/user. However, as 'phenomena,' the product of fossilization and L2 attrition would be, by definition, 'that which is not there,' since fossilization is said to prevail when the L2 learner stagnates in a *permanent state of not attaining a desired L2 native state*, and L2 attrition results from the *permanent loss of some level of L2 competence that the L2 user reportedly had acquired at an earlier stage*. As long as fossilization and L2 attrition are viewed as phenomena, this 'not-there' essential feature of their products would constitute a major roadblock to empirical research. This chapter defends the point of view that fossilization and L2 attrition are hypotheses that have been formulated by language acquisition scholars about L2 learner/user behavior and about L2 learning and retention outcomes, and rejects their characterization as observable phenomena whose existence can be demonstrated or proven by identifying and measuring their product through longitudinal research. It discusses fossilization and L2 attrition as hypotheses about 'within-learner' outcomes manifested as failure in reaching native-like L2 competence. Such failure, the chapter assumes, varies from individual to individual not only in terms of the linguistic elements affected but also in terms of the degree of failure relative to success. It attempts, in partial response to invitations to embark on empirical studies on fossilization (e.g. Selinker and Han, 2001; Han, 2003) and L2 attrition (e.g. Nakuma, 1997a, 1997b), to explain why empirical studies of these concepts have 'not thrived in L2 research,' as Han (2003) puts it, and why the few attempted investigations have produced questionable and inconclusive results (see Han's 2003 discussion of typical studies of fossilization). It suggests that the way forward, as far as research on these hypotheses is concerned, would be for SLA scholars to engage in hypothesis testing, rather than attempt to prove the reality or otherwise of fossilization and L2 attrition.

Assuming (as this author no longer does) that fossilization and L2 attrition are phenomena, what SLA scholars should at least know about them is how widespread and far-reaching they are among the general L2 learners/users population. It would require a comprehensive survey of a good sample of L2 learners/users to obtain that information. Scholars have insinuated that they are widespread and far-reaching phenomena, but no one knows for certain that they are. The first easy question that this chapter asks is whether or not fossilization and language attrition constitute legitimate fields of investigation in their own right outside the domain of second language acquisition theory.

Uses and Abuses of Fossilization and L2 Attrition

Within the field of SLA studies, fossilization and L2 attrition can be characterized as hypotheses about L2 learner/user behaviors (as well as the outcomes of L2 learning) that have been formulated on the basis of anecdotal reports of observed L2 learner behaviors, and which scholars have evoked in support of other assumptions and hypotheses about L2 learning behavior when there has been some advantage in doing so. For example, Schachter (1988, 1990, 1996) evoked fossilization and three other variables (previous knowledge, completeness and equipotentiality) to support the 'incompleteness hypothesis' stating that efforts by adult L2 learners to acquire native competency in L2 are doomed to result in incomplete success. Bley-Vroman (1989) employed essentially the same *modus operandi* in developing the 'fundamental difference' hypothesis. These examples are not intended as a critique of these scholars or their ideas; they are provided here to illustrate the uses to which untested hypotheses like fossilization and L2 attrition have been subjected.

Fossilization and L2 attrition have played a major role in keeping SLA scholars *wondering and debating whether or not adult second language learners can attain native-like competency in a second language.* Some SLA scholars have insinuated that fossilization in particular affects most, if not all, L2 learners/users. A statement like 'It has long been noted that foreign language learners reach a certain stage of learning – a stage short of success – and that learners then permanently stabilize at this stage' (Bley-Vroman, 1989: 46) illustrates how generalization and vagueness can be used to insinuate the existence of a widespread 'phenomenon.' Similarly, Schachter (1996), in trying to account for why adult L2 learning is not likely to result in native-like L2 competence, makes a series of assertions as follows:

- 'The ultimate attainment of most, if not all, of adult L2 learners is a state of incompleteness with regard to the grammar of the L2.'
- 'Long after the cessation of change in the development of their L2 grammar, adults will variably produce errors and non-errors in the same linguistic environments.'
- 'The adult's knowledge of a prior language either facilitates or inhibits acquisition of the L2, depending on the underlying similarities or dissimilarities of the languages in question.'
- 'The adult learner's prior knowledge of one language has a strong effect, detectable in the adult's production of the L2.'

Though Schachter did not explicitly state that most, if not all, adult L2 learners are affected by fossilization, the insinuation is there through the juxtaposition of the statements concerning L2 learning behavior.

Current thinking on adult L2 learning behavior and on the outcome of such learning has been informed by either controversial hypotheses like the 'critical age hypothesis,' or untested ones like the 'incompleteness hypothesis' or 'fundamental difference hypothesis.' These hypotheses have conditioned the thinking of scholars about adult L2 acquisition as being an event continuum that begins at point L1/zero L2 and progresses through varying degrees of interlanguage development up to a potential maximum point of L1/near-native L2, where 'near-native' rather than 'native-like' is considered as the highest level of acquisition possible for adult learners. The term 'native L2' rings suspicious in the current SLA climate, unless it is specifically limited in its domain of validity to the non-adult L2 learner population.[1]

In the presumed L2 acquisition continuum from L1/zero-L2 to L1/ near-native, it would be tempting to imagine that fossilization (if taken as a phenomenon) is manifested at the front end (i.e. during the phase of active interlanguage acquisition and use), and L2 attrition (also viewed as a phenomenon) at the back end (i.e. during the post-active-acquisition and post-active-use phase, following a relatively 'long-term cessation of interlanguage development' and usage). The rationale for inviting reflection on fossilization and L2 attrition in tandem is that

bringing into sharper focus the two ends of this presumed SLA continuum is more likely to inform SLA theorization better than otherwise.
This point will be discussed later in the chapter, at which point the characterization of fossilization and L2 attrition as 'phenomena' will be rejected
more categorically in favor of their characterization as 'hypotheses.'

Assuming that there is indeed any need for further investigation into
these 'phenomena' beyond the comprehensive survey to determine how
widespread and far-reaching they are, another easy question to address
would be how one must go about proving that 'that which is not there'
is actually there. In other words, how can one successfully identify and
measure the product of fossilization and L2 attrition? Since we reject the
'phenomenon' view of these concepts, we do not consider this question
any further. Only if their products can be identified and measured will
longitudinal research on these 'phenomena' be feasible. In that event,
the researcher of attrition, for example, would have to be able to anticipate
fully and accurately, and from the onset of research, the potential 'losable
linguistic items' of each research participant in order to be able to show
later that those items have subsequently been lost permanently.

Aspects of Fossilization and L2 Attrition

Han's (2003) comprehensive review of the literature on fossilization led
her to the remark that 'fossilization is no longer a monolithic concept as it
was in its initial postulation, but rather a complex construct intricately
tied up with varied manifestations of failure' (p. 106). This remark
invites comment, because although the concept is indeed no longer as
monolithic as it was in the early 1970s, a factor that contributed immen-
sely to the loss of its monolithic character was the broadening of the definition of 'fossilization' to include manifestations of non-failure as well.
When Selinker (1972) coined the term 'fossilization' to denote a combi-
nation of different aspects of L2 failure that scholars like Weinreich
(1953) and Nemser (1971) had observed and described under the labels
of 'permanent grammatical influence' and 'permanent intermediate
systems and subsystems' respectively, he had tied fossilization directly
to the manifestation of 'failure in L2.' Thereafter, Selinker (Selinker and
Lamandella, 1978) participated in reinterpreting the term more loosely
to make it possible for manifestations of 'non failure' as well to be associated with the term. Nakuma (1998) discussed the implications of that conceptual shift, noting that all manifestations of 'stabilized interlanguage'
would thereby logically qualify as a 'giant fossil' that would have both
positive (success) and negative (failure) aspects. The proliferation of

viewpoints and accounts of fossilization that ensued (see Han's 2003 review for details) highlights the desire of scholars to imbue the concept with greater precision. Attempts to distinguish more clearly between 'stabilization' and 'fossilization,' for example (e.g. Han, 1998; Selinker and Han, 2001) have, arguably, fallen short of their goal, but have highlighted the nature of fossilization as a hypothesis.

Selinker and Han (2001: 202) identify three possible cases that could qualify as instances of 'stabilization,' and they argue that 'fossilization,' which is preceded by stabilization, is necessarily marked by 'long-term cessation of interlanguage development,' whereas some instances of stabilization are not. They acknowledge that when stabilization is manifested as long-term cessation of interlanguage development, it is indistinguishable from fossilization. Basically, their distinction could be stated simply as 'all instances of fossilization qualify as stabilization, but not all instances of stabilization qualify as fossilization.' Their distinction is anchored on the condition of 'long-term cessation of interlanguage development,' a concept which raises questions about what exactly fossilization is, and whether it can happen. Restated differently, is fossilization a 'phenomenon' or is it an assumption, a hypothesis?

'Long-term cessation of IL development,' if it were to occur, would imply that there is no point for the L2 learner to persist henceforth in trying to attain native-like competence in L2. (There is the nagging question of why L2 development would progress steadily and then suddenly stop so completely and permanently, though the learner has not been affected by a debilitating learning impairment and continues to make efforts to learn the L2.) If it were truly to happen at any point in a person's lifetime, long-term cessation of IL development would also imply, in light of the prevailing view of language as being dynamic and constantly evolving, that such a person would necessarily become out of touch with the language as it evolves, and thereby become progressively less native-like over time when (s)he uses the L2. Moreover, given another prevailing view that language development takes a lifetime and is never really complete in anyone, the notion of permanent cessation of IL development sounds questionable.

In light of these observations, one would have to presume that L2 learners would continue to strive for (and make some degree of progress towards?) native-like competence throughout their existence. It could indeed be argued that what makes 'fossilization' such an intriguing concept for SLA scholars is the presumption that *fossilization strikes and persists in spite of the learner's efforts to progress to native L2 competence*. If L2 interlanguage were ever to cease developing, therefore, and if it was the learner who voluntarily triggered such cessation, there would be no case of fossilization; there would be only an instance of outright discontinuation of L2 learning. In other words, fossilization, properly speaking, could not be said to have 'happened' if the L2 learner voluntarily or consciously discontinued developing the L2. What this brief discussion is intended to highlight is that the condition of 'long-term cessation of interlanguage development,' which is considered as a defining feature of fossilization, cannot include instances of voluntary cessation of IL development. Fossilization therefore would prevail only if interlanguage ceases permanently to develop, despite conscious and continuing efforts by the learner to develop it. Thus, fossilization as process or product necessarily results from the permanent, imperceptible cessation of IL development. If so, how should the learner know that fossilization has struck? Usually, learners do not know it, but they are told so by some SLA researcher, who makes them conscious of their L2 'deficiency.' And how permanent can cessation be if the learner is capable of responding to corrective feedback, even if for a brief moment, or if (s)he can produce the native-like L2 target under more relaxed and carefully considered production situations? It is a lot easier to ask these questions than to answer them!

Let us assume now, for the sake of argument, that cessation of IL development happens, but the L2 continues to be used actively. Such cessation could affect the totality of the learner's interlanguage generally or only part of it, differentially. These views have been expressed or implied by different scholars in the literature.

If such cessation affects the totality of the learner's interlanguage, then the learner is bound to experience, under the circumstances, a progressive 'decline' in L2 competence over time due to not keeping up with changes occurring in L2 through the natural process of language change. Although such decline would not qualify, strictly speaking, as an instance of L2 attrition, since the affected linguistic elements would never have been learned, it would nonetheless look like a case of attrition if reported. Remembering that L2 attrition studies are predicated on the notion that a language that is not kept active will eventually atrophy, 'long-term cessation of (inter)language development' that triggers a decline in L2 competence over time by keeping the learner out of touch with the evolving language, could cause the L2 user to report the occurrence of 'L2 attrition.' Indeed, it has often been commented that fossilization (when perceived as failure in L2 learning, that is) persists despite the availability of good opportunities for the L2 learner to make progress towards the desired L2 target. 'Staying out of touch' with the evolving target language would surely result in the perception of 'failure' on the part of the L2 learner, a failure resulting from the L2 learner not keeping up with language change. Thus, if considered from the perspective that cessation of development affects the totality of a learner's interlanguage, fossilization could indeed trigger some 'look-alike' form of L2 attrition. Furthermore, the notion of 'permanent cessation' would be within the realm of logical possibility, but the nagging question that such a perspective would pose would be why L2 development would have progressed steadily up to the point of onset of fossilization and then suddenly stopped so completely and permanently, even though the learner, who is not affected by a debilitating learning impairment, would have continued to make efforts to learn the L2.

If development ceases permanently for some elements but not all of a learner's interlanguage, then there must be something about those elements affected by fossilization that would explain why the given L2 learner cannot acquire them well. SLA scholars have looked generally to L1 influence, avoidance, and other factors to explain such cases of differential success or failure. Differential success or failure implies that IL development continues to be possible for non-fossilized elements. And as long as IL development continues to be possible for any L2 component, then the notion of 'permanent cessation of development' has a rather weak logical foundation, given that the learner is still theoretically able to acquire new L2 input, which could result from language change. The ability to acquire new L2 input, whatever that input is, theoretically makes the cessation of interlanguage development potentially reversible, and therefore 'non-permanent.' For example, if change happens in L2 affecting a fossilized element for a given L2 learner, such a learner could acquire properly the new form resulting from the change. If all fossilized elements underwent change to forms that the learner could properly acquire, such a learner would eventually no longer exhibit any manifestations of failure in L2.

The point about developing these scenarios is to highlight the implications of different accounts of fossilization, and to argue next that fossilization is not a phenomenon (in the sense of something that happens) but rather a hypothesis (in the sense of an assumption) formulated by SLA scholars about L2 learning behaviors and outcomes.

If one holds the view that fossilization affects an individual's entire interlanguage, then the notion of permanent cessation of interlanguage development would have a strong logical foundation, but the view itself would be at odds with observable L2 learner behaviors which indicate that different learners manifest different degrees of approximation to native L2 competence. On the other hand, if one holds the view that cessation affects only a part of the learner's interlanguage, then the logical foundation for 'permanent cessation of IL development' would be weakened, and the concept of fossilization itself as a phenomenon would be put to question, especially as long as permanent cessation is considered a critical feature of its definition.

In closing this discussion, it should be remarked that the 'long-term cessation of interlanguage development' condition that is built into the definition of 'fossilization' constitutes also one of the most problematic aspects of the concept. If interlanguage development never ceases permanently (as would be the case if cessation happens for some but not all of a learner's interlanguage), then 'fossilization' will never happen, at least not according to the definition given to it. If the 'phenomenon' never happens, then it becomes a myth that should be treated as such. On the other hand, if permanent cessation of IL development can and does happen (as is logically possible if permanent cessation affects the totality of a learner's interlanguage), then fossilization could be widespread and far-reaching among L2 learners/users. The logical endpoint of fossilization, under this scenario, would be a state of loss of L2 competence due to the learner/user staying out of touch with the evolving L2. Is fossilization a myth or is it a widespread 'phenomenon' that manifests itself as 'foreigner speech'? We argue that it is neither myth nor phenomenon, just a hypothesis.

Is Empirical Research on Fossilization and L2 Attrition Feasible?

Han (2003: 99) implicitly argues that empirical research on fossilization would be facilitated by the existence of a more precise definition of the concept. She offers a two-tier 'definition,' but immediately points out its many weaknesses. Her two-tier definition reads as follows:

COGNITIVE LEVEL: Fossilization involves those cognitive processes, or underlying mechanisms that produce permanently stabilized IL forms.

EMPIRICAL LEVEL: Fossilization involves those stabilized interlanguage forms that remain in learner speech or writing over time, no matter what the input or what the learner does. (Han, 2003: 99)

What is striking about these 'definitions' is that they are formulated as null hypotheses that could, with some deconstruction, lend themselves to empirical testing. It is also interesting that Han retains the broadened view of fossilization by not explicitly tying the term to 'failure.' Finally, it is significant that fossilization is cast as a process at the cognitive level, but as a product at the empirical level. The views reflected in these 'definitions' ('null hypotheses' would be our preferred choice of terminology) are widely expressed and discussed in the literature on fossilization, where it is viewed and treated as a phenomenon.

Focused attempts to account for fossilization from a theoretical and empirical standpoint include, to-date, at least four unpublished doctoral dissertations (e.g. Han, 1998; Lin, 1995; Thep-Ackrapong, 1990; Washburn, 1991) and numerous journal articles (e.g. Hawkins, 2000; Hylthenstam, 1988; Long, 2003; Lowther, 1983; Nakuma, 1998; Schnitzer, 1993; Selinker, 1993; Selinker and Han, 2001; Selinker and Lakshmanan, 1992; Selinker and Lamandella, 1978, 1979). Larry Selinker, who coined the term 'fossilization' in 1972, has been one of the most prolific and pioneering scholars on the subject. Other studies have evoked the concept but not really focused on it. Such interest in fossilization, as we have discussed earlier, tends to be largely tangential, in the sense that the concept is evoked usually within the context of hypotheses or discussions focusing on much broader questions pertaining to adult second language acquisition.

Underlying the direct interest in fossilization on the part of scholars is the presumption that understanding how fossilization is triggered and what L2 targets are most susceptible to the 'phenomenon' would enable SLA scholars, (barring individual differences affecting L2 learning), to help L2 learners to avoid or overcome it and progress better towards native-like L2 competence. Such a presumption is reminiscent of the presumption underlying the Contrastive Analysis Hypothesis, which was so influential in SLA theorization in the 1970s. Tangential or focused, the interest in fossilization has not resulted in much empirical research on the subject. Is fossilization researchable empirically?

To be researchable empirically, a phenomenon or issue must be 'capable of being confirmed, verified or disproved by observation or experiment' (Webster's Third International Dictionary). A major challenge posed by concepts like fossilization and L2 attrition for SLA scholars is that, because they have been misconstrued as 'phenomena,' their product is essentially nihilistic and their process of self-actualization is imperceptible to the affected subject. One concludes that fossilization has happened after observing a second language learner manifest repeatedly and for a prolonged period of time either an inability to produce a native-like L2 target,[2] and despite the fact that the learner makes an effort and has a good opportunity not to fail. Similarly, one concludes that L2 attrition has occurred when a second language learner reports the permanent loss of some L2 competency level claimed to have been acquired at an earlier point in life. By their nature, therefore, if one considers fossilization and L2 attrition as 'happenings' or 'phenomena,' then their products 'exist' only as logical constructs through assumption and deductive thinking. 'Evidence' to validate the existence of these 'phenomena' is obtained from L2 learners/users presumed to be affected by them. One difference between fossilization and attrition is perhaps that fossilization is necessarily beyond the learner's awareness, whereas attrition appears to be a conscious process for the learner. In other words, fossilization as product already is the product of much hypothesizing on the part of the second language acquisition researcher who reports its existence. The conclusion that fossilization prevails in the case of a given L2 user's IL results from an intellectual leap from event (failure) to state (permanence). Fossilization, properly speaking, is an assumption (or hypothesis) formulated about how L2 learners/users progress towards native-like L2 competence, which states that adult L2 learners especially will not attain native-like competence for a whole array of reasons. What remains to be done, by way of research, is to test the hypothesis so formulated.

Researching fossilization and L2 attrition can be likened methodologically to the work of a psychiatrist or psychologist. The psychiatrist (SLA researcher) proceeds by formulating an assumption (formulates fossilization hypothesis) about what is happening in the mind of the patient (about how L2 learning is proceeding) based on information solicited from the patient (by seeking confirmation from the presumed affected L2 learner), and confirms or modifies the assumption based on goodness-of-fit. The research that is yet to be done on fossilization will be about testing the fossilization and L2 attrition hypotheses. Because these hypotheses were formulated as offshoots of second language acquisition theories, it is within that framework that the relevant research questions can be formulated. The concept of 'fossilization' was coined within the context of trying to account for how L2 acquisition happens, and it retains its interest within that context as one of several competing hypotheses about how and why second language acquisition differs from first language acquisition.

As a concluding remark, we contend that Schachter's 'incompleteness hypothesis' is a misnomer in the sense that it is not a single hypothesis but rather a composite of different hypotheses used to account for the larger issue of L2 acquisition. Schachter, like Bley-Vroman, evoked the fossilization hypothesis along with a version of the contrastive analysis hypothesis and other hypotheses to make the incompleteness argument. What we have tried to argue up to this point is that the difficulty of researching fossilization and L2 attrition empirically has arisen from the misunderstanding of their true nature as hypotheses (rather than as phenomena), from the lack of a precise definition, and from their true nature as hypotheses about L2 learner/user behaviors and learning outcomes.

Research on Fossilization and L2 Attrition: Which Way Forward?

Hypothesis testing is the way forward. Assumptions made about happenings are either maintained or discarded over time depending on how useful they prove to be in helping to 'account for' the happenings about which they are made. The same would be true of fossilization and L2 attrition, which we have characterized as hypotheses about L2 learner/user behavior that are overlaid with anecdotal reports of observed L2 learner behavior. It needs to be acknowledged upfront that not all issues lend themselves to empirical investigation. More importantly, not all issues need to be proven empirically in order to influence human existence. Testing hypotheses is done routinely, so it should be possible to test the fossilization and L2 attrition hypotheses as well. These hypotheses might lend themselves to investigation, but being the complex constructs that they are, they will need to be deconstructed in order to identify researchable strands from the complex maze of issues.[3]

Some of the easy questions that this chapter has asked include:

- How widespread and far-reaching are fossilization and L2 attrition among L2 learners/users, if they are considered as phenomena affecting L2 learners? (A comprehensive survey of L2 learners/users will be necessary to answer this question. We have argued that they are hypotheses rather that phenomena.)
- 'Long-term cessation of interlanguage development' is considered as a necessary feature of the definition of fossilization. But can and does interlanguage ever cease developing permanently in the L2 learner? If so, under what conditions and for what reasons would such cessation happen? (Answering this question could shed new light on adult second language acquisition, the broader topic that the fossilization hypothesis was intended to help address.)
- How must one go about proving that 'that which is not there' is actually there. In other words, how can one successfully identify and measure the product of fossilization and L2 attrition? (We have argued that such measurement is not feasible, given the nihilistic essence of the product of fossilization-as-phenomenon.)

- Do fossilization and language attrition constitute legitimate fields of investigation in their own right outside the domain of second language acquisition theory?
- Is fossilization a 'phenomenon' or is it an assumption, a hypothesis?
- How 'permanent' can cessation be if the learner is capable of responding to corrective feedback, even if for a brief moment, or if (s)he can produce the native-like L2 target under more relaxed and carefully considered production situations?

These questions are meant to provoke thought and generate more ideas on these concepts.

Notes

1. Thanks are due to one of the anonymous reviewers for drawing our attention to the following article, whose very title says it all: Han, Z.-H. (2004b) To be a native speaker means not to be a non-native speaker. *Second Language Research*, 24 (2), 166–187.
2. 'Inability to produce a native-like target' is to be understood here as including both instances where a Japanese learner of English may exhibit persistent difficulty in differentiating /r/ from /l/ and as a result pronounces 'pray' as 'play' and vice versa, or where the English learner of French may systematically pronounce /ky/ 'cul' (bottom) as /ku/ 'cou' (neck), for example, because they cannot produce a rounded high front vowel, and instances where IL forms such as 'I don't know what are you saying' or 'He go to school everyday' persist in spite of optimal learning conditions. In both types of examples, the learner has been unable to produce the desired target form. Instead, the learner persists in producing a form that deviates from the 'target.'
3. For some thoughts on this issue, see Han (2004a).

References

Bley-Vroman, R. (1989) What is the logical problem of foreign language learning? In S. Gass and J. Schachter (eds) *Linguistic Perspectives in Second Language Acquisition* (pp. 41–68). Cambridge: Cambridge University Press.

Han, Z.-H. (1998) Fossilization: An investigation into advanced L2 learning of a typologically distant language. Unpublished doctoral dissertation, University of London.

Han, Z.-H. (2003) Fossilization: From simplicity to complexity. *International Journal of Bilingual Education and Bilingualism* 6 (2), 95–128.

Han, Z.-H. (2004a) *Fossilization in Adult Second Language Acquisition*. Clevedon: Multilingual Matters.

Han, Z.-H. (2004b). To be a native speaker means not to be a non-native speaker. *Second Language Research* 20 (2), 166–187.

Hawkins, R. (2000) Persistent selective fossilization in second language acquisition and the optimal design of the language faculty. *Essex Research Reports on Linguistics* 24, 74–90.

Hylthenstam, K. (1988) Lexical characteristics of near-native second language learners of Swedish. *Journal of Multilingual and Multicultural Development* 9, 67–84.

Lin, Y.-H. (1995) An empirical analysis of stabilization/fossilization: Incorporation and self-correction of Chinese learners. Unpublished doctoral dissertation. Universitat de Barcelona.

Long, M. (2003) Fossilization and stabilization in interlanguage development. In C. Doughty and M. Long (eds) *Handbook of Second Language Acquisition*. Oxford: Blackwell.

Lowther, M. (1983) Fossilization, pidginization and the monitor. In L. Mac-Mathuna and D. Singleton (eds) *Language Across Cultures*. Dublin: Irish Association for Applied Linguistics.

Nakuma, C. (1997a) Cleaning up spontaneous speech for use in L2 attrition research: A proposal. *Journal of Multilingual and Multicultural Development* 18, 135–144.

Nakuma, C. (1997b) A method for measuring sttrition of communicative competence: A pilot study with Spanish L3 subjects. *Applied Psycholinguistics* 18, 219–235.

Nakuma, C. (1998) A new theoretical account of 'fossilization': Implications for L2 attrition research. *IRAL (International Review of Applied Linguistics in Language Teaching)* 36 (3), 247–256.

Nemser, W. (1971) Approximative systems of foreign language learners. *International Review of Applied Linguistics in Language Teaching* 9, 115–123.

Schachter, J. (1988) Second language acquisition and universal grammar. *Applied Linguistics* 9, 219–235.

Schachter, J. (1990) On the issue of completeness in second language acquisition. *Second Language Research* 6, 93–124.

Schachter, J. (1996) Maturation and the issue of universal grammar in second language acquisition. In W. Ritchie and T. Bathia (eds) *Handbook of Second Language Acquisition* (pp. 159–193). San Diego: Academic Press.

Schnitzer, M.L. (1993) Steady as a rock: Does the steady state represent cognitive fossilization? *Journal of Psycholinguistic Research* 22 (1), 1–20.

Selinker, L. (1972) Interlanguage. *IRAL* 10 (2), 209–231.

Selinker, L. (1993) Fossilization as simplification? In M. Tickoo (ed.) *Simplification: Theory and Application* (Anthology series 21). Singapore: Southeast Asian Ministers of Education Organization.

Selinker, L. and Lamandella, J. (1978) Two perspectives on fossilization in second language learning. *Interlanguage Studies Bulletin* 3 (2), 143–191.

Selinker, L. and Lamandella, J. (1979) The role of extrinsic feedback in interlanguage fossilization: A discussion of 'rule fossilization'. *Language Learning* 29 (2), 363–375.

Selinker, L. and Lakshmanan, U. (1992) Language transfer and fossilization: The multiple effects principle. In S. Gass and L. Selinker (eds) *Language Transfer in Language Learning* (pp. 197–216). Amsterdam: John Benjamins.

Selinker, L. and Han, Z.-H. (2001) Fossilization: Moving the concept into empirical longitudinal study. In C. Elder, A. Brown, E. Grove, K. Hill,

N. Iwashita, T. Lumpley, T. McNamara and K. O'Loughlin (eds) *Studies in Language Testing: Experimenting with Uncertainty* (pp. 276–291). Cambridge: Cambridge University Press.

Thep-Ackrapong, T. (1990) Fossilization: A case study of practical and theoretical parameters. Unpublished doctoral dissertation, Illinois State University.

Washburn, G. (1991) Fossilization in second language acquisition: A Vygotskian perspective. Unpublished doctoral dissertation, University of Pennsylvania.

Weinreich, U. (1953) *Languages in Contact.* Publication of the Linguistic Circle of New York (No 1).

Chapter 3
Establishing Ultimate Attainment in a Particular Second Language Grammar

DONNA LARDIERE

In this chapter I present findings which corroborate the conclusions drawn in a previous study (Lardiere, 1998b), using a different kind of data from that used in the earlier study. Both studies (1998b and the one reported here) are part of an ongoing longitudinal project investigating various characteristics of the 'steady state' L2 English idiolect of Patty, a native speaker of Hokkien and Mandarin Chinese who acquired English as an adult. Specifically, this chapter investigates the stability of Patty's knowledge of verb and adverb placement in English, as articulated within a generative UG framework that posits the raising of verbs (over negation and adverbs) in some languages but not others, as a function of inflectional 'strength'.

Lardiere (1998b) argued that Patty had nativelike knowledge of (verbal) inflectional feature strength in English despite her fossilized omission of the actual inflectional morphology associated with this feature, on the basis of near-perfect (unraised) verb placement found in her naturalistic, spoken production data. Given that the main theoretical issue investigated in that study was whether Patty *knows* that there is a constraint prohibiting thematic verb-raising in English, however, the fact that she merely does not produce raised verbs in English is suggestive but not necessarily conclusive. The naturalistic data needed to be supplemented with a task that would actually test her ability to reject ungrammatical English sentences with raised verbs. This chapter reports the results of two such tasks, both of them grammaticality judgment tasks with slightly different methodologies, each administered 18 months apart. The results indicate that Patty indeed knows that thematic verbs cannot raise in English. Moreover, the results show an interesting pattern regarding adverb placement which does not come from knowledge of her L1(s). The ultimate attainment of abstract principles thought to govern word order appears to be quite nativelike in Patty's representation of English, despite the overall impression of fossilization in the morphological domain.

In many ways, Patty is an ideal candidate for research into the L2 steady state, given her long length of residence in the United States and near-total immersion and active engagement in a native-English speaking environment for many years. Patty was exposed to some English in high school in Hong Kong after she arrived there via mainland China around the age of 16; however, the language she acquired and primarily used in Hong Kong was Cantonese. After immigrating to the United States at the age of 22, she enrolled in a small junior college where she took two semesters of ESL in addition to her other classes, transferring in her second year to a four-year college where she completed an undergraduate degree in accounting. She also eventually completed an MBA program in the United States, and became a naturalized U.S. citizen. During the first several years of her life in the United States she lived in a mixed-language environment, speaking both Cantonese and English at home with her first husband and his family, English at school and English at work. At the time of the first recorded interview with her, she had lived in the United States for about 10 years, had divorced her first husband and was completely immersed in a near-exclusively English-speaking environment. Her immersion in this English-speaking environment has continued from then until the present. She remarried shortly after this project began, speaking only English at home with her second husband, who is a native-English-speaking American who does not speak any variety of Chinese. With the exception of a few Chinese songs and vocabulary items she has taught to her daughter, she speaks English to her daughter. Her work environment is still exclusively English-speaking. The period over which both spoken and written L2 data have been collected now extends to approximately 16 years. The data reported on here were collected at two intervals 18 months apart, approximately 22–23 years after Patty's arrival in the United States and about 12 years after the first recorded interview with her which initiated this project.

It is clear to anyone looking at Patty's data that her English is in some respects clearly non-nativelike and appears to have fossilized. Some grammatical elements that tend to be omitted from her spoken production data include verbal inflections for regular past tense marking (at about only 6% suppliance in obligatory contexts[2]) and nonpast third singular agreement (at about 4% suppliance) (see examples (1a) and (1b) below). The data also exhibit the omission of past participle forms (1c), the occasional overuse or omission of the present participle -_ing_ form (1d–e) and the omission of copula and auxiliary _be_ (1f–g), and for nouns, the occasional omission of regular plural (1 h) and possessive -_s_ marking (1i).

1. (a) _I call Bill this morning and nobody answer_
   (b) _because he understand better now_
   (c) _yeah but we haven't look at it carefully_
   (d) _so he make me spending money_
   (e) _I was stay by myself in the dormitory_
   (f) _he around adult a lot_
   (g) _she just hanging around_
   (h) _I borrow a lot of book from her_
   (i) _Debbie brother was very rich_

On the other hand, looking more carefully, we also find some aspects of the data that are indeed quite nativelike, and which moreover cannot necessarily be explained in terms of facilitative transfer from the L1. These acquired elements include knowledge of overall pronominal case-marking, case-marking on subjects in particular as a function of clausal finiteness (see 2a below), and various word-order-related phenomena such as the placement of verbs and adverbs (2b), robust relative clause formation, and _wh_-movement in general including the appropriate stranding of prepositions (2c) and subject-auxiliary inversion/ _do_-support in questions (2d). Her use of determiners, while not completely nativelike, is surprisingly proficient (2e–f).

2. (a) _maybe they don't want us to use it after office hour_
   (b) _B. didn't really say much about his brother_
   (c) _you don't know who you should associate with_
   (d) _didn't he know that it will get back to me?_
   (e) _our hostess J. and her family_
   (f) _say, um, he have a beer . . . when A. repeat the story to us the other day about the beer_

In the following sections, I review the findings of Lardiere (1998b), briefly sketching the theoretical assumptions and some other recent SLA literature in this area. Then I provide a description of the two grammaticality judgment tasks used to test Patty's knowledge of verb-(non-)raising in English. After that, I present and discuss the results. Finally, I conclude with some thoughts regarding the nature of the construct of fossilization as illustrated within the context of this particular study.

Verb-Raising Features in SLA

Within generative syntactic theory, the position of verbs in relation to adverbs, negation, and inversion with the subject in questions has been tied over the past decade to features of finiteness in INFL, particularly 'rich' or morphologically complex subject-verb agreement. Compare the (well-known) examples of French vs. English in (3) below (from White, 1992b: 121; following Pollock, 1989):

3. (a)   Jean n'aime pas Marie
          *John likes not Mary
          John does not like Mary
    (b)   Aime-t-elle Jean?
          *Likes she John?
          Does she like John?
    (c)   Jean regarde souvent la télévision
          *John watches often television
          *Marie souvent regarde la télévision
          Mary often watches television

In the French examples in (3), the thematic verb precedes (i.e. has raised over) the negation element *pas* (3a), the pronominal subject *elle* (3b), and the adverb *souvent* (3c). In contrast, the raising of verbs over these elements is ungrammatical in English, which must instead rely on *do*-support in (3a–b); (3c) illustrates the contrast in verb-adverb placement with respect to transitive verbs.[3] The raising of verbs has been correlated with agreement, such that languages with rich agreement are hypothesized to have a 'strong' feature which requires movement (raising) to INFL to 'check' the feature; English, on the other hand, with its impoverished agreement on 3sg nonpast forms only, has 'weak' agreement and thus verbs do not raise. Note that copula *be*, with its richer suppletive subject-verb agreement paradigm, is exceptional in that it does not rely on *do*-support and does appear to raise, as shown in (4) (compare with the examples in (3) above):

4. (a)   John is not a good student.
    (b)   Is John a good student?
    (c)   John is often late for class.

Finally, it should be mentioned that the precise nature of the relationship between verb-raising and rich agreement has recently been questioned and has not been truly satisfactorily explained (Chomsky, 1995: 277 notes the correlation as a 'tendency'; see Bobaljik, 2002; Lardiere,

2000; Sprouse, 1998 for some discussion). Nonetheless, whatever the ultimate formal explanation, the empirical facts do suggest the presence of fairly systematic differences between French-type and English-type languages with respect to verb-raising that must be somehow recognized in the language acquisition process.

For second language acquisition, investigations into verb-raising have been widely used for well over a decade as a window onto the learner's grammatical representation of the target language, especially regarding the issue of whether functional categories are present in the L2 initial state and/or whether learners could acquire targetlike feature settings such as 'strong' vs. 'weak' (see, for example, Beck, 1998; Eubank, 1993/1994, 1996; Eubank & Grace, 1998; Eubank, Bischoff *et al.*, 1997, Eubank, Cliff *et al.*, 1998; Lardiere, 1998b; Schwartz & Gubala-Ryzak, 1992; Schwartz & Sprouse, 1996; Vainikka & Young-Scholten, 1994, 1996; White, 1990/1991, 1991, 1992a, 1992b; Yuan, 2001).[4,5]

Here, I would like to focus in particular on the series of papers by Eubank and colleagues cited above, which constituted the primary point of departure for Lardiere (1998b). Assuming the hypothesized theoretical link between rich agreement paradigms and feature strength triggering verb-raising, as outlined above, Eubank (1993/1994, 1996) proposed his *valueless features hypothesis*, such that learners who had not yet acquired the subject-verb agreement paradigm in their L2 would have an 'inert' value for feature strength – neither strong nor weak – and thus would optionally allow verb-raising even in those languages (such as English) which prohibit it. For English, this would mean testing to see whether learners had acquired regular nonpast 3sg -*s* marking, and whether this could be tied to learners' knowledge that agreement is 'weak' in English and therefore thematic verbs do not raise.

Using different methodologies – an on-line sentence-matching procedure (Eubank & Grace, 1998), a truth-value judgment task (Eubank *et al.*, 1997) and a grammaticality judgment task (Eubank *et al.*, 1998), Eubank and colleagues tested native Chinese-speaking learners of English on their knowledge of the constraint prohibiting thematic verb-raising over adverbs in their L2 English. Chinese was chosen as the L1 because it is also a non-raising language, and thus any acceptance of verb-raising by the participants could not be attributed to their L1. In all three studies, all Chinese participants were also administered an oral translation task testing their production of sentences requiring regular nonpast 3sg -*s* marking on verbs; performance on this test determined whether learners would be grouped into an 'Agreement' or

'No-Agreement' group, employing a 70%-correct criterion. The verb-raising tasks tested Eubank's prediction that the 'Agreement' group would (correctly) reject verb-raising over adverbs whereas the 'No-Agreement' group would exhibit optionality in accepting such verb-raising, because the former but not the latter group would have acquired the agreement paradigm needed to determine the 'weak' feature value of English.

The results from all three of these studies were mixed and rather inconclusive. Contrary to prediction, Eubank and Grace found that the (presumed) lower-proficiency No-Agreement group performed more like the native-speaker controls than did the higher-proficiency Agreement group. Eubank *et al.* (1997) found that both Chinese groups appeared to accept some verb-raising over adverbs, suggesting that even the acquisition of 3sg agreement marking did not appear to result in a switch from an 'inert' to a 'weak' value for feature strength. On the basis of these results, Eubank *et al.* (1997) concluded that adult second language learners had an apparently permanent (one might say fossilized), selectively impaired representation of INFL feature strength, following Beck's (1998) *local impairment hypothesis*. However, even some native controls accepted some verb-raising in this task, and some Chinese speakers from each group performed like native speakers. (See White (2003) for a detailed critique of the conceptual basis and methodology of these studies.) Finally, Eubank *et al.* (1998) found no significant difference in verb-raising among all the groups they tested – both groups of native Chinese speakers and their native English speaker controls. This was attributed to the fact that their native-English speaker controls did not perform as expected, raising doubts about the validity of the task they designed.

Against this backdrop, Lardiere (1998b) carried out a detailed analysis of Patty's naturalistic, spoken production data from three transcribed recordings that spanned a period of about eight and a half years, for any evidence of verb-raising over negation or adverbs. Previous research (Lardiere, 1998a) had suggested that, contra Eubank (and others, such as Vainikka & Young-Scholten (1994, 1996)), the acquisition or omission of inflectional morphology was independent of knowledge of underlying syntactic features and functional categories, such as those related to verb-raising. And Patty was a good test case for examining the hypothesized link between agreement morphology and knowledge of verb-raising, since she clearly appeared to have fossilized with respect to regular nonpast 3sg -*s* agreement marking, supplying it in less than 5% of obligatory contexts across the three recordings referred to above.

Like the participants in Eubank and colleagues' studies, her native L1 was Chinese, so that any acceptance of verb-raising could not be due to L1 transfer. Finally, whereas Eubank's studies looked only at ('short') verb-raising over a tiny set of adverbs (e.g. only *slowly* and *quietly* in Eubank *et al.* (1997)), Patty's data yielded findings for both short verb-raising over (a wider variety of) adverbs as well as 'long' verb-raising over NEG [compare with example (3a) above].

The results showed that Patty did not raise verbs in her spoken production over the entire time covered by the data collection period, neither over NEG (0/112 contexts = 0.0%) nor adverbs (1/122 contexts = 0.8%). Some examples of correct verb placement with respect to NEG are shown in (5), and with respect to adverbs in (6) (from Lardiere, 1998b: 368):

5. (a) *I do not write in Chinese*
   (b) *he did not try to do it anymore*
   (c) *I do not like to play in front of people*

6. (a) *I already took uh # eight credit*
   (b) *so she perform and always send me the picture*
   (c) *I just barely pass the # uh # the minimum*

To summarize, the findings from Lardiere (1998b) indicate that, despite Patty's near-total absence of agreement marking on thematic verbs in the data, she appears to know that verbs cannot raise in English, suggesting that fossilization in one domain (inflectional morphology) does not preclude development in another (knowledge of syntactic features and word order).

More Evidence

As mentioned earlier, although the spontaneous production data reported in Lardiere (1998b) are highly suggestive of a constraint prohibiting verb-raising in Patty's grammatical representation of English, they do not conclusively show that she *knows* that verb-raising in English is ungrammatical. Rather, that study shows only that she does not raise verbs in her spoken production of English. In order to reinforce the conclusions from that study regarding Patty's knowledge of this constraint in English, acceptability judgments for both grammatical and ungrammatical sentences involving adverb placement (or so-called 'short' verb movement) were elicited, following Eubank and colleagues. This section describes two tasks which were administered to Patty 18 months apart. The second of these tasks was also given to 25 native speaker controls.

Test 1

The first task, which I will refer to as Test 1, was an untimed, written, binary forced-choice test in which Patty was asked to rate sentences using either 'Y' ('yes') for acceptable or 'N' ('no') for unacceptable. For those sentences she rated 'N' or unacceptable, she was asked to provide what she considered to be a more acceptable version. (The test sentences are shown in the Appendix.) There were a total of 40 sentences, consisting of 10 ungrammatical *Subject-Verb-Adverb-Object (SVAO) sentences, as shown in example (7a), 10 grammatical SAVO sentences (as in 7b), 10 ungrammatical distracters (7c) and 10 grammatical distracters (7d).

7. (a) The chef cooked slowly the meat.
   (b) The maid carefully ironed the shirt.
   (c) The old guy forgot his umbrella to take.
   (d) The artist painted a very lovely picture.

The crucial condition for demonstrating knowledge of the ungrammaticality of verb-raising in English was for sentences of type (7a), the ungrammatical *SVAO pattern. The prediction was that if the findings from Lardiere (1998b) were indeed indicative of Patty's knowledge of this constraint (or feature-value) in English, then she would also correctly reject *SVAO sentences of the type shown in (7a). The motivation for asking her to provide correction for sentences she considered ungrammatical was to ensure she was disqualifying them for relevant reasons. As we shall see from the results presented in the next section, this component of the task turned out to be quite important.

Test 2

A second written follow-up test, Test 2, was administered 18 months later. This time Patty was asked to judge the items on a scale from '1' (unacceptable) to '5' (acceptable), and to provide a more acceptable version for any item she ranked '3' or lower. This test was also untimed and consisted of the same 40 items used a year-and-a-half earlier in Test 1, presented in reverse order, with the addition of five grammatical SVAP(reposition phrase) sentences of the type shown in (8a) interspersed among the other 40 items. The SVAP sentence type shown in (8a) was added because findings from previous research (White, 1991) had indicated that classroom francophone learners of English who were explicitly instructed on the ungrammaticality of *SVAO sentences (compare with (8b)) failed to distinguish these two sentence types; i.e. both were rated unacceptable.

8. (a) The child walked slowly to school.
   (b) *The child ate slowly her lunch.

In other words, as discussed in (White, 1991: 148–149) it appeared that the participants in White's study who were instructed on adverb placement in English were not able to differentiate between permissible adverb positions in sentences with transitive vs. intransitive verbs, and instead incorrectly overgeneralized aspects of their instruction to the SVA(P) word order. Moreover, although White's study showed that those learners who were explicitly instructed on adverb placement performed significantly better than those students who were not, a follow-up study conducted one year later showed that the effects of the instruction were apparently not retained: there was no significant difference between those students' original pre-test and follow-up test scores, as well as no significant difference between their follow-up scores and scores from an additional uninstructed group.

It is thus largely on the basis of White's results that it seemed necessary to add the SVAP sentences, to test whether Patty distinguished between sentences such as those in (8a) and (8b), and also to conduct a long-term follow-up study, to ensure that Patty's intuitions from the initial task (Test 1) were indeed stable (compare with Han, this volume: chap. 4). Additionally for Test 2, to help ensure its validity, 25 adult native-English speakers were added as a control group. These NS controls were also asked to provide more acceptable versions for any sentence they ranked at '3' or lower.

Again, the prediction was that if Patty had (stable) knowledge of the feature(s) related to verb-raising in English, as suggested by her naturalistic production data, she would correctly reject *SVAO sentences. Furthermore, if Patty had succeeded in acquiring a nativelike representation of verb-raising (and/or adverb placement) as opposed to, say, an overgeneralized learning strategy that simply prohibited post-verbal adverbs as White (1991) seems to have found, then we would also expect her to accept grammatical SVAP sentences while still rejecting ungrammatical *SVAO sentences.[6]

Results

Test 1

Recall that our expectation for Test 1 was that Patty would reject ungrammatical *SVAO sentences, in line with her naturalistic production data in which such sentences were never produced. The results strongly confirm this prediction, as she correctly rejected all 10 of these, a finding which converges completely with the results based on her spoken data reported in Lardiere (1998b). These findings indicate that for her, there is clearly no thematic verb-raising in English.

However, there is an interesting wrinkle in the results. For the grammatical SAVO sentences, Patty spontaneously created an intermediate category 'Y/N' to express a preference for postposing most of the manner adverbs to the end of the sentence, outside of the VP (which of course is also grammatical in English). For example, she rewrote grammatical sentences such as *The kids quickly finished breakfast* to *The kids finished breakfast quickly.* In correcting the ungrammatical *SVAO sentences, she also tended to place the adverb in sentence-final position; for example, a sentence like *The chef cooked slowly the meat* was rewritten to *The chef cooked the meat slowly* (instead of the expected *The chef slowly cooked the meat*). At the bottom of the test sheet, she provided the following notation:

9. 'Y/N = could be either way, prefer to put adverb at the end (conversation) & writing (modify noun) in the front.'

This notation reveals a quite sophisticated sensitivity to adverb placement in English. Even if the formulation of her metalinguistic 'rule' is a bit clumsy, Patty's intuition regarding a preference for manner adverbs to follow the VP is one that I as a native speaker of the variety of English she is exposed to would agree with. Interestingly, White (1991: 145) had also found that many students in the instructed adverb group of her study did the same, and so did her native speaker control group.

Even more striking, Patty (correctly) did not postpose those adverbs that resist such extraposition, such as *barely* or frequency adverbs like *always*; for example, her response to the test item *The receptionist always reads magazines* was a straightforward accept ('Y') and *The gardener wears always gloves* was marked 'N' and corrected to *The gardener always wears gloves.* The results indicate that Patty has acquired knowledge of the placement possibilities for different types of adverbs.[7] In sum, all grammatical SAVO sentences were judged as either 'Y' (='yes, OK') or 'Y/N'; none were rejected outright as all of the *SVAO sentences were.

Test 2

The results of the second test taken by Patty 18 months later confirmed the findings of the first. For the ungrammatical *SVAO items, Patty again correctly and decisively rejected all 10 of them (on the scale of 1–5, mean = 1). For every one of the 10 ungrammatical sentences, the native speakers' group mean score was <2, as expected. The native speakers' overall mean across all 10 *SVAO sentences was 1.49 on the scale of 1–5.[8]

For the grammatical SVAP sentences, Patty correctly judged these to be acceptable (mean = 4.8), clearly showing that she distinguishes between the ungrammatical *SVAO and the grammatical SVAP sentences. Her mean for the grammatical SAVO sentences was 3.7. Once again, Patty assigned the middle point on the scale ('3') to nearly the very same SAVO sentences she had 18 months earlier assigned her 'Y/N' rating in the first test, and again rewrote them with the adverb in the (also correct) sentence-final position. Thus, it appears from this consistency in her responses to both tests that the stability of her knowledge of English verb and adverb placement is not in doubt. For each of the grammatical SAVO and SVAP sentences, the native speaker group mean score was >4, as expected. Similar to what White (1991) reported, some of the native speakers also preferred adverb extraposition: 14 out of 16 NS responses rating a grammatical sentence as ≤3 rewrote the test item postposing the adverb to sentence-final position just as Patty had done. The overall native speaker mean for the SAVO sentences was 4.61, and for the SVAP sentences 4.59, on a scale of 1–5. The NS means for the grammatical SAVO and SVAP sentences were each significantly higher than that for the ungrammatical *SVAO sentences ($p < 0.001$ on paired t-tests).

Discussion

The results of both of the acceptability tasks converge with the production data reported in Lardiere (1998b), and allow us to draw the conclusion with some confidence that there is no optional verb-raising in Patty's grammatical representation of English, *contra* the predictions of the local impairment hypothesis. In this discussion section I would like to touch on two main issues, one primarily methodological, and the other concerning the possible role of persistent L1 influence in Patty's English idiolect.

Confirming a steady-state representation

As discussed in Long (2003) and Selinker and Han (2001), a claim of fossilization (more on the term *fossilization* below as it applies to Patty) must be based on longitudinal study of enough duration to demonstrate a persistent lack of change in (some area of) the learner's grammar. Of course, the duration of Patty's case-study meets this criterion, as do two other studies cited by Long (Han, 1998, 2000; Long, 1997). As mentioned in the introduction, the period over which both spoken and written L2 data have been collected for Patty now extends to approximately 16 years. The findings reported here were collected at two intervals 18 months apart, approximately 23 years after Patty's arrival in the United States and about 12 years after the first recorded interview which provided naturalistic spoken production data for the results reported in Lardiere (1998b). The follow-up period for Test 2 was six months longer than the one-year period after which White (1991) found that her study participants had 'reverted' to their pre-test knowledge status, suggesting that, unlike the subjects in White's study, Patty has clearly internalized the knowledge she has acquired of English in this regard. The durability of such convergent findings from different kinds of evidence over this length of time appears to provide us with a picture of real ultimate attainment in a particular L2 steady-state in a particular grammatical domain.

The main finding, of course, is that the similarity of the results across both tests 18 months apart indicates that Patty's knowledge of feature-strength (or whatever constrains verb-movement in UG) and of adverb placement in English is indeed remarkably stable. This similarity of results at each time period also provides some measure of reliability for the grammaticality judgment task (McDonough, 2001, 2002). Additionally, at least in this case, the exact nature of each task – namely, binary forced-choice vs. a five-point scale, appears not to have yielded different results, keeping in mind, however, that Patty added her own intermediate category for the binary choice task.

Finally, in this study, eliciting participant correction of perceived ungrammaticality has allowed us to see more clearly what motivated this intermediate category choice for Patty, opening a window onto additional information that reveals more about what she has actually acquired in English. For the native speaker controls, such correction allowed judgments for particular responses based on irrelevant factors (as revealed in the correction provided, see note 8) to be set aside, thus ensuring cleaner quality of the data.

Is Patty representing 'English' or 'Chinese'?

One of the main arguments of Lardiere (1998b) was that the productive acquisition of inflectional morphology on verbs was not directly linked to knowledge of feature-strength or verb-raising in the way argued for by Eubank, at least in Patty's case and most likely in general in SLA (see also some discussion in Lardiere, 2000). This is because, *contra* the predictions of either the valueless features or local impairment hypotheses mentioned earlier, Patty's rate of verbal inflectional marking was extremely low whereas associated syntactic properties as reflected, for example, in correct verb and adverb placement, were near-perfect. However, since Chinese has no verbal agreement inflection, and like English, disallows verb-raising, one might well ask if Patty isn't simply representing a Chinese-like grammar in her English idiolect, given that she produces almost no agreement inflection and categorically rejects verb-raising. There are several reasons to doubt this.

First, consider the findings from another recent study, that of Yuan (2001), who investigated optional verb-raising among L2 acquirers of Chinese at varying proficiency levels whose native languages were English, French or German. As might be expected, the native English speakers neither produced nor accepted raised verbs; however, neither did the native French or German speakers, whose L1s do raise verbs.[9] Not only did Yuan find that his study results also ran counter to the predictions of the valueless features and local impairment hypotheses, but there were no apparent L1 transfer effects, either. This of course is not to suggest that L1 influence plays no role at any point in the L2 acquisition of knowledge of verb-raising (compare with White 1990/1991, 1991, 1992a, who shows that it does), but Yuan concludes instead that such transfer is not inevitable, perhaps depending on the kind of positive evidence available in the input for whether verbs raise or not in the target language. Let us turn to consider such evidence.

For English, positive evidence is indeed available in the input and crucially is quite different from that in Chinese, such as the presence of *do*-support. It is clear that Patty has productively acquired *do*-support and thus could be expected to know consequently that thematic verbs do not raise in English:

10. (a) *we do not need to arrange any play date at all*
    (b) *I did not want to hurt your feeling*
    (c) *it doesn't stick anymore*
    (d) *did you watch Olympic?*
    (e) *didn't he know that it will get back to me?*

Patty also knows that, unlike thematic lexical verbs, finite forms of *be* do in fact raise over adverbs and NEG in English, as shown in the examples in (11) below from her data. Examples (11d–e) in particular contrast the position of *be* relative to adverbs with Patty's production of the same adverbs occurring with thematic verbs. Again this distinction is not available in Chinese.[10]

11. (a) *my family was not rich*
    (b) *she's not moving away*
    (c) *isn't it generous gift?*
    (d) *although it was never obvious* (compare with *his brother never came here*)
    (e) *because it is always there* (compare with *I always love to be a dancer*)

Finally, as observed above, Patty has acquired knowledge of placement possibilities for adverbs in English that are disallowed in Chinese. Some examples from the data are shown below in (12). In each case, the equivalent Chinese adverb could not appear in sentence-final position as they can in English.

12. (a) *there were some changes in my life recently*
    (b) *it was nice to hear from you finally*
    (c) *he did not try to do it anymore*
    (d) *J. told me afterward*
    (e) *cause his father drink a lot too sometime*

In sum, it is clear that Patty is not relying on a Chinese-type grammar but rather has acquired an English-like representation of the features governing verb-movement and adverb placement.

Conclusion: On 'Fossilization'

Finally, in conclusion, I would like to offer some thoughts on what it might mean to say that Patty's English has *fossilized*. The results from previous studies including Lardiere (1998b), taken together with the findings from this study, tell us that we certainly cannot speak of fossilization in any global sense. Patty's data show that in some respects her grammar clearly diverges from that of the native English speakers whose linguistic environment she shares and fully engages in. On the other hand, there are other aspects of her grammatical knowledge which do indeed appear quite nativelike, and hopefully, this study has contributed to more firmly establishing nativelike competence which may have otherwise been obscured by some across-the-board application of the term 'fossilization.'

Hawkins (2000) has referred to this sort of divergence and convergence in relation to native speaker grammars as 'persistent *selective* fossilization' (emphasis added). Although the characterization of fossilization as 'persistent' is perhaps obviously redundant, the point about selectivity is important and not as obvious or uncontroversial. Consider the following discussion in Long (2003), who would presumably disagree with Hawkins:

> ... Fourth, at what level does fossilization supposedly occur? What is the appropriate *unit of analysis*: the whole IL, the module, the linguistic rule, particular forms, words, meanings, collocations, form–function relationships, ranges of variation, all of these, or something else? ...
>
> Fifth, is fossilization a matter of *deviance* only, or, as might reasonably be supposed, of correct, nativelike rules and forms, too? A cognitive mechanism that could differentiate nativelike from non-nativelike elements and apply only to the latter requires some imagination. Yet, given that many target-like, as well as non-target-like, rules and forms are acquired early, even by ultimately unsuccessful learners, and remain unchanged 'permanently,' belief in such an uncannily sophisticated device is what acceptance of the construct entails. Conversely, positing that target-like forms fossilize, too, increases plausibility, but creates another problem, for what kind of cognitive mechanism could simultaneously apply and not apply to different structures, 'freezing' grammatical ones while allowing ungrammatical ones to continue to develop...? [emphasis in original]. (Long, 2003: 491–492)

However, Long's apparent reservations about 'fossilization' quoted above raise something of a strawman argument, resting explicitly on an unnecessary and incorrect premise that elevates and ascribes to fossilization the status of a theoretical 'construct' or, worse yet, a 'cognitive mechanism' or 'device'. (I suspect Long would agree with the 'unnecessary and incorrect' part.) In reality, there exists – to whatever extent this is true for a speaker of any language, native or not – a grammatical 'steady state' or 'endstate,' likely idealized from the researcher's point of view, that is the state of ultimate attainment. The 'cognitive mechanisms' are those that result in ultimate attainment of an I-language, regardless of whether this endstate is nativelike or not.

There are of course several ways in which the L2 endstate could differ from the NS endstate, including, for example, in the degree of variability vs. categoricalness in the representation and/or production of inflectional morphology. However, 'fossilization' as a theoretical construct can only be interpreted within the broader context of ultimate attainment, and certainly not as a cognitive mechanism. What we mean when we say that we would like to 'explain' fossilization is simply that we would like to account for why L2 endstates differ in some (clearly defined) respects from native speaker endstates, and from each other. Trying to account for that which is likely or not likely to fossilize is typically done post-hoc after observing what *has* fossilized, and must necessarily be informed by a reasonably accurate description of the grammar. The first step, however, which constituted one of the specific goals of this study, is to establish methodologically the likelihood of Patty's having actually arrived at 'ultimate attainment' in particular grammatical domains.

To claim that some area of the grammar has fossilized – and Long is absolutely right to insist on well-motivated and defined units of analysis upon making such a claim – is, in my view, simply a useful and convenient descriptive shorthand for indicating that some part of the L2 end-state grammar deviates in some particular ('selective') respect from that of a typical or idealized native-speaker and is unlikely to change. What makes the claim of *selective* fossilization (in the sense intended by Hawkins) interesting is its implicit commitment to the possibility or indeed likelihood of some type of modularity within the language faculty. In that sense, another goal of this study has been to establish such domains, or 'units of analysis.' The fact that Patty has been able to so perfectly acquire apparently nativelike knowledge in one domain (verb and adverb placement) despite considerable deviance from native-speaker norms in another (in her radical omission of verbal agreement morphology), indicates that these domains are probably not linked in the way that previous linguistic theory has suggested.

Notes

1. This chapter is based on a talk first presented at the Generative Approaches to Second Language Acquisition (GASLA) Conference at MIT, April 2000. I thank that audience as well as students in the Language Acquisition Seminar at Georgetown University for helpful comments and assistance, particularly Myong-Hee Choi and Joaquim Kuong.
2. In Lardiere (1998a) I reported that Patty's spoken production rate for past tense marking had remained stable at approximately 34% suppliance over a period of nearly nine years. This figure included irregular verbs and copula/auxiliary *be*, for which past tense marking rates were considerably higher than for regular verbs. See also Lardiere (1999, 2000) for some discussion of regular vs. suppletive verb inflection, and Lardiere (2003) for an analysis of past tense marking by individual verb type (which Long, 2003 refers to as verb 'token'; in contrast, I use 'token' to mean the number of instances of occurrence of each type).
3. Odlin (2003: 460) provides internet-attested examples of raised verbs over adverbs in English as in the following example: (i) Read *carefully* everything

received from the Office of Admissions. In cases such as these, however, the direct object is typically quite 'heavy' (as in this example as well). Note that the 'lighter' the direct object NP, the worse such adverb placement becomes: (ii) ??Read *carefully* the label. (iii) *Read *carefully* it.

Such 'heavy NPs' have traditionally been analyzed as requiring object-postposing (i.e. rightward adjunction) rather than verb-raising. Haegeman (1994) notes, 'A precise definition of the concept of heaviness has not been formulated, but the intuitive idea is clear' (p. 421).

4. Some important seminal research in verb and adverb placement in SLA was carried out by White (1989) under different theoretical assumptions, namely in terms of case adjacency within the context of the Subset Principle (following Stowell, 1981). Within this framework, francophone learners of English faced a learnability problem in that English – the more restrictive language, in subset terms – provided no evidence that could indicate the ungrammaticality in English of the *SVAO word order that is acceptable in French (compare with example (3c) in the text). In other words, there was no way on the basis of positive evidence alone for French speakers to de-learn their L1 word order.

5. An anonymous reviewer opines that Vainikka and Young-Scholten (1994, 1996) (cited above) 'have made an irresponsible claim about the non-transferability of functional projections' and cites research showing, for example, that there is a lot of empirical evidence for the positive transfer of functional elements such as articles from L1s that have them (Odlin, 2003: 461). I do not agree that their claim is 'irresponsible' (although I also don't agree with the assumptions on which their claim is based, as I have made clear elsewhere, e.g. Lardiere 1998a, 1998b, 2000). Rather, the claim of non-transferability of functional projections in the L2 initial state is an interesting and strong hypothesis subject to empirical disconfirmation. It is not clear to what extent the body of research cited in Odlin (2003) investigates L2 grammatical knowledge at the *initial state* or the earliest stages of L2 development. However, see also Schwartz and Sprouse's Full Transfer/Full Access Hypothesis (1994, 1996) and much related research in the L2-UG literature which specifically address Vainikka & Young-Scholten's claim.

6. Although not discussed in Lardiere (1998b), Patty's production data give no indication that she has any problem representing SVA(P) sentences, as indeed, she produces them, as shown by the examples in (i) below:

(i) a. *so I wrote and speak fluently in Indonesia*
   b. *I did so poorly in my math*
   c. *Chinese speak differently from English*

7. An anonymous reviewer points out that the post-positioning of manner adverbs could reflect a 'transfer-of-training effect' in that 'EFL teachers tend to teach their students to postpose adverbs.' Although this is possible, note that at the time Patty completed the grammaticality judgment tasks, she had not received ESL instruction in over 20 years. Moreover, as mentioned above, it is not clear how or whether such instruction on adverbs (if she ever received it – we simply do not know) would account for her intuitions about adverb placement according to the task or stylistic register (i.e. in

conversation vs. writing) and to what extent such instruction ('postpose adverbs') would differentiate among types of adverbs.

8. Native-speaker scores on test sentences which were rejected for irrelevant reasons, as revealed by the corrected revisions they provided, were not included in the calculation of means. For example, one native speaker gave a '2' rating to the test item 'The kids quickly finished breakfast' and corrected it to 'The CHILDREN quickly finished breakfast.'

9. An anonymous reviewer wonders whether the results for the native French and German speakers in Yuan's study might have been affected by their knowledge of English (if any). Yuan explicitly considers and rejects this possibility based primarily on two factors: first, the French and German speakers had only "limited" knowledge of English, particularly the French speakers 'most of whom had difficulty understanding English or communicating in English' (p. 267); second, since persistent optional verb raising had previously been found in particular for native French speakers acquiring L2 English (by White, 1990/1991, 1991), Yuan claims that native French speakers (at least) would be expected to show similar optionality in verb-raising in their (L3) Chinese if they were influenced by their (L2) English. However, such optionality was not found in any of the L1 language groups tested, including the native French speakers.

10. Chinese has a copula *shi* 'be' which is used in predicate nominal constructions. Note that the position of NEG is the same before *shi* as before thematic verbs, such as 'know' *zhidao* (examples from Li & Thompson, 1981: 422):

(i) women bu   zhidao ta   zai nar
     we   not   know   s/he at   where
     'We don't know where s/he is.'

(ii) ta   bu   shi   xiaozhang
     s/he not   be   school-chief
     'S/he is not the principal.'

References

Bobaljik, J.D. (2002) Realizing Germanic inflection: Why morphology does not drive syntax. *Journal of Comparative Germanic Linguistics* 6, 129–167.

Beck, M.-L. (1998) L2 acquisition and the obligatory head movement; English-speaking learners of German and the local impairment hypothesis. *Studies in Second Language Acquisition* 20, 311–348.

Chomsky, N. (1995) *The Minimalist Program*. Cambridge, MA: MIT Press.

Eubank, L. (1993/1994) On the transfer of parametric values in L2 development. *Language Acquisition* 3, 183–208.

Eubank, L. (1996) Negation in early German-English interlanguage: More value-less features in the L2 initial state. *Second Language Research* 12, 73–106.

Eubank, L., Bischoff, J., Huffstutler, A., Leek, P. and Wiest, C. (1997) 'Tom eats slowly cooked eggs': Thematic verb-raising in L2 knowledge. *Language Acquisition* 6, 171–199.

Eubank, L., Cliff, S., Collins, G., Ellis, M., Seo, E.-J., Tamura, A. and Yates, K. (1998) Grammaticality judgments and verb raising: if it feels good, raise it. Paper presented at the Second Language Research Forum (SLRF), University of Hawaii, October 1998.

Eubank, L. and Grace, S. (1998) V-to-I and inflection in non-native grammars. In M.-L. Beck (ed.) *Morphology and its Interfaces in L2 Knowledge* (pp. 69–88). Amsterdam: John Benjamins.

Haegeman, L. (1994) *Introduction to Government & Binding Theory*. Cambridge, MA: Blackwell.

Han, Z.-H. (1998) Fossilization: An investigation into advanced L2 learning of a typologically distant language. Unpublished doctoral dissertation, Birkbeck College, University of London.

Han, Z.-H. (2000) Persistence of the implicit influence of NL: The case of the pseudo-passive. *Applied Linguistics* 21, 55–82.

Hawkins, R. (2000) Persistent selective fossilization in second language acquisition and the optimal design of the language faculty. *Essex Research Reports in Linguistics* 34, 75–90.

Lardiere, D. (1998a) Case and tense in the 'fossilized' steady state. *Second Language Research* 14, 1–26.

Lardiere, D. (1998b) Dissociating syntax from morphology in a divergent L2 end-state grammar. *Second Language Research* 14, 359–375.

Lardiere, D. (1999) Suppletive agreement in second language acquisition. In A. Greenhill, H. Littlefield and C. Tano (eds) *BUCLD 23 Proceedings* (pp. 386–396). Somerville, MA: Cascadilla Press.

Lardiere, D. (2000) Mapping features to forms in second language acquisition. In J. Archibald (ed.) *Second Language Acquisition and Linguistic Theory* (pp. 102–129). Malden, MA: Blackwell.

Lardiere, D. (2003) Second language knowledge of [±past] vs. [±finite]. In J.M. Liceras, H. Zobl and H. Goodluck (eds) *Proceedings of the 6th Generative Approaches to Second Language Acquisition Conference (GASLA 2002)* (pp. 176–189). Somerville, MA: Cascadilla Press.

Lardiere, D. (in press) Knowledge of definiteness despite variable article omission in SLA. *BUCLD 27 Proceedings*. Somerville, MA: Cascadilla Press.

Lardiere, D. (forthcoming) *The Endstate Grammar in Second Language Acquisition: A Case Study*. Ms, Georgetown University (to be published by Lawrence Erlbaum).

Li, C.N. and Thompson, S.A. (1981) *Mandarin Chinese: A Functional Reference Grammar*. Berkeley, CA: University of California Press.

Long, M.H. (1997) Fossilization: Rigor mortis in living linguistic systems? Plenary address to the EuroSLA 97 Conference. Universitat Pompeu Fabra, Barcelona, May 1997.

Long, M.H. (2003) Stabilization and fossilization in interlanguage development. In C.J. Doughty and M.H. Long (eds) *Handbook of Second Language Acquisition* (pp. 487–535). Malden, MA: Blackwell.

McDonough, K. (2001) Investigating the reliability and validity of grammaticality judgment tests. Unpublished Ms, Georgetown University.

McDonough, K. (2002) Reconceptualizing the validity of grammaticality judgment tests. Paper presented at AAAL, Salt Lake City, UT, March 2002.

Odlin, T. (2003) Cross-linguistic influence. In C.J. Doughty and M.H. Long (eds) *Handbook of Second Language Acquisition* (pp. 436–486). Malden, MA: Blackwell.

Pollock, J.-Y. (1989) Verb movement, Universal Grammar and the structure of IP. *Linguistic Inquiry* 20, 365–424.

Schwartz, B.D. and Gubala-Ryzak, M. (1992) Learnability and grammar reorganization in L2A: Against negative evidence causing the unlearning of verbmovement. *Second Language Research* 8, 1–38.

Schwartz, B.D. and Sprouse, R.A. (1994) Word order and nominative case in nonnative language acquisition: A longitudinal study of (L1 Turkish) German interlanguage. In T. Hoekstra and B.D. Schwartz (eds) *Language Acquisition Studies in Generative Grammar*. Amsterdam: John Benjamins.

Schwartz, B.D. and Sprouse, R.A. (1996) L2 cognitive states and the full transfer/full access model. *Second Language Research* 12, 40–72.

Selinker, L. and Han, Z.-H. (2001) Fossilization: Moving the concept into empirical longitudinal study. In C. Elder, A. Brown, E. Grove, K. Hill, N. Iwashita, T. Lumpley, T. McNamara and K. O'Loughlin (eds) *Studies in Language Testing: Experimenting with Uncertainty* (pp. 276–291). Cambridge: Cambridge University Press.

Sprouse, R.A. (1998) Some notes on the relationship between inflectional morphology and parameter setting in first and second language acquisition. In M.-L. Beck (ed.) *Morphology and its Interfaces in Second Language Knowledge*. Amsterdam: John Benjamins.

Stowell, T. (1981) *Origins of Phrase-Structure*. Unpublished doctoral dissertation, Massachusetts Institute of Technology.

Vainikka, A. and Young-Scholten, M. (1994) Direct access to 'X'-theory: Evidence from Turkish and Korean adults learning German. In T. Hoekstra and B.D. Schwartz (eds) *Language Acquisition Studies in Generative Grammar*. Amsterdam: John Benjamins.

Vainikka, A. and Young-Scholten, M. (1996) Gradual development of L2 phrase structure. *Second Language Research* 12, 7–39.

White, L. (1989) *Universal Grammar and Second Language Acquisition*. Amsterdam: John Benjamins.

White, L. (1990/1991) The verb-movement parameter in second language acquisition. *Language Acquisition* 1, 337–360.

White, L. (1991) Adverb placement in second language acquisition: Some effects of positive and negative evidence in the classroom. *Second Language Research* 7, 133–161.

White, L. (1992a) Long and short verb movement in second language acquisition. *Canadian Journal of Linguistics* 37, 273–286.

White, L. (1992b) On triggering data in L2 acquisition: A reply to Schwartz and Gubala-Ryzak. *Second Language Research* 8, 120–137.

White, L. (2003) *Second Language Acquisition and Universal Grammar*. Cambridge: Cambridge University Press.

Yuan, B. (2001) The status of thematic verbs in the second language acquisition of Chinese. *Second Language Research* 17, 324–340.

Appendix

*SVAO test sentences:

(1) The girls played happily checkers.
(2) The doctor examined carefully Bob.

(3) The cat saw suddenly the bird.
(4) The students passed barely the exam.
(5) The teacher explained clearly the poem.
(6) The chef cooked slowly the meat.
(7) The secretary ate quickly lunch.
(8) The road workers stop often traffic.
(9) The woman recognized immediately the man.
(10) The gardener wears always gloves.

SAVO test sentences:

(1) The boys happily built a treehouse.
(2) The maid carefully ironed the shirt.
(3) The scientist suddenly realized the answer.
(4) The salesman barely caught the last flight.
(5) The witness clearly repeated her statement.
(6) The hikers slowly climbed the mountain.
(7) The kids quickly finished breakfast.
(8) The neighbor often mows the lawn.
(9) The waiter immediately brought some water.
(10) The receptionist always reads magazines.

SAVP test sentences:

(1) The child walked slowly to school.
(2) The police shouted harshly at the homeless guy.
(3) The students performed poorly on the test.
(4) The farmers prayed harder for some rain.
(5) The wife reacted immediately to the bad news.

Chapter 4

Fossilization: Can Grammaticality Judgment Be a Reliable Source of Evidence?

ZHAOHONG HAN

Key to any investigation of fossilization is to find a reliable way to *establish* that a steady state has been reached for interlanguage-particular features. Traditionally, researchers have sampled learners' naturalistic production data over an extended period of time (e.g. Han, 1998; Lardiere, 1998, this volume: chap. 3; Schumann, 1978). Few have resorted to experimental tasks (see, however, Long, 2003; Lardiere, this volume: chap. 3). Recently, however, White (2003) speculated that 'longitudinal data involving testing and retesting on a variety of experimental tasks would provide another means of determining whether or not a steady state has been reached' (p. 244). Much in alignment with the suggestion, this chapter reports on a seven-year longitudinal study of the reliability of grammaticality judgments. The study was designed to test out the grammaticality judgment (GJ) methodology as an alternative method of investigating fossilization. In the sections that follow, I first will review major arguments for and against the GJ methodology, isolating epistemological differences between naturalistic data and GJs. Then, I will examine a number of empirical studies of the reliability of the GJ methodology. After that, I will present my own study, which involves longitudinal cross-comparisons of elicited grammaticality judgments with naturalistic production data, and subsequently discuss its findings.

Grammaticality Judgments or Naturalistic Production

Throughout the history of SLA, the issue of what kind of data constitutes a valid basis for investigating interlanguages has been cause of much concern and controversy among researchers. For quite a long time, naturalistic production data were thought to be the only relevant data. Selinker (1972: 213), for example, suggested that researchers should focus their analytical attention on 'the only observable data to which [they] can relate theoretical predictions: the utterances which are produced when the learner attempts to say sentences of a language.' Many years later, Klein and Perdue (1997) still maintained that naturalistic (longitudinal) production data are the only window onto two kinds of systematicity inherent in interlanguages: *horizontal systematicity* (i.e. the internal systematicity of an interlanguage or a learner variety at a given time), and *vertical systematicity* (i.e. the systematic transition from one variety [of an interlanguage] to the next over time). Similarly, pointing to the 'chameleon-like' nature of interlanguages (Tarone, 1979), other researchers have argued that naturalistic data are a better reflection of an interlanguage in that they embody real-life conditions under which the interlanguage is used.

While earlier L2 studies saw an exclusive reliance on naturalistic production data for inferring systematicity, the goal for some researchers was gradually changed from understanding such systematicity to making claims about L2 competence. Influenced by Chomskyan theories of language and grammar, these researchers argued that an interlanguage is a natural language, and as such it has the dual dimension of performance and of competence (e.g. Adjemian, 1976). Under this view, naturally-occurring interlanguage production data pertain only to interlanguage performance, and hence are not an adequate manifestation of interlanguage competence. The premise of this view is that interlanguage competence is tacit, and as such, it needs to be probed through specially designed tests (see e.g. Schachter *et al.*, 1976). However, the question is: Are grammaticality judgments reliable?

Two decades ago, Chaudron (1983), after reviewing 39 studies employing or investigating the grammaticality judgments of native and non-native speakers, concluded that 'given appropriate controls and validation procedures, metalinguistic judgments can play a useful role in language acquisition studies' (p. 343), and thus that 'we would be doing ourselves a disservice to neglect them when attempting to expand our knowledge of language teaching and learning' (p. 372). Chaudron's conclusion, however, rather than eliminating doubts, served to accentuate the need for further examination. Indeed, in the ensuing years, researchers continued to investigate the reliability of the methodology, yet again offering mixed findings, to which I now turn.

Are Grammaticality Judgments Reliable?

Ellis (1991) addresses the issue of reliability through examining the theoretical assumptions underlying GJ tasks, taking as a point of departure the differences – revealed by published studies – in the results obtained from GJ tasks as opposed to from other, production-based tasks. The inquiry leads him to claim that grammaticality judgment tasks are, in nature, performance-oriented in that (a) learners adopt a variety of strategies to arrive at their answers – as if they were solving problems, and (b) learners' judgments display both inter- and intra-learner variation. To ascertain the basis of learner judgments, Ellis administered a grammaticality judgment task to 21 adult advanced Chinese learners of English to test their knowledge of dative alternation. A week later he administered a reduced version of the same test to eight of the subjects as a think-aloud task. The results showed that although the participants relied primarily on implicit knowledge when judging sentences – suggesting that grammaticality judgment tasks can be used to investigate competence – they were inconsistent in a considerable portion of their judgments, as a result of *erratically and inconsistently* using various strategies (i.e. using 'feel,' 'rehearsing,' 'rehearsing alternative version,' 'trying to access explicit knowledge,' 'using analogy,' 'evaluating a sentence,' and 'guessing'). Another relevant observation is that the participants made little use of the option of 'not sure,' which was given to them for coping with uncertainty; instead, they used a number of test-taking strategies to arrive at a definite judgment.

For Ellis, the use of strategies as a result of indeterminate knowledge invalidates grammaticality judgments. He argues that:

> A grammaticality judgment test may turn out to be a useful instrument in SLA research, but the confidence placed in it by some researchers is not yet justified. In particular, there is a need to recognize the problems that result from the way learners deal with indeterminacy and to find solutions to these problems. (Ellis, 1991: 181)

Since Ellis's study, there have been several other attempts to examine 'the way learners deal with indeterminacy.'

A noteworthy study is that of Davies and Kaplan (1998) which investigates if native speakers use the same strategies as non-native speakers when performing GJ tasks. Two versions of a grammaticality judgment task were created, one in the L1 and one in the L2, to ensure comparability. Data consisted of group oral protocols that participants generated while performing the tasks. Results of analyses showed an important difference in strategy use. Specifically, when operating in the L1, the participants used 'feel,' 'meaning-based,' 'repair,' and 'learned,' whereas they, in addition to these, used three more strategies when operating in the L2: 'translation,' 'analogy,' and 'guess.' Moreover, there was a difference in the rate of particular strategies. For example, in the L2 context, the participants used more 'learned' and 'meaning' than in the L1 context, where they predominantly used 'feel.' This difference, Davies and Kaplan argue, was due to the fact that in the L2 context, the participants experienced more indeterminacy when making judgments than in the L1 context. Thus, similarly to Ellis (1991), the erratic and inconsistent use of strategies was ascribed to uncertainty or indeterminate knowledge.

The crux of the reliability issue, then, lies in indeterminacy, which, as Sorace (1988) defines it, is 'the absence of a clear grammaticality status for particular linguistic constructions in the speaker's competence, and which manifests itself either in the speaker's lack of intuitions or in variability at the intuition level' (p. 166). Davies and Kaplan note that 'grammaticality judgements are not reliable if the subjects are faced with sentences for which they have indeterminate grammatical knowledge' (p. 199; compare with Gass, 1994). Interestingly, the researchers alluded to lack of proficiency as a potential source of indeterminacy:

> ... it is incumbent upon researchers using this methodology to demonstrate that the sentences subjects judge are not so far beyond the level of the subjects that indeterminacy becomes a debilitating factor and that the [subjects] are proficient enough in the L2 to ensure that the strategies used in rendering judgments parallel those used in judging their L1. (Davies and Kaplan, 1998: 200)

Two implications can be deduced from this statement. The first is that GJ tasks should be matched to subjects' proficiency. The second is that less than advanced learners are likely to exhibit indeterminate judgments, but that as their proficiency develops relative to a particular structure, their knowledge may show a gradual departure from indeterminacy, and a corresponding approximation to certainty.

This line of reasoning, though intuitively appealing, does not take account of two concerns. The first is what if indeterminacy persists into the very advanced stage, as shown in Sorace (1993, 2003; see also Johnson *et al.*, 1996), in which case are indeterminate judgements still considered unreliable? Related to the first, a second concern is what if indeterminacy is the norm, rather than a transient feature, of the interlanguage (compare with Adjemian, 1976). Would indeterminate judgments still be considered unreliable? Answers to these questions must be hard to come by, without any longitudinal studies.

Additionally, there is a third question to ask, namely, what is the source of indeterminacy (compare with Birdsong, this volume: chap. 9)? The discussion so far has assumed indeterminacy to be knowledge-related. But could it also be performance-related? Put differently, could indeterminate judgments be prompted by subject-external factors such as the format of the test, the instructions given to test takers, the lack of focus in test sentences, the nature of grammatical constructions tested, and order and length of presentation of test items (for a description of the design features or rather, sources of variation across GJ tasks, see Ellis, 1991; also Chaudron, 1983; Gass, 1994; Mandell, 1999; Sorace, 1996a)? Apparently, should any such externally driven indeterminacy arise, it would only be an artefact of the task.

Following from these concerns, it would seem necessary that researchers, when invoking indeterminate behaviors as evidence against the reliability of GJ tasks, tease out those that are induced by lack of knowledge from those that are artefacts of the tasks. As Gass (1994) aptly points out, 'what we want to know is which sentences actually represent those sentences that are part of a learner's grammatical knowledge and which ones do not' (p. 306).

GJ tasks can be reliable, as has been explicitly argued by some researchers. To illustrate, I will cite three empirical studies: Gass (1994), Leow (1996), and Mandell (1999), all of them exploring grammaticality judgments in contrast with production data. Gass's (1994) study employed a GJ task to test the prediction on a group of L2 learners of Keenan and Comrie's (1977) *Noun Phrase Accessibility Hierarchy*. The test was administered twice to the subjects with a one-week interval in between. On each administration, the subjects were first asked to provide a categorical answer and then assess the degree of confidence they had in their judgments. Statistical analyses of the judgments showed a significant correlation between Time 1 and Time 2. This, however, is just one facet of reliability. Additionally, Gass found that the reliability manifested itself as a function of relative clause positions. In particular, the subjects' judgments were the most consistent on the type of relative clauses that were the highest in the hierarchy, and less consistent on the ones that were lower. This result therefore largely matched the theoretical prediction.

Leow's (1996) study investigated two specific issues. The first is the correlation between grammaticality judgments and L2 production, and the second the correlation between grammaticality judgments and production of different modalities. Thirty undergraduate students of

Spanish were subjected to three tasks – a grammaticality judgment task, a written production task, and an oral production task – twice,[1] first in the third week and then in the 14th week of classes. For all three tasks, the researcher's linguistic target was noun–adjective/past participle agreement. Statistical analyses yielded significant correlations between the GJ and the production data at both times, thereby confirming Gass's (1994) finding of grammaticality judgments as a reliable reflection of L2 knowledge. Leow's study, moreover, provides evidence that 'modality may play a role in the relationship between grammaticality judgments and production tasks' (p. 135). Specifically, it was found that the subjects' grammaticality judgments correlated more with their written production data than with their oral production data.

In a similar thrust, Mandell (1999) examined the reliability issue by comparing GJ data with dehydrated sentence (DS) test[2] data from the same learners, considering the correlation between the two an indicator of reliability. A GJ test and a DJ test, targeting several V-movement-related syntactic properties in Spanish, were administered, in one packet, to 204 university students of L2 Spanish who were respectively in their second, fourth and sixth semester of study. The results revealed consistent and cross-sectional correlations between the two types of data, thereby showing that the GJ task did provide a reliable measure of interlanguage competence. This led Mandell to conclude that 'the grammaticality judgments of L2 learners, though indeterminate, are consistent' (p. 93).

In summary, research to date on the reliability issue of L2 grammaticality judgments have yielded mixed results. Nevertheless, it is clear that the incongruence stemmed, at least in part, from a difference in the approach adopted. Researchers who employed a process-oriented approach by *qualitatively* examining think-aloud protocols of test-takers have provided evidence that (a) learner judgments are different, in nature, from those of native speakers, (b) learner judgments tend to be indeterminate, and (c) learners tend to approach GJ tasks as if they were problem-solving tasks, hence using a variety of strategies including those that are not pertinent to the deployment of linguistic knowledge (e.g. guessing). On the other hand, evidence supporting the reliability of GJ tasks has been made available by researchers adopting what seems to be a product-oriented approach, that is, by *quantitatively* analyzing the judgments per se and validating them with other comparison measures (e.g. a production task). Clearly in favor of the latter approach, Chaudron (1983: 369) asserts that 'judgments should be validated by other measures on the same or comparable items and subjects,' and recommends that 'they be obtained as independently as possible from the judgment measures' (p. 369).

Researchers who use GJ tasks generally believed that the methodology allows for (a) a focused scrutiny on specific linguistic features, and (b) a determination of knowledge of what is, and more importantly, what is not, grammatical – a crucial index of the nature of L2 knowledge. For them, naturalistic data are inadequate for these purposes: during naturalistic production, learners can avoid producing structures they have difficulty with (Hyltenstam & Abrahamsson, 2003; Long, 1993; Schachter, 1974); by the same token, naturalistic production often involves limited use of a given grammatical structure. However, what the researchers seem to have failed to recognize is that that these limitations may be characteristic of 'synchronic' production (i.e. production at one point in time), and not of 'diachronic' production (i.e. production over an extended period of time). Indeed, any type of one-time data – naturalistically produced or elicited – are accidental in nature.

In their typical applications, GJ tasks are synchronic in nature; that is, they are administered to subjects once, at one point in time. In a few reported cases so far that attempted to examine the reliability of the methodology, researchers administered a GJ task more than once but with a relatively short time interval in between, in the range of weeks (see, e.g. Ellis, 1991; Johnson *et al.*, 1996), revealing much instability (inconsistency) of the interlanguage knowledge in question.[3] What remains to be seen is whether the picture can change when grammaticality judgements are studied over a significantly longer time scale of years, rather than weeks or months, and when the judgments are made by L2 advanced users. This line of inquiry,[4] I believe, may not only shed further light on the reliability of the GJ methodology but also on fossilization, one facet of a steady state.

In the study reported below, I adopted a longitudinal comparative approach whereby a grammaticality judgment task was administered twice – six years apart – and the data thereby elicited were compared with concurrent, naturalistic production data, the goal being to ascertain similarities and discrepancies both within and across the two types of data, at one time as well as over time. The research questions were as follows:

(1) Does the GJ task yield consistent results over time?
(2) Do the naturalistic production data yield consistent results over time?
(3) Do the GJ task and the naturalistic production yield consistent results at each time?

Method

Participants

This study is part of an on-going longitudinal inquiry into fossilization which was started in 1995 (Han, 1998, 2000). Participants were therefore the same two adult, male native speakers of Chinese, pseudo-named Geng and Fong, who served as subjects in Han (1998, 2000). In addition, one adult male native speaker of American English, pseudo-named Peter, served to provide the baseline data for the GJ test. As described elsewhere previously, Geng and Fong were both advanced users of English. By the first data collection for the present study, both had lived in an English-speaking country for five years, where they first studied for their doctorate and then worked as postdoctoral fellows. For personal and professional reasons, both were highly motivated to improve their English. Peter was, for several years, a colleague of Geng at a U.S. university.

Linguistic focus

The focus in the present study was on Geng and Fong's mental representations of English unaccusatives (e.g. *happen, arrive, occur, break*). The choice of this linguistic focus was largely motivated by a number of L2 studies (e.g. Balcom, 1995, 1997; Hirakawa, 1995, 1997; Hwang, 1997; Ju, 2000; Juffs, 1996; Montrul, 1999, 2000, 2001; Oshita, 2000, 2001; Sorace, 1993, 1995; Yip, 1995; Zobl, 1989) which, collectively, reveal a general tendency among L2 learners of English, regardless of their L1 backgrounds and levels of proficiency, to passivize unaccusatives,[5] as shown in [1] and [2] below:

[1] The accident *was happened* yesterday.
[2] I threw the plate against the wall, and it *was broken*.

[1] and [2] illustrate, respectively, the passivization of a non-alternating and an alternating unaccusative. [1] involves an unaccusative verb without a transitive counterpart, hence non-alternating (henceforth '[−T]'), and [2] an unaccusative verb with a transitive counterpart, hence alternating (henceforth '[+T]'). Each, as represented in [3], has an internal argument, Theme, which, as shown in [4], is encoded as the D-structure object, and under case-assigning constraints, moves to the subject position in the S-structure (Burzio, 1986).

[3] ((x))
     Theme
          (Grimshaw, 1990)

[4]   [$_{VP}$ V NP]
        (Burzio, 1989)

In the present study, I investigated whether or not the phenomenon of passivized unaccusatives (see [1] and [2] above) existed in Geng and Fong's L2 English, and if it did, whether or not it changed over time. Because the study was methodological in nature, here I will not provide a review of studies of L2 acquisition of unaccusatives (for review, see Montrul, 2001).

Procedure

Two types of data, grammaticality judgments and naturalistic production, were collected at two times over a period of seven years. First in September 1997, a GJ test (see description below) was administered individually to Geng, Fong, and Peter, and the test was repeated, six years later, in May 2003. For each administration, each participant was given 20 minutes to complete the test, on which they not only had to discriminate the stimulus sentences but also to locate and correct the perceived errors. Research has suggested that judging plus correcting offers a more sensitive measure of L2 competence than judging alone. While grammaticality judgments were collected at two times (hereafter Sample$_{GJ\ 1997}$ and Sample$_{GJ\ 2003}$), naturalistic written production data, which consisted of first drafts of academic papers and letters to friends, were also collected from Geng and Fong, thereby resulting in four sub-corpora of comparable size (mean = 20,000 words),[6] as follows:

Sample$_{naturalistic\ 1997}$ for Geng

Sample$_{naturalistic\ 2003}$ for Geng

Sample$_{naturalistic\ 1997}$ for Fong

Sample$_{naturalistic\ 2003}$ for Fong

The Grammaticality Judgment Test

The grammaticality judgment test used in the study was borrowed from Balcom (1997). The test contained 35 stimulus sentences, 20 of which were grammatical and 15 ungrammatical, showing inappropriate use of passive morphology. Among the 35 sentences, eight were included as distracters. Out of the 27 sentences containing unaccusatives, eight were unaccusatives (−T) and 19 were unaccusatives (+T)[7] (see Appendix A for the test).

Analysis

The GJ data were dual coded with a high inter-rater reliability (Cronbach's alpha = 0.92), and were subsequently subjected to the

McNemar test. The statistic was considered fit for addressing the first research question: the subjects served in this case as their own controls. With time an independent variable, and judgments a dependent variable, it was possible to calculate whether $Sample_{GJ\ 1997}$ and $Sample_{GJ\ 2003}$ were homogeneous or not. The significance level was set at $p \leq 0.05$. A statistically significant difference between the two samples would mean that a significant change had occurred from 1997 to 2003; otherwise, the change (if any) was negligible, indicating that the subjects' judgments had stabilized.

To address the second research question, the naturalistic production data ($Sample_{naturalistic\ 1997}$ and $Sample_{naturalistic\ 2003}$) were analyzed qualitatively, with the focus on identifying (a) passivized unaccusatives and their non-passivized counterparts, and (b) differences and similarities, at the level of types, between the two samples across time.

The third research question was addressed through a qualitative comparison between the GJ and naturalistic production data, the focus being on discerning, again at the level of types as opposed to tokens, how consistent the two types of data were at one time as well as across time.

Results

GJ test

Given in Tables 4.1, 4.2, and 4.3 below are tokens of Geng, Fong, and Peter's judgments on the GJ task in 1997 and 2003.

Table 4.1 Grammaticality judgments for Geng by time

Time	Passivized form			Non-passivized form	Total verbs
	Unacc. (+T)	Unacc. (−T)	Other		
1997	8	1	0	26	35
2003	14	1	2	18	35

Table 4.2 Grammaticality judgments for Fong by time

Time	Passivized form			Non-passivized form	Total verbs
	Unacc. (+T)	Unacc. (−T)	Other		
1997	13	0	0	22	35
2003	8	0	1	26	35

Table 4.3 Grammaticality judgments for Peter by time

Time	Passivized form			Non-passivized form	Total verbs
	Unacc. (+T)	Unacc. (−T)	Other		
1997	7	0	0	28	35
2003	6	0	0	29	35

As shown in Table 4.1, on the GJ test administered in 1997, Geng accepted nine passivized verbs, all of which were unaccusatives; on the test administered in 2003, he accepted 17 passivized verbs, 15 of which were unaccusatives. The McNemar test showed that a significant change ($p = 0.02$) had occurred from 1997 to 2003. This, however, is but a coarse-grained picture. A close scrutiny of the passivized verbs from each time reveals a strong stability, as can be seen in Figure 4.1.

In Figure 4.1, the upper panel of checks marked the verbs that were passivized. As shown, there was consistency over time such that the passivized verbs from 2003 overlapped – with the exception of one verb (i.e. *close*[a]) – with those from 1997.

Table 4.2 shows that in 1997, Fong accepted 13 passivized verbs, all of which were unaccusatives; in 2003, he accepted nine passivized verbs,

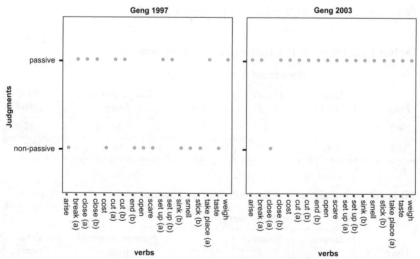

Note: (a) and (b) represent, respectively, the first and second time the verb appeared in the GJ stimuli.

Figure 4.1 Geng's passivized verbs in 1997 vs. 2003.

eight of which were unaccusatives. The McNemar test showed an insignificant but quite a meaningful change ($p = 0.21$) over time. Figure 4.2 provides a detailed comparative view on the passivized verbs. As shown in the upper panel in Figure 4.2, the number of passivized verbs went down from 1997 to 2003 for Fong, thereby indicating progress. But similarly to what we see in Geng's profile, eight of the 13 passivized verbs from 1997 remained unchanged in 2003, thus indicating considerable stability.

Turning now to Peter's profile, Table 4.3 shows that in 1997 he accepted seven passivized verbs, all of which were unaccusatives, and six in 2003.

The McNemar test shows neither a significant nor a meaningful change ($p = 0.00$) over time. Figure 4.3 gives a detailed comparative view of the passivized verbs. As shown in Figure 4.3, six of the seven passivized verbs in 1997 remained unchanged in 2003, thus indicating the stability of Peter's judgments over time.

Naturalistic production

The analysis of the naturalistic production data focused on identifying passivized unaccusatives and their non-passivized counterparts in Geng's and Fong's Sample $_{naturalistic\ 1997}$ and Sample $_{naturalistic\ 2003}$. Specifically,

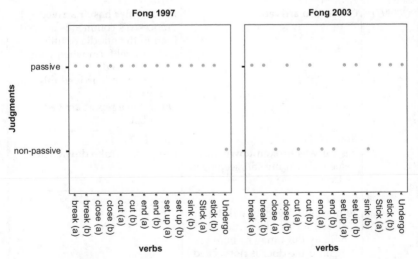

Note: (a) and (b) represent, respectively, the first and the second time the verb appeared in the GJ stimuli.

Figure 4.2 Fong's passivized verbs in 1997 vs. 2003.

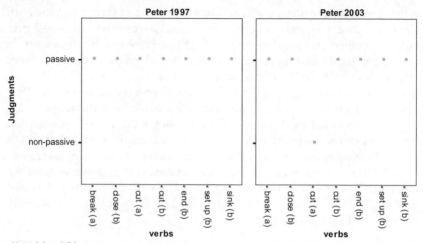

Note: (a) and (b) represent, respectively, the first and the second time the verb appeared in the GJ stimuli.

Figure 4.3 Peter's passivized verbs in 1997 vs. 2003

Table 4.4 Geng's naturalistic production

Time	Passivized unaccusatives	Non-passivized counterparts
Geng (1997)	*Arrive* (−T) Gas is also **arrived**.	*Arrive* (−T) Italian letter **hasn't arrived** yet. Francesco's commends arrived. I am in the middle of filling the travel form when your mail **arrived.** Our phone bill **arrived** this morning. Our referee report **arrived**, not bad.
	Break (+T) His car **was broken down** and spend $1000, but still sleeping in street	*Break* (+T) Feng's car **broke down** again.
	Close (+T) Tomorrow university **will be closed** for thanks giving holiday but I may be here again if the door is not locked.	

(continued)

Table 4.4 *Continued*

Time	Passivized unaccusatives	Non-passivized counterparts
	Pile (+T) I will wash my cloth after shopping, dirty cloths **are piled up**. Sorry for writing you now, as things **were piled up** after a long period of absence from the institute.	
Geng (2003)	*Disappear* (−T) Some of them are from outsiders against ON-web, but we have two level protection there, i.e. IIS itself and ISS. Relay event against Listserv **is** now **disappeared**, I expect the same will happen with ON-web	*Disappear* (−T) This info might be distributed among Spammers. We expect that this **will** gradually **disappear**.
	Stop (+T) Thanks to John's blocking, the event **were stopped** after 3/7/03. For last two days the listsv database was not refreshed, Jobs **were stopped**.	*Stop* (+T) The action already **stopped** on 1/6 probably after receiving our mail. (1/03) It turns out that OPS **stopped** during the weekend. Since the service **stopped** on the server and ISS reported the clients contact as suspicious WWW activities. It could be that B.I **stopped** due to the reboot process. Most of Unicode-Translation were done by 345.236.101.25. Many servers were among the targets, but the event **stopped** within a few hours on 5/27, probably after failed attempts.

verbs in finite forms were examined, yielding the results displayed in Tables 4.4 and 4.5.

As shown in Table 4.4, both Sample $_{naturalistic\ 1997}$ and Sample $_{naturalistic\ 2003}$ provided evidence of Geng passivizing unaccusatives. Similarly, evidence

Table 4.5 Fong's naturalistic production

Time	Passivized unaccusatives	Non-passivized counterparts
Fong (1997)	*Close* (+T) Fanta is expanding at present (close connection with ACDB). But it **may be closed down** in future, and I have to prepare for the worst because I stay in a company not a university. Recently a big steel manufacture compnay **was closed** here and lots of workers lost their job the country's industry is hopeless. But as you know, every company **may be closed** in future.	
	Change (+T) I am rather busy since my family joined me. My routine timetable **is changed**. My thinking way **has been changed** a lot since joining Fanta. I am reforming my mind recently. At least the presonal views on some issues **is being changed**.	
	Improve (+T) Anyway, I believe that my background **will be improved** to a significant extent becuase I am reponsible for the development of a medium package. My background **has been** highly **improved** since I joined Fanta.	
	Increase (+T) If Fanta's revenue **is** consectively **increased**, it will be on the stock market.	
Fong (2003)	*Eject, Freeze, Cool* (+T) When a part (midplane/fusion/3D model) **is ejected** before it **is** completely **frozen** (some hot unfrozen spots exit), the current calculation method in the midplane/fusion does not use free-quenching approach. The mechanism of free-quenching part is very different from the residual stress build-up in the constrained part if the fluid inside **is** gradual **frozen and cooled down**.	

(continued)

Table 4.5 *Continued*

Time	Passivized unaccusatives	Non-passivized counterparts
	The algorithm is carried on with the assumption that the part remain constrained in the mould when the part **is cooled down** from ejecting temperature to room temperature.	
	Improve (+T) My English **was not improved.** What I am working on at the moment is to filter these noise. After several days' work, the results **are improved.**	
	Increase (+T) Number of nodes **will be increased** by 6–7 times when the tetrahedral elements are upgraded from the first order form to the second-order form.	
	Prove (+T) For typical-size of shell models, the direct solver **is proved** very effective.	
	Slow (+T) However, if the virtual memory is used, the speed **will be slowed down** significantly.	

was found of passivized unaccusatives in Fong's Sample $_{\text{naturalistic 1997}}$ and Sample $_{\text{naturalistic 2003}}$, as shown in Table 4.5.

Discussion

The study set out to examine the reliability of GJ data for the ultimate purpose of finding an alternative route to investigating fossilization. To that end, synchronic and diachronic comparisons were carried out of GJ data and naturalistic production data. To its first research question (i.e. *Does the GJ test yield consistent results over time?*), the study appears to have generated an affirmative answer, as explained below, case by case.

First of all, for Geng, there was a significant change from Sample$_{\text{GJ 1997}}$ to Sample$_{\text{GJ 2003}}$. Thus, on the face of it, there was little consistency between the two samples. However, a closer look focusing on the passivized unaccusatives did show a great deal of consistency. Among other things, the passivized verbs in Sample $_{\text{GJ 1997}}$ stayed unchanged in Sample$_{\text{GJ 2003}}$, thereby showing the stability of Geng's knowledge vis-à-vis *those* unaccusatives.

Second, although Fong's Sample$_{GJ\ 1997}$ and Sample $_{GJ\ 2003}$ revealed a meaningful change vis-à-vis passivized unaccusatives, it was also noted that, as in Geng, some of the passivized verbs in Sample$_{GJ\ 1997}$ remained unchanged in Sample $_{GJ\ 2003}$. This thus likewise constitutes evidence for the stability of Fong's knowledge of *those* unaccusatives.

Third, Peter's Sample$_{GJ\ 1997}$ and Sample$_{GJ\ 2003}$ offered the most revealing evidence of consistency. As reported earlier, statistically, there was no change between the two samples. Nearly all that was accepted as grammatical in 1997 remained so in 2003.

It may be recalled from the earlier review of studies that lack of consistency, which is generally considered a manifestation of indeterminate knowledge (Ellis, 1991), has been a major source of doubts about the reliability of grammaticality judgments. Following that same logic, consistency between Sample$_{GJ\ 1997}$ and Sample$_{GJ\ 2003}$ should be taken as evidence for the reliability of grammaticality judgments. In some sense, this study corroborates Davies and Kaplan's (1998) hypothesis, namely that as proficiency grows, indeterminacy decreases. As described in the earlier section 'Participants,' both Geng and Fong were advanced users of L2 English and their length of residence in an English-speaking environment had exceeded five years. By the 'criterion' posited in the SLA literature (see, e.g. DeKeyser, 2000; Johnson & Newport, 1989; Oyama, 1976), Geng and Fong had been in the L2 environment long enough for their L2 grammars to reach their end state. But the question is: Has such a state indeed been reached?

The results have shown that in terms of unaccusatives, the two grammars, while displaying long-term (i.e. at least seven years) stability, exhibited idiosyncratic changes over time. Specifically, Geng's Sample$_{GJ\ 2003}$ manifested deterioration in knowledge in that he accepted more passivized unaccusatives than he did in Sample$_{GJ\ 1997}$. Thus, extended exposure did not seem to have led to any knowledge improvement. Fong's Sample$_{GJ\ 2003}$, on the other hand, showed that he accepted fewer passivized unaccusatives, thereby suggesting progress. Thus, based on the GJ data alone, one tentative conclusion we can draw is that part of the subsystem (i.e. unaccusatives) in the two grammars reached its end state and part of it did not, an issue to be discussed later in the section. For now, let us turn to the second research question: *Does the naturalistic production yield consistent results across time?*

As reported earlier in the 'Results' section, both Geng and Fong passivized unaccusatives in 1997 and 2003; there was therefore at least a broad consistency over time. This said, it is worth noting that the number of passivized unaccusatives was rather low for both Geng and Fong (see

Tables 4.4 and 4.5), considering the size of the data samples. It would be mistaken, however, to interpret this as Geng and Fong having largely acquired the unaccusatives, with the few passivized ones only being residual. For one thing, the low number was attributable to the uncontrolled nature of naturalistic data. In the mode of naturalistic production, the discourse topics could dictate the use of some linguistic constructions to the exclusion of others, and even when the discourse itself compels the use of a particular type of linguistic construction, one always has the option of not producing it – 'avoidance' in Schachter's (1974) term. Thus, as Long (1993: 209) cautions, 'it would be unwarranted to assume either (a) lack of knowledge on the basis of non-use, or (b) that error-free performance on what the learner did say or write can be interpreted as nativelike competence in all unobserved domains, as well.' With that in mind, I should like to argue (a) that the few passivized unaccusatives notwithstanding, Geng and Fong's acquisition of unaccusatives was item-based rather than rule-based (for discussions of the two types of learning, see Birdsong & Flege, 2001; Ellis, 1999; Pinker, 1999; Skehan, 1998), and (b) that they had not fully acquired the underlying semantic and syntactic constraints. Both of my arguments will become clear as we discuss the third research question: *Do the GJ task and the naturalistic production yield consistent results at each time?*

Findings from the study show that there was an overall consistency between the GJ samples and the naturalistic production samples for both Geng and Fong at each time. Geng's Sample$_{GJ\ 1997}$ and Sample$_{GJ\ 2003}$ both show that he accepted passivized unaccusatives (+T; −T), and that for certain verbs, he variably accepted the passivized and the non-passivized form. This corresponds with his Sample$_{naturalistic\ 1997}$ and Sample$_{naturalistic\ 2003}$ (see Table 4.4). For example, in his Sample$_{GJ\ 1997}$, Geng was seen variably accepting [5a] and [5b], and similarly, in his Sample$_{naturalistic\ 1997}$, he produced [6a] and [6b]:

[5a] The bottle **was broken** when Bill threw it on the road.
[5b] The glass **broke** when the child dropped it on the floor.

[6a] His car **was broken down** and spend $1000, but still sleeping in the street.
[6b] His car **broke down** again.

Fong's Sample$_{GJ\ 1997}$ and Sample$_{GJ\ 2003}$, on the other hand, consistently indicate that his passivized unaccusatives were restricted to unaccusatives (+T). While this was corroborated by his Sample$_{naturalistic\ 1997}$ and Sample$_{naturalistic\ 2003}$, the latter two provided additional passivized unaccusatives (+T) to those exhibited on the GJ test (see Table 4.5). Of note also is that in spite of the broad consistency, Fong's acceptance and use of unaccusatives exhibited intra-task variability. For instance, his Sample$_{GJ\ 1997}$ shows that he variably accepted [7a] and [7b], as does his Sample$_{GJ\ 2003}$, as in [8a] and [8b]:

[7a]   The boat **sank** when it hit an iceberg near Newfoundland.
[7b]   The ship **was sunk** when the captain crashed it onto the rocks.

[8a]   The door **closed** quietly because the hinges were well-oiled.
[8b]   The door **was closed** smoothly because Mary had remembered to oil the hinge.

Interestingly, the intra-task variability, which shows that Fong's knowledge was not well-defined with regard to these unaccusatives, was consistently unattested in Fong's Sample$_{Naturalistic\ 1997}$ and Sample$_{Naturalistic\ 2003}$. This, in my view, bears out the inadequacy of naturalistic data which I commented on earlier.

In summary, a broad consistency, or rather, systematicity, was observed for (a) the GJ data over time, (b) the naturalistic production data over time, and last but not least, (c) the two types of data at each time, which attests to the reliability of the GJ task. However, some issues remain that warrant further discussion. In the remainder of the section, I will discuss two: indeterminacy and end state, both having high relevance to research on fossilization.

Indeterminacy

The intra-task variability noted above, albeit concerning individual unaccusatives, gives evidence of indeterminacy. Importantly, that the variability was seen at both times (i.e. 1997 and 2003) for Geng and Fong suggests that indeterminacy *as a phenomenon* may fossilize in the interlanguage (compare with Sorace, 1996b, 2003). This finding creates problems for Long's (2003) view that stability and variability must be mutually exclusive, and that if fossilization is an outcome of long-term stabilization, then it must not exhibit variability (compare with Birdsong, this volume: chap. 9). What the current study has shown is that variability can stabilize and possibly fossilize.

The observed stabilized variability also invites a re-evaluation of the prevailing suspicion of the GJ methodology that ties lack of consistency with lack of reliability. Lack of consistency may be the norm of inter-language, and as such, it speaks nothing to the reliability of the GJ methodology. Indeed, as Schachter *et al.* (1976) long noted, determinacy and indeterminacy are both a natural part of the interlanguage system. In this conceptualization, the lack of consistency documented in the earlier GJ studies could, in fact, be a true, as opposed to an unreliable, reflection of the status of L2 knowledge. This, of course, is a far more complex issue than a few lines of discussion can do justice to. Clearly, further empirical studies are warranted.

Another finding from the current study that is worth discussing here concerns Peter's performance on the GJ test. As shown in Table 4.3 and Figure 4.3, Peter, a native-speaker of American English, accepted seven passivized unaccusatives (+T) in 1997 and six in 2003. What is of relevance to note is that unlike Geng and Fong, whose judgements seemed highly dichotomous and clear-cut,[8] Peter's judgments appeared to be 'indeterminate'; he seemed to simultaneously tolerate both passivized and non-passivized forms vis-à-vis a few alternating unaccusatives ('+T'). An example is given in [9a, b].

[9a] Prompt
The bottle **was broken** when Bill threw it on the wall.

[9b] Peter's response
'This is possibly true and is grammatical, although it's far more likely that' "The bottle broke when Bill...."'

Such kind of 'indeterminacy' was entirely consistent through Peter's Sample$_{GJ\ 1997}$ and Sample$_{GJ\ 2003}$, giving a robust enough reason to raise a larger theoretical question: Are all linguistic structures appropriate targets for GJ tests? It is by now a well-accepted understanding that linguistic structures can differ from one another in terms of their formal and/or semantic complexity, and of their dependence on discourse context (see, e.g. DeKeyser, 1994; Hulstijn, 1995; Schmitt & Zimmerman, 2002; VanPatten, 1996). Yet, as noted earlier, standard GJ tests typically comprise decontextualized stimuli. As such, they may not be sensitive to mental representations of those linguistic structures whose grammaticality is context-dependent (compare with Chaudron, 1983; Sorace, 1996a; 2003). When those structures are detached from their required contexts, as were the unaccusatives (+T) in the GJ test in the current study, they evoke ambivalence. Following from this line of reasoning, a non-differentiated use of GJ tests can potentially be a source of lack of reliability.

End State

An issue brought up earlier was whether or not the L2 grammars of Geng and Fong had reached an end state. Judging from the GJ data, both Geng and Fong's knowledge of unaccusatives appeared to be in a state of flux: Geng exhibited deterioration and Fong exhibited progression. This, however, was the picture obtained through a quantitative analysis; a qualitative look at each passivized verb indicated that some passivized unaccusatives had undergone no change over time. Thus, it can be claimed that the subjects' knowledge of those had reached an end state (i.e. they had fossilized). Another facet of the end state can be seen in the fact that Geng's passivization of unaccusatives consistently involved U (+T) and U (−T) while Fong's was confined to U (+T) (see Tables 4.1, 4.2, 4.4, and 4.5), although both Geng and Feng variably accepted and used, simultaneously and over time, the passivized and non-passivized forms for certain unaccusatives (see Figures 4.1 and 4.2). The intra-subject variable performance can be interpreted such that the subject's knowledge of those unaccusatives was as yet non-categorical and might still undergo restructuring. Thus, it appears that even within a subsystem (e.g. unaccusatives), it is possible that part of it fossilizes, and part of it may still be open to change, in a target-like or a non-target-like direction. This kind of evidence falsifies two popular assumptions in SLA research: the first is that five years of length of residence in a target-language environment defines the L2 end state. The second is that just as there is a global end state for first language acquisition, there is one for L2 development (passim the SLA literature on maturational constraints and L2 ultimate attainment; see also discussion in the first chapter). I should argue, based on the findings from this study and a growing number of others, that linguistic properties are unequal in L2 learning, hence their differential outcomes. L2 development, therefore, defies a global end state, but compels local end states, some of which conform to the target, and some of which deviate from it (i.e. fossilize).

Conclusions

The study reported above, by virtue of its multi-way comparison of GJ and naturalistic production data, demonstrates that the GJ methodology is a viable alternative for studying fossilization. In terms of tapping into L2 knowledge of English unaccusatives, the GJ data appeared to be more sensitive and effective than the naturalistic production data inasmuch as they provided a more sophisticated picture. One clear example is that the GJ test identified that Geng and Fong had a greater problem with unaccusatives (+T) than with unaccusatives (−T). Another example is that Fong's GJ data, but not his naturalistic production data, provided evidence of the indeterminacy of his knowledge of unaccusatives (+T).

Indeterminacy, as I have argued, can be a true reflection of the status of L2 knowledge, rather than a threat to the reliability of the GJ methodology. Nevertheless, this should not be taken for granted without a careful examination of the source of indeterminacy. As the present study revealed, indeterminacy may stem from lack of pertinent knowledge, or it may be an artefact of the design of a GJ task (compare with Sorace, 1996). Clearly, it should be the latter that speaks to the reliability issue, not the former.

As may be recalled, Ellis (1991) discussed a number of common problems with the design of GJ tasks, viewing them as sources of lack of reliability. To his list, the present study adds one more problem, namely that the across-the-board application of the standard format of GJ tasks to any linguistic structure may induce indeterminate judgments. In particular, providing isolated stimulus sentences, while sufficient for the linguistic structures that can be reliably judged in isolation (e.g. U [−T]), may nevertheless be inadequate for others that must be judged in context (e.g. unaccusatives [+T]). Judging the latter in isolation evokes ambivalence or forces the subjects to conjure up their own contexts, thereby giving the false impression of indeterminacy. 'The importance of context for certain kinds of constructions is often underestimated,' as Sorace (1996a: 377) has aptly noted.

The view on linguistic structures as unequal predicts that there are differential end states vis-à-vis different parts of the interlanguage system (and its subsystems). Thus, for each and every individual L2 learner or user, there is not likely to be a global end state, as generally assumed in the SLA literature; rather, there can be multiple local end states to be reached at different points in time, with some showing fossilization (i.e. incomplete acquisition) and others complete acquisition (compare with Han, 2004; Han & Odlin, this volume: chap. 1; Lardiere, this volume: chap. 3).

Notes

1. The procedures were similar with only a few minor changes at the second time such as randomizing the order of items on the GJ task.
2. A dehydrated test, also known as a slash-sentence test, is typically composed of constituents separated by slashes, and subjects are required to combine them to construct what they consider to be acceptable sentences.
3. Sorace (1996a) notes also that a short time interval may potentially produce a learning effect in the subjects.

4. Chaudron (1983) offers a similar view on the necessity to study 'the development or operation of an individual's metalinguistic awareness' (p. 346).
5. The studies, in fact, noted a distinct pattern vis-à-vis L2 acquisition of two types of intransitive verbs, unergatives and unaccusatives: learners across various L1 backgrounds have no difficulty mastering unergatives, but they do acquiring unaccusatives, with passivized unaccusatives one of many manifestations thereof.
6. Because the focus of my data analysis was not on identifying context-induced differences in output/production, I collapsed the two types of writings into one general (sub) corpus for each subject.
7. Included in this category were also middle constructions (e.g. *This bread cuts easily when it isn't frozen solid*). For discussion of English middles, see Levin and Rapport Hovav (1995) and Bassac and Bouillon (2002).
8. On the GJ task, the subjects were offered three options: (1) correct, (2) incorrect, and (3) not sure. With the exception of one instance, Geng and Fong's responses were dichotomous and certain (compare with Ellis, 1991); that is, they only chose between (1) and (2). Sorace (1996a) offers the insight that determinate judgments may entail *Divergence*, and indeterminate judgments *incompleteness*. Indeed, both divergence and incompleteness were implicated in Geng's and Fong's judgments, with the former seen in some of their consistent yet deviant judgments, and the latter in their variable judgments.

References

Adjemian, C. (1976) On the nature of interlanguage systems. *Language Learning* 26 (2), 297–30.

Balcom, P. (1995) Argument structure and multi-competence. *Linguistica Atlantica* 17, 1–17.

Balcom, P. (1997) Why is this happened? Passivized morphology and unaccusativity. *Second Language Research* 1, 1–9.

Bassac, C. and Bouillon, P. (2002) Middle transitive alternations in English. In P. Boucher (ed.) *Many Morphology* (pp. 29–47). Somerville: Cascadilla Press.

Burzio, L. (1986) *Italian Syntax*. Dordrecht: Reidel.

Chaudron, C. (1983) Research in metalinguistic judgments: A review of theory, methods and results. *Language Learning* 33, 343–377.

Davies, W. and Kaplan, T. (1998) Native speaker vs. L2 learner grammaticality judgements. *Applied Linguistics* 19 (2), 183–203.

DeKeyser, R. (1994) How implicit can adult second language learning be? *AILA Review* 11, 83–96.

DeKeyser, R. (2000) The robustness of critical period effects in second language acquisition. *Studies in Second Language Acquisition* 22, 499–533.

Ellis, R. (1991) Grammaticality judgments and second language acquisition. *Studies in Second Language Acquisition* 13, 161–186.

Ellis, R. (1999) Item vs. system learning: Explaining free variation. *Applied Linguistics* 20 (4), 460–480.

Gass, S. (1994) The reliability of second-language grammaticality judgements. In E. Tarone, S. Gass and A. Cohen (eds) *Research Methodology in Second-Language Acquisition* (pp. 303–322). Hillsdale, NJ: Lawrence Erlbaum Associates.

Grimshaw, J. (1990) *Argument Structure.* Cambridge, MA: The MIT Press.

Han, Z.-H. (1998) *Fossilization: An Investigation into Advanced L2 Learning of a Typologically Distant Language.* Unpublished doctoral dissertation. Birkbeck College, University of London.

Han, Z.-H. (2004) *Fossilization in Adult Second Language Acquisition.* Clevedon: Multilingual Matters.

Hirakawa, M. (1995) L2 acquisition of English unaccusative constructions. *Proceedings of BUCLD* 19, 291–302.

Hirakawa, M. (1997) On the unaccusative/unergative distinction in SLA. *JACET Bulletin* 28, 17–27.

Hwang, J.B. (1997) Implicit and explicit instruction for the L2 acquisition of English unaccusative verbs. Ms, University of Oregon.

Hulstijn, J. (1995) Not all grammar rules are equal: Giving grammar instruction its proper place in foreign language teaching. In R. Schmidt (ed.) *Attention and Awareness in Foreign Language Learning* (pp. 359–386). University of Hawaii at Manoa: Second Language Teaching & Curriculum Center.

Hyltenstam, L. and Abrahamsson, N. (2003) Maturational constraints in SLA. In C. Doughty and M. Long (eds) *Handbook of Second Language Acquisition* (pp. 539–587). Oxford: Blackwell.

Johnson, J. and Newport, E. (1989) Critical period effects in second language learning: The influence of maturational state on the acquisition of English as a second language. *Cognitive Psychology* 21, 60–99.

Johnson, J., Shenkman, K., Newport, E. and Medin, D. (1996) Indeterminacy in the grammar of adult language learners. *Journal of Memory and Language* 35, 335–352.

Ju, M. (2000) Overpassivization errors by second language learners: The effects of conceptualizable agents in discourse. *Studies in Second Language Acquisition* 22, 93–123.

Juffs, A. (1996) *Learnability and the Lexicon: Theories and Second Language Acquisition Rresearch.* Amsterdam: Benjamins.

Keenan, E. and Comrie, B. (1977) Noun phrase accessibility and Universal Grammar. *Lingusitic Inquiry* 8, 63–99.

Klein, W. and Perdue, C. (1997) The basic variety (or: couldn't naturalistic languages be much simpler?). *Second Language Research,* 13 (4), 301–347.

Lardiere, D. (1998) Dissociating syntax from morphology in a divergent l2 end-state grammar. *Second Language Research* 14 (4), 359–375.

Leow, R. (1996) Grammaticality judgment tasks and second-language development. *Georgetown University Round Table on Languages and Linguistics* (pp. 126–139). Washington, DC: Georgetown University Press.

Levin, B. and Rappaport Hovav, M. (1995). *Unaccusativity at the Syntax-Lexical Semantics Interface.* Cambridge, MA: The MIT Press.

Long, M. (1993) Second language acquisition as a function of age: Research findings and methodological issues. In K. Hyltenstam and Å. Viberg (eds) *Progression and Regression in Language* (pp. 196–221). Cambridge: Cambridge University Press.

Long, M. (2003) Stabilization and fossilization in interlanguage development. In C. Doughty and M. Long (eds) *The Handbook of Second Language Acquisition* (pp. 487–536). Oxford: Blackwell.

Mandell, P.B. (1999) On the reliability of grammaticality judgement tests in second language acquisition research. *Second Language Research* 15, (1), 73–100.

Montrul, S. (1999) Causative errors with unaccusative verbs in L2 Spanish. *Second Language Research* 15, 191–219.

Montrul, S. (2000) Transitivity alternations in L2 acquisition: Toward a modular view of transfer. *Studies in Second Language Acquisition* 22, 229–273.

Montrul, S. (2001) (ed.) Representational and developmental issues in the lexico-syntactic interface: Acquiring verb meaning in a second language. *Studies in Second Language Acquisition* 23 (2).

Oshita, H. (2000) What is happened may not be what appears to be happening: A corpus study of 'passive' unaccusatives in L2 English. *Second Language Research* 16, 293–324.

Oshita, H. (2001) The unaccusative trap in second language acquisition. *Studies in Second Language Acquisition* 23 (2), 279–304.

Oyama, S.C. (1976) A sensitive period for the acquisition of a nonnative phonological system. *Journal of Psycholinguistic Research* 5 (3), 261–283.

Schachter, J. (1974) An error in error analysis. *Language Learning* 24, 205–214.

Schachter, J, Tyson, A. and Diffley, F. (1976) Learner intuitions of grammaticality. *Language Learning* 26, 67–76.

Selinker, L. (1972) Interlanguage. *International Review of Applied Linguistics* 10 (2), 209–231.

Skehan, P. (1998) *A Cognitive Approach to Language Learning.* Oxford: Oxford University Press.

Schmitt, N. and Zimmerman, C. (2002) Derivative word forms: What do learners know? *TESOL Quarterly* 36 (2), 145–171.

Schumann, J. (1978) *The Pidginization Process: A Model for Second Language Acquisition.* Rowley, MA: Newbury House.

Sorace, A. (1988) Linguistic intuitions in interlanguage development: The problem of indeterminacy. In J. Pankhurst, M. Sharwood Smith and P. Van Buren (eds) *Learnability and Second Languages: A Book of Readings* (pp. 167–190). Dordrecht: Foris.

Sorace, A. (1993) Incomplete vs. divergent representations of unaccusativity in non-native grammars of Italian. *Second Language Research* 9 (1), 22–47.

Sorace, A. (1995) Acquiring linking rules and argument structures in a second language: The unaccuasative/unergative distinction. In L. Eubank, L. Selinker and M. Sharwood Smith (eds) *The Current State of Interlanguage: Studies in Honor of William E. Rutherford* (pp. 153–176). Amsterdam: John Benjamins.

Sorace, A. (1996a) The use of acceptability judgments in second language acquisition research. In W. Ritchie and T. Bhatia (eds) *Handbook of Second Language Acquisition* (pp. 375–412). New York: Academic Press.

Sorace, A. (1996b, May) Permanent optionality as divergence in non-native grammars. Paper presented at *EUROSLA 6*, Nijmegen.

Sorace, A. (2003) Near-nativeness. In C. Doughty and M. Long (eds) *The Handbook of Second Language Acquisition* (pp. 130–152). Oxford: Blackwell.

Tarone, E. (1979) Interlanguage as Chameleon. *Language Learning* 29 (1), 181–191.

VanPatten, B. (1996) *Input Processing and Grammar Instruction: Theory and Research.* Norwood, NJ: Ablex.

White, L. (2003) Fossilization in steady state l2 grammars: Persistent problems with inflectional morphology. *Bilingualism: Language and Cognition* 6, 129–141.

Yip, V. (1995) *Interlanguage and Learnability: From Chinese to English.* Amsterdam: John Benjamins.

Zobl, H. (1989) Canonical typological structures and ergativity in English L2 acquisition. In S. Gass and J. Schachter (eds) *Linguistic Perspectives on Second Language Acquisition* (pp. 203–221). Cambridge: Cambridge University Press.

Appendix

Grammaticality Judgement Task (Balcom, 1997)

Read the following sentences. Put a (in the brackets beside the sentences which you think are grammatical. Put an X in the brackets beside the sentences which you think are NOT grammatical. Put a ? in the brackets if you are not sure. For all of the sentences you marked with an X, provide a correct version in the space provided. You will have 20 minutes to complete this task.

(1) The child underwent the operation, even though it was expensive.

(2) The gum stuck to the wall where Mary had placed it.

(3) The results pleased the students, although the professor was unhappy.

(4) These events were taken place after she had registered at the university.

(5) The test scared the students, although they were well-prepared.

(6) The riot occurred after the police officers had been acquitted.

(7) The package was weighed 6 kilograms, although Mike had removed one book.

(8) The door closed quietly because the hinges were well-oiled.

(9) The students met with many adventures while they were travelling.

(10) This story took place before the couple got married.

(11) The bottle was broken when Bill threw it on the road.

(12) Osmosis is occurred when solvents diffuse into a more concentrated solution

(13) The door was closed smoothly because Mary had remembered to oil the hinges.

(14) A verb ends with the suffix 'ed' when the action is in the past.

(15) This bread cuts easily when it isn't frozen solid.

(16) These socks were smelled bad before Jim washed them.

(17) Many people like their coffee before they get out of bed.

(18) The boat sank when it hit an iceberg near Newfoundland.

(19) The problem arose because no one was responsible for checking for errors.
(20) This tent sets up easily when you follow the instructions.
(21) This soup was tasted good after the cook had added some salt.
(22) This dress was only cost $40, because Janet bought it on sale.
(23) Many teachers experience feelings of anticipation before they meet their students.
(24) The fight was happened because they had too much to drink.
(25) This meat was cut easily when Jane used a sharp knife.
(26) The accident happened because they driver forgot to stop.
(27) Pronouns are ended with the suffix '-self' when they are reflexive.
(28) This stereo system is set up easily once you have read the instructions.
(29) Some children fear monsters when they are alone in bed.
(30) The key will open the door if you insert it properly.
(31) 3The glass broke when the child dropped it on the floor.
(32) The ship was sunk when the captain crashed it onto the rocks.
(33) The poster was stuck to the wall when Susan put it there.
(34) These scissors won't cut the paper because Mary didn't sharpen them.
(35) The disagreement was arisen after Stella borrowed John's car.

Chapter 5
Fossilization in L2 and L3

TERENCE ODLIN, ROSA ALONSO ALONSO and
CRISTINA ALONSO-VÁZQUEZ

Two of the classic problems of second language acquisition, transfer and fossilization, have often been considered in isolation from each other, but few if any researchers in either area would fail to acknowledge that the two research problems are interdependent. In fact over a decade ago Larry Selinker (1992) posited an explicit linkage between fossilization and transfer, and he formulated a Multiple Effects Principle in the following terms:

> It is a general law in SLA that when two processes work in tandem, there is a greater chance for stabilization of forms leading to possible fossilization. (Selinker, 1992: 262)

In addition, he postulated the following corollary: 'In every instance of the multiple effects principle, language transfer will be involved' (1992: 263). In a reconsideration, Selinker and Lakshmanan (1993) acknowledge that there are possible strong and weak versions of this corollary, the latter formulated accordingly: 'language transfer is a *privileged* co-factor in setting multiple effects' (1993: 198, emphasis in the original). If this contention of Selinker and Lakshmanan is correct, we should expect there to be a wealth of relevant examples.

Yet however many instances we may hope to find, we still have to acknowledge that many theoretical and methodological issues arise in the study of transfer as well as of fossilization. With no pretense of trying to address all of those issues, this chapter focuses on the following two research questions: (1) What parallels are there in second and third language acquisition with regard to the problems of transfer and fossilization? (2) What methodologies are appropriate to study the acquisition of tense and related verb categories?

Before considering the specific problems that our research addresses, we will also state our assumptions concerning fossilization. Long (2003) has noted an ambiguity common in the way second language researchers use the term 'fossilization,' in that it can indicate either a product (or, explanandum) or a process (or, explanans) or both. Our chapter focuses on a structure that might be considered fossilized (and thus a product): the present perfect, where the target language is English, and with the other languages relevant to the study being Spanish and Galician. The English present perfect is appropriate to study in relation to fossilization since, as Bardovi-Harlig (2001) observes, it is a structure that emerges relatively late in acquisition. Indeed, it is arguably a structure that many learners never succeed in acquiring. Before further discussion of the perfect in English, however, it will be necessary to discuss similar considerations with the perfect in a bilingual situation in Spain where there is likewise evidence that the perfect might be viewed as a structural area where the notion of fossilization is relevant. Later in the chapter we will return to the distinction made by Long and address the problematic notion of fossilization in relation to transfer.

Bilingualism in Galicia

For many learners in Spain as in the central region of Castile, English is a second language, but for many in other regions it is a third language as in the area of northwest of Spain known as Galicia. The traditional language of this area, Galician, is distinct from Portuguese and from Castilian (which is more commonly called Spanish), although all three languages belong to the Iberian subfamily of Romance languages. For about a century many Galicians have been learning Spanish as a second language, which not surprisingly takes on a distinctive shape in Galicia (Hermida, 2001). The widespread acquisition of Spanish indicates that the overall sociolinguistic environment is changing, and both the social and the structural characteristics of the local Spanish fit the pattern that Thomason and Kaufman (1988) denote with the term 'shift.' Many people who regard themselves as Galicians now use Spanish as their primary language, according to Hermida, although many others still speak Galician as their first language, with yet another sizeable part of the population considering themselves equally proficient in both languages. The great similarity of Castilian and Galician makes at least a passive bilingualism rather easy to attain. In research cited by Hermida, 97% of the Spanish speakers surveyed in the region report having a good comprehension of Galician and some 86% report a similar proficiency in spoken Galician. A smaller number, however, report having Galician as their first language: 60% of the total population, and only 36% of the generation aged 16 to 25 (a clear indicator of the pattern of language shift).

Although Galician has some constructions comparable to the perfect of Castilian (C), the present perfect is conspicuous by its absence as in the following Galician (G) sentence:

(1)   G: non che estuvo nunca en Lugo
        Not dative (I) was-1st never in Lugo

      = C: nunca he estado en Lugo
          never I have been in Lugo

      = I have never been in Lugo (Carballo Calero, 1979: 286)

The dative pronoun *che* in the Galician should not be confused with the auxiliary *he* in the Castilian translation given by Carballo Calero. From a historical point of view transfer has made the Galician variety of Spanish distinctive. One study of written language in the region (Goyanes *et al.*, 1996) notes that the difference between simple and periphrastic tenses in Galician and Castilian leads to errors in the latter due to influences from the former. Thus in a Castilian sentence where the perfect is the norm, a variant common in Galician Spanish uses instead the simple past:

(2) Ricardo Portabales se paseó [past simple] esta semana por Vigo. (Spanish outside of Galicia: Ricardo Portabales se ha paseado [present perfect] esta semana por Vigo. ('Ricardo Portabales has put in an appearance this week in Vigo.')

Although it is possible to argue that such use of the past simple is merely the outcome of a process of 'simplification,' Jarvis and Odlin (2000) cite evidence to support the likelihood that when a structure in the interlanguage is compatible with a structure in the native language, simplification and transfer actually work in tandem. Along with structural patterns that mirror the Galician substrate, there are cases of hypercorrection in which the present perfect is used but where a past simple would be the norm in Castilian:

(3) Tales escritos se han enviado [present perfect] en días pasados. (Spanish outside of Galicia: Tales escritos se enviaron [past simple] hace unos días. 'Such writings were sent some days ago.')

Apart from the hypercorrect perfect in #3, there is also, we should note, something that appears to be more a Galician expression of time than a Castilian: *en días pasados*. Goyanes *et al.* give no information as to how fluent in Galician the writers were, and so it is not necessarily the case that these sentences are interlanguage productions. That is, the authors might have been monolingual speakers of Spanish living in Galicia. However, one plausible interpretation of the facts is to say that the infrequent use of the present perfect in Galicia reflects an incomplete acquisition of Castillian norms and thus reflects a widespread stabilization that contributed to the current characteristics of Spanish as used in Galicia. A similar analysis is necessary to explain certain structures common in Hiberno-English, the vernacular of Ireland greatly influenced by Irish Gaelic. Although it would be fatuous to talk about transfer and stabilization in the speech of monolinguals, their English does show characteristics that resulted from the widespread acquisition of English in the 19th century (compare with Filppula, 1999).

Some might argue that cases of language shift in places such as Galicia and Ireland are irrelevant to the study of second language acquisition. Dulay and Burt (1974), for example, claimed that language contact situations such as those studied by Weinreich (1953/1968) are different in kind from second languages. Their claim of a difference in kind is mistaken, however. First, Weinreich made no such distinction in his study of transfer (which he called 'interference'), and he cited quite a few studies where second language acquisition had helped shape the patterns of bilingualism found (Odlin, 1989). Second, when a region undergoes language shift and becomes bilingual, the first stages of the shift invariably entail second language acquisition, and the effects of transfer seen in the second language acquisition of early generations often linger well beyond the period when the bilinguals can be viewed as non-native speakers of one of the languages in the contact situation; indeed, the effects can linger into a period where the bilingualism disappears, and the shift to a monolingual community has been completed (Odlin, 1997, 2003a).

One limitation of the current study is that we did not focus on the degree of bilingualism of the Galician students who took part in our research project. We assume, however, that most had at least a passive knowledge of both Galician and Castilian (as Hermida's discussion of surveys of bilingualism, as noted above, makes clear that passive bilingualism is nearly universal). We also assume that the bilingual environment helps to account for the differences seen in their performance in comparison with Castilian students in Madrid, regardless of whether the Galicians were fluent in both Castilian and Galician or whether their competence in either language was non-native. As will be seen, there are indeed differences between the performance in Galicia and Madrid with regard to the English perfect.

Stabilization and the English Perfect

Like Castilian Spanish – yet unlike Galician or Galician Spanish – English makes considerable use of both the present and past perfect. Yet the similarity of English and Spanish does not mean that speakers of Castilian Spanish have no problems with the English perfect, as the following example from a Spanish speaker shows:

> By the time I reached the Art Museum, the noise from the street *has gone* from us. We contacted our guide, and our outside class began ... (Bardovi-Harlig, 2001: 243, emphasis in the original)

In both English and Castilian the perfect is something of a semantic hybrid. Comrie (1976) lists four meanings common in English and some other languages using the perfect: result (*He has arrived*), experience (*Bill has been to America*), persistent situation (*I've shopped there for years*), and perfect of recent past – also known sometimes as 'hot news' (*Bill has just arrived*). The present tense of the *have* auxiliary suggests a current state of affairs whereas the perfective form of the verb suggests either completion or location in the past (or both). The phrase 'current relevance' is often used to characterize perfect constructions although the pragmatic conditions of such relevance may not always be transparent. The four meanings given by Comrie also are evident in the Castilian perfect although current relevance will often be expressed with an ordinary present tense (e.g. *Vivo aquí*, literally, 'I live here') instead of the perfect (*He vivido aquí* 'I have lived here'). The semantics of the perfect in the two languages are thus not identical, but even where a similarity could lead to positive transfer, there are other factors that might impede learners taking advantage of the similarity, and some of those factors will be discussed later in this chapter. Apart from production errors, another manifestation of the difficulty of the perfect might arise from a problem of comprehension of the special meanings of the perfect. Even so, it is the difficulty of producing the perfect that seems to be more salient in the observations of teachers.

Unless difficulties of using the perfect in speech and writing are overcome, the structure is an area where stabilization (and possibly fossilization) can occur. In the longitudinal research of Bardovi-Harlig, speakers of Arabic, Japanese, Korean, and Spanish all had difficulties with the present perfect, and while all the learners in the investigation had begun to use the perfect in the 15-month duration of the study (and often use it accurately), there is no indication that any had achieved complete mastery. Indeed, one Japanese learner (TO) was producing more errors in the later months than in the earlier months (2001: 248). Although any strong claim about fossilization would be unwarranted in view of the background of the learners and the duration of the study, the findings in the Bardovi-Harlig investigation make it natural to wonder just how many learners ever do acquire a fully accurate use of all of the meanings of the perfect.

Teachers in Galicia likewise have the impression that the perfect is an exceptionally difficult area for their students. However, in contrast to the developmental focus in the research of Bardovi-Harlig, transfer is emphasized. Conversations we have had with teachers suggest that many of them assume, correctly or not, that the present perfect in Castilian fosters positive transfer and the scarce use of the structure in Galicia contributes to negative transfer. Research on the use of the perfect by Spanish-speaking learners does not give unequivocal support to assuming transfer, however. At least two studies (Russell & Snow, 1977; Heckler, 1983) indicate little if any positive transfer from the perfect in Spanish although there have also been claims that positive transfer occurs (Espinoza, 1997). One empirical study of bilingual speakers of Spanish and Quechua (Klee & Ocampo, 1995) indicates the use of present and past perfect verb phrases in Spanish that reflect a semantic influence from the evidential category of Quechua verbs. While this study cannot be construed as a case of positive transfer, it nevertheless shows that periphrastic perfect tenses are, as Schachter (1993) terms it, a 'domain' subject to interlingual identifications and thus to language transfer. Moreover, research by Collins (2002) on the use of the English perfect by L1 French learners indicates positive and negative transfer from the native language, which frequently uses perfect constructions.

Clearly, the issue of transfer and the perfect is an empirical one, and our study may offer some support for both transfer and developmental approaches to research on the acquisition of tense, aspect, and other categories of the verb. Our analysis suggests that incomplete attainment of the perfect (and thus a possible instance of fossilization) may arise from difficulties learners have in noticing the necessary semantic and pragmatic conditions that warrant the present perfect. Moreover, such difficulties of noticing seem to be related to cross-linguistic influence. If our analysis is correct, it suggests an interaction between stabilization and transfer similar to what is envisioned in Selinker's Multiple Effects Principle.

Testing and the Present Perfect

Apart from the theoretical question of whether transfer is involved at all, there is the practical question of a methodology to get at the verification problem: how can we elicit occasions for learners to use – or not use – the perfect? The difficulty arises largely from the hybrid nature of the perfect in English. On the one hand a sentence such as *Sally has been in Cairo* indicates an event that happened in the past, yet on the other hand, it suggests some 'current relevance' as discussed in the preceding section. The challenge for test makers therefore lies largely in trying to provide discourse contexts where the perfect will be much more likely than either the past simple or the present simple tense. Providing such contexts for a production task is by no means easy, however. One possible elicitation device might be to try to elicit a specialized use of the perfect, such as what Comrie (1976) calls 'the experiential perfect.' A test developer might try, for instance, to ask learners to speak or to write about cities or countries they have visited. However, it is easy enough to describe such experiences with little or no use of the present perfect (or the past perfect). Although the two sentences *I have been in Cairo* and *I was once in Cairo* are not totally synonymous, either one would certainly meet the demands of an essay prompt asking for discourse about personal experiences. [Bardovi-Harlig (2001) discusses advantages of naturalistic data but also acknowledges the difficulty of comparing individual learners' performances.]

If elicitation of natural discourse is unpromising, the only recourse seems to be some kind of test that provides contexts which are uniform for all learners and which are numerous enough to compare performances of different groups. Accordingly, the elicitation device we have used in this study is a passage correction exercise, essentially a kind of proofreading test that allows investigators to choose the kind of errors they wish to insert in a paragraph or longer passage. This testing format has proved valid for other investigations (e.g. Odlin, 1986), and it enabled us to construct a passage in which there were several obligatory uses of the present perfect.

Sample Errors

PR item: From the twentieth century onwards, archeologists <u>find</u> a wide variety of prehistoric artifacts such as stone tools and pottery in a variety of sites on the island. (Correct: <u>have found</u>)

PA item: No doubt the Ice Age glaciers that once <u>covered</u> most of the British Isles <u>made</u> it nearly impossible now to <u>detect</u> human remains or artifacts before the Mesolithic. (Correct: <u>have made</u>)

Distractor: Although Gaelic <u>is</u> <u>spoke</u> on Tiree even now, the language <u>is</u> much more widely <u>used</u> in the Outer Hebrides. (Correct: <u>spoken</u>)

The passage that we wrote specifically for this test had about 550 words and about 60 verbs. Twenty errors, all involving verbs, were then inserted in the passage. Ten of the errors replaced uses of the present perfect with present tense (items PR 1–5) and past tense verbs (items PA 1–5). An example of each kind of item appears in the boxed inset. Ten other errors did not involve the perfect at all but served two purposes: (1) to distract test takers from thinking only about uses of the perfect, and (2) to get an estimate of the relative proficiency of the groups taking the test, an estimate that would be independent of their performance on the perfect. The errors in the distractors involved problems such as number agreement and irregular verb forms as in the one seen in the boxed inset. The passage described the current state of the Hebrides Islands in Scotland, as this topic allowed for frequent uses of the present perfect. To create contexts where the perfect was obligatory, we sometimes used adverbials and sometimes other structures to make the discourse context one having 'current relevance.' The test had the five dozen verb phrases underlined, and test takers were instructed not to correct anything other than verbs. They were given nearly an hour to make 20 and, they were told, only 20 corrections.

Two groups in Spain took the test, along with one group of 18 native speakers of English in the United States; in all three groups the individuals were university students generally in their early twenties. One group in Spain consisted of 28 more or less bilingual in Galician and Spanish (whether the variety of Castile or of Galicia), while the other group, with 46 students, knew Castilian but not Galician.

Predictions

We made the following predictions:

(1)   The Galician group would have greater difficulty than the Castilian group in attempting corrections of errors involving the present perfect.
(2)   There would be differences between the Galicians and Castilians in their ability to detect and change errors where the present perfect was replaced with an anomalous use of the past tense. That is, we expected that the Galicians would have an especially hard time with items PA 1–5.
(3)   Native speakers of English would perform more successfully in attempting to change errors involving the present perfect as well as other errors in the test.

It should be noted that the first two predictions do not consider whether or not the attempts of learners are successful but instead whether they attempt corrections involving the present perfect and whether they attempt any correction at all. In effect, we were more interested in ascertaining how aware learners were of semantic and pragmatic conditions warranting the present perfect than we were in how accurate the actual corrections were.

Scoring

Our scoring procedures naturally reflect our predictions. We tallied any and all cases of where test takers attempted a correction involving the present perfect, which we defined as any form of a *have* auxiliary plus a main verb, whether or not the auxiliary showed appropriate number agreement or whether the verb was in a standard perfective form (i.e. the so-called past participle). Thus, for example, we counted both *has encouraged* as well *have encouraged* as uses of the perfect in attempts to correct the tense problem in . . . *schools in the Hebrides encourage the use of the [Gaelic] language in the last twenty years* . . . , even though only the latter change (*have encouraged*) is completely accurate. We scored each of the 10 items not only for whether it showed an attempt at using the perfect but also for whether it showed any attempt to change the error at all. The scoring of the distractors was somewhat different in order to give a clear sense of the relative proficiency of the three groups. Each answer was distinguished in terms of whether or not it was a completely acceptable correction. There was also a count similar to those for items involving errors with the present perfect as to whether any attempt to correct the error was made.

Results

Table 5.1 indicates that native speakers had little difficulty in spotting the problems in the distractor items or in making acceptable changes. There was a statistically significant effect in a one-way analysis of variance for items successfully corrected as the dependent variable ($F = 31.23$, $p < 0.01$), and post-hoc tests (Tukey HSD) showed the inter-group differences significant in all cases ($p < 0.05$). In other words, the evidence indicates that the native speakers were more proficient than the non-natives, and it also indicates that the Galician group was more proficient than the Castilian. The native speakers in this study were mainly undergraduate English majors taking an upper-division course in the structure of the English, and it is an open question as to whether other native speaker groups would have similar success with the distractors.

Table 5.2 corroborates such evidence about proficiency as it shows that the native speakers very rarely ignored the errors in the distractors (even though not every attempt they made to correct the problem was successful). In contrast, both the Galician and Castilian groups had considerable difficulty with the items, although there was also a great deal of individual variation. In any case, there was also a statistically significant effect for items completely ignored as the dependent variable ($F = 27.28$, $p < 0.01$), and post-hoc tests (Tukey HSD) again showed the inter-group differences significant in all cases ($p < 0.05$). As with

Table 5.1 Successful corrections of distractor items

Galicians (n = 28)	Castilians (n = 46)	Native speakers (n = 18)
55% (162)	42% (197)	90% (162)

Table 5.2 Cases of *no* attempted correction of any kind on distractor items

Galicians (n = 28)	Castilians (n = 46)	Native speakers (n = 18)
24% (68)	36% (165)	3% (6)

Table 5.1, Table 5.2 indicates both that the native speakers were more proficient than the non-natives and that the Galician group was more proficient than the Castilian (with their greater proficiency perhaps explainable in terms of their majors: languages in the case of the Galicians, and economics in the case of the Castilians). While it might seem preferable to have two non-native groups with the same proficiency, the greater general proficiency of the Galicians will be shown to corroborate the evidence for transfer discussed in relation to Table 5.4.

Table 5.3 gives results relevant to the first prediction, indicating attempts at using the present perfect. Contrary to what we expected, the Galicians did somewhat better than the Castilians, who did not attempt more corrections of the errors of either kind; furthermore, while the native speakers did make somewhat more attempts at using the perfect, the total of 35% is hardly different from the performance of the two non-native groups. It should be noted, however, that some of the attempts of both the non-native and the native speakers to change errors used other corrections besides the present perfect. In some cases these attempts were successful, while in some they were not. In any event, relatively few of the attempts to correct errors employed a present perfect verb phrase.

Despite the infrequent use of the perfect, Table 5.3 does show something consistent with our expectations: namely, the striking difference in the Galicians' attempts to use the perfect in items PR 1–5 and items PA 1–5. Items PR 1–5, it will be recalled, were those in which the error inserted was a present simple tense in a context calling for the present perfect, while items PA 1–5 were those in which the error inserted was a past simple in a context calling for the present perfect. In other words, the errors where the Galicians attempted fewer changes involving a perfect were those compatible with the infrequent use of the perfect in the Spanish of Galicia, where a past simple is the tense used where Castilian and English would use a present perfect construction.

Table 5.3 Attempted corrections using perfect verb phrases. Percentages (with raw figures in parentheses)

	Items PR 1–5	Items PA 1–5	Total
Galicians ($n = 28$)	42% (59)	22% (31)	32% (90)
Castilians ($n = 46$)	27% (63)	21% (48)	24% (111)
N. speakers ($n = 18$)	46% (41)	24% (22)	35% (63)

Table 5.4 Cases of *no* attempted correction of any kind on items where the present perfect would be acceptable. Percentages (with raw figures in parentheses)

	Items PR 1–5	*Items PA 1–5*	*Total*
Galicians ($n = 28$)	31% (44)	57% (80)	44% (124)
Castilians ($n = 46$)	37% (84)	41% (94)	39% (178)
N. speakers ($n = 18$)	14% (13)	46% (42)	31% (55)

Table 5.4 also shows results consonant with the second prediction. Despite their greater proficiency in English (as seen in more successful corrections of distractors), the Galicians made fewer attempts than did the Castilians to correct errors involving items PA 1–5, that is, the substitution of a past tense form for a present perfect verb. On a repeated-measures analysis of variance with item type (PR and PA items) as the dependent variable and group (Galicians and Castilians) as the independent variable, there was a statistically significant effect ($F = 12.23$, $p < 0.01$) for item type and also for the interaction of group with the item type $F = 5.76$, $p < 0.02$). In other words, problems in PA items proved harder to detect, and there was a significantly greater difficulty for the Galicians as opposed to the Castilians in detecting the problems in PA items. What is especially interesting in these results is the fact that the results involving the distractor items (Tables 5.1 and 5.2) indicate that the Galicians were more proficient than the Castilians overall. Nevertheless, cross-linguistic influence from Galician or from Galician Spanish (or from both) seems to have made it much harder (as stated in Prediction 2) for the Galician group to notice problems with PA items.

The native speakers showed behavior partly congruent with the third prediction and partly divergent. On the one hand, they frequently attempted corrections of errors involving the substitution of a present tense form (PR items), but on the other hand, they also resembled the Galicians in attempting relatively few changes of items PA 1–5.

The biggest surprise in our results is clearly how the native speakers did. Part of this unexpected turn can probably be attributed to the demands of the test itself. To note the problems of items PR 1–5 and PA 1–5, test takers have to pay very close attention to the discourse constraints. Yet along with the attention problem, variation in native speaker norms is perhaps an even more important factor. Although the NS group seemed very tolerant of the errors in items PA 1–5, their tolerance is actually comparable to the results of a study by Sheen (1984). In our study exactly half of the native speakers made no attempt of any kind to correct item PA 1, which appears in the boxed inset. The use of the adverb *now* indicates that a situation that still holds true. yet only half the NS group attempted to change the verb tense (and in this case, all the changes happened to be acceptable). In Sheen's study, however, the native speakers were even more tolerant: 74% of his raters found the following sentence acceptable: *The guards were made hostage this morning and now one was released* (emphasis added). Sheen notes that the presence of *now* made this sentence less acceptable than many others in the judgments of the native speakers in his study. This example is also notable because it comes from actual native speaker usage as recorded by Sheen. Interestingly, he observes that such uses of a past simple with the adverb *now* were very rare in his database. Thus even though native speakers proved to be tolerant of such cases, there does not seem to be any direct relation to its frequency in actual usage, though it is possible that such tolerance is a harbinger of ongoing linguistic change, that is, of further mergers of uses of the past simple and the present.

Discussion

We will summarize the results of our study before considering their implications for fossilization and for transfer in L3 settings. Tables 5.1 and 5.2 indicate that the Galician group had a greater proficiency in English than did the Castilian group, as measured by their abilities in correcting errors in a passage (and as validated against a group of native speakers of English who were very successful in detecting and correcting the errors). Table 5.3 indicates that, contrary to our expectations, the Galician group surpassed the Castilian group in attempting corrections of PR and PA items in the passage. Nevertheless, the results of Table 5.4 indicate that the Galician group had significantly more difficulty in noticing problems in the PA items than did the Castilian group. This finding is consistent with our prediction that influence from Galician and/or Galician Spanish would impede the detection of problems in PA items. Even so, native speakers of English also had considerable difficulty in spotting problems in the PA (but not the PR) items.

Our results offer some intriguing hints about how transfer can contribute to stabilization and perhaps to fossilization. Most importantly, Galicians were the group which ignored the largest number of problems involving the past verb forms where a perfect is required (as seen in Table 5.4). In effect, the Galicians' performance supports an explanation that the infrequency of perfect in the local form of Spanish (influenced directly or indirectly by Galician) often induces them to ignore the particular semantic and pragmatic conditions compatible with the perfect. Transfer thus seems to contribute to a failure to 'notice,' this latter verb being one well known in the investigation of focus on forms (e.g. Hulstijn, 2003). Such a failure to notice is also consistent with the characterization of Schachter (1993) of transfer being a constraint on the hypotheses that a learner may construct of the target language.

By the logic of our argument, fossilization may arise from a stabilization in production patterns linked to a tendency to use the past simple instead of the present perfect or to produce hypercorrect uses of the perfect. Such a tendency is evident in the historical pattern of Galician speakers of Spanish using a past simple where a present perfect is obligatory in Castilian; it is likewise evident in the hypercorrect present perfect in a syntactic environment calling for the past simple. The observations of teachers about the difficulties of Galician learners of English suggest a similar pattern in third language acquisition. Both patterns are, we believe, closely linked to difficulties occasioned by the native language of Galicians (whether Galician itself or the local form of Spanish), which induces them to overlook the semantic and pragmatic conditions that warrant the use of the perfect. By this interpretation, a previously acquired language (or languages) can bias assessments of what is acceptable though it does not determine such assessments. Our findings support such an interpretation and accordingly, they provide some indirect evidence for fossilization of production patterns in L3 analogous to patterns seen in a bilingual language contact setting.

As the word 'indirect' in the preceding sentence suggests, there are reasons to be cautious. First our test really only looks at sensitivity to a grammatical norm, not at production per se – and methodological problems already described make clear why it is very hard to elicit satisfactory production data for the perfect. Second, our results proved a bit surprising. Even though neither the native speakers of English nor the Castilians experienced the same degree of difficulty as the Galicians did with items PA 1–5, all three groups often ignored semantic and pragmatic conditions compatible with the use of the present perfect.

There thus seems to be a bias in the test that induces many readers to equate the semantics of the past tense with the semantics of the present perfect. In the case of the native speakers, the predilection for the past simple may be related to specific factors in American English which have been observed by Comrie (1976) and Sheen (1984), and corroborated to some extent by the corupus research of Biber *et al.* (1999). Perhaps, however, such results have to do less with the test itself or with the peculiarities of American English and more to do with the semantics of the perfect in English. At this stage in our research, the best explanation for the varied nature of our results remains unclear.

We should also note the possibility of some positive transfer in the Galician group since all have more experience with Spanish than with English. Our test cannot really shed much light on the possibility, but we nevertheless think it likely that Castilian provided some facilitating influence. Many studies of transfer in L3, such as those in the recent volume edited by Cenoz *et al.* (2001) show instances of where L2 aids in the acquisition of L3.

The range of methodological problems we have considered in this chapter shows that there exist some formidable challenges for those who study third as well as second language acquisition. However, the difficulties should not make us lose sight of the hope that further work will shed light on the study of transfer involving tense, aspect, and other categories of the verb. So far, the categories of the noun have been more intensively studied in the search for evidence of syntactic transfer, as seen in work on relative clauses and articles (as reviewed by Odlin, 2001, 2003b). Nevertheless, some evidence indicates that the verbal categories of tense, aspect, and mood are likewise transferable (e.g. Klee & Ocampo, 1995; Sabban, 1982; Wenzell, 1989).

The interpretive problems of the study are as formidable as the methodological ones and, of course, related to them. The quite tolerant intuitions of native speakers with items PA 1–5 do not show a straightforward relation to actual usage, as both this study and Sheen's indicate. Accordingly, a satisfactory understanding of native speaker norms, a prerequisite for any thorough account of either stabilization or fossilization, remains to be achieved.

As noted in the introduction, the concept of fossilization itself is controversial, with skeptics such as Long (2003) questioning the very need for the concept in a viable theory of second language acquisition. Yet whatever judgments the research community may reach about the necessity of the concept, sociolinguistic environments such as Galicia make clear the need to explain stabilization resulting in a permanent divergence from the norms of one variety (Castilian Spanish) in a variety that arises from language contact (Galician Spanish). Even though stabilization may not invariably imply a permanent cessation of learning (i.e. fossilization), stabilization can be not only a concomitant of transfer in the acquisition of a second language but also itself a cause of transfer in the acquisition of a third language.

Acknowledgement

We would like to thank Jan Hulstijn, Diane Larsen-Freeman, and an anonymous referee for their comments on earlier versions of this chapter.

References

Bardovi-Harlig, K. (2001) Another piece of the puzzle: The emergence of the present perfect. *Language Learning* 51 (supplement 1), 215–264.
Biber, D., Johansson, S., Leech, G., Conrad, S. and Finegan, E. (1999) *Longman Grammar of Spoken and Written English*. London: Longman.
Carballo Calero, R. (1979) *Gramática Elemental del Gallego Común*. Vigo: Galaxia.
Cenoz, J., Hufeison, B. and Jessner, U. (eds) (2001) *Cross-Linguistic Influence in Third Language Acquisition: Psycholinguistic Perspectives*. Clevedon, UK: Multilingual Matters.
Collins, L. (2002) The roles of L1 influence and lexical aspect in the acquisition of temporal morphology. *Language Learning* 52, 43–94
Comrie, B. (1976) *Aspect*. Cambridge: Cambridge University Press.
Dulay, H. and Burt, M. (1974) Natural sequences in child second language acquisition. *Language Learning* 24, 37–53.
Espinoza, A.M. (1997) Contrastive analysis of the Spanish and English passive voice in scientific prose. *English for Specific Purposes* 16 (3), 229–243.
Filppula, M. (1999) *The Grammar of Irish English*. London: Routledge.
Goyanes, H., Núñez, C., Romero, P. and Túñez, M. (1996) *A Información en Galego*. Santiago de Compostela: Lea.
Heckler, E. (1983) The acquisition of the auxiliary by ESL learners. ERIC ED240878.
Hermida, C. (2001) The Calician speech community. In T. Turrel (ed.) *Multilingualism in Spain: Sociolinguistic and Psycholinguistic Aspects of Linguistic Minority Groups* (pp. 110–140). Clevedon: Multilingual Matters.
Hulstijn, J. (2003) Incidental and intentional learning. In C. Doughty and M. Long (eds) *Handbook on Second Language Acquisition* (pp. 349–381). Oxford: Blackwell.
Jarvis, S. and Odlin, T. (2000) Morphological type, spatial reference, and language transfer. *Studies in Second Language Acquisition* 22, 535–556.
Klee, C. and Ocampo. A. (1995) The expression of past reference in Spanish narratives of Spanish-Quechua bilingual speakers. In C. Silva-Corvalán (ed.) *Spanish in Four Continents* (pp. 52–70). Washington, DC: Georgetown University Press.
Long, M. (2003) Stabilization and fossilization in interlanguage development. In C. Doughty and M. Long (eds) *Handbook on Second Language Acquisition* (pp. 487–535). Oxford: Blackwell.
Odlin, T. (1986) Another look at passage correction tests. *TESOL Quarterly* 20, 123–130.
Odlin, T. (1989) *Language Transfer: Cross-Linguistic Influence in Language Learning*. Cambridge: Cambridge University Press.
Odlin, T. (1997) Bilingualism and substrate influence: A look at clefts and reflexives. In J. Kallen (ed.) *Focus on Ireland* (pp. 35–50). Amsterdam: John Benjamins.
Odlin, T. (2001) Language transfer and substrate influence. In R. Mesthrie (ed.) *Concise Encyclopedia of Sociolinguistics* (pp. 499–503). Amsterdam: Elsevier.
Odlin, T. (2003a) Language Ecology and the Columbian Exchange. In J. Brian, J. DeStefano, N. Jacobs and I. Lehiste (eds) *When Languages Collide: Perspectives*

on *Language Conflict, Language Competition, and Language Coexistence* (pp. 71–94). Columbus: Ohio State University Press.

Odlin, T. (2003b) Cross-linguistic influence. In C. Doughty and M. Long (eds) *Handbook on Second Language Acquisition* (pp. 436–486). Oxford: Blackwell.

Russell, W. and Snow, D. (1977) A bilingual study of selected syntactic skills in Spanish-speaking children. *SWRL Technical Report* 60. ERIC ED174002.

Sabban, A. (1982) *Gälisch-Englischer Sprachkontakt*. Heidelberg: Julius Groos.

Schachter, J. (1993) A new account of language transfer. In S. Gass and L. Selinker (eds) *Language Transfer in Language Learning* (pp. 32–46). Amsterdam: John Benjamins.

Selinker, L. (1992) *Rediscovering Interlanguage*. London: Longman.

Selinker, L. and Lakshmanan, U. (1993) Language transfer and fossilization: The Mulitple Effects Principle. In S. Gass and L. Selinker (eds) *Language Transfer in Language Learning* (pp. 197–216). Amsterdam: John Benjamins.

Sheen, R. (1984) Current usage of the simple past and present perfect and its relevance for teaching English as a foreign language or second language. *The Canadian Modern Language Review/La Revue canadienne des langues vivantes* 40, 374–385.

Thomason, S. and Kaufman, T. (1988) *Language Contact, Creolization, and Genetic Linguistics*. Berkeley: University of California Press.

Wenzell, V. (1989) Transfer of aspect in the English oral narratives of native Russian speakers. In H. Dechert and M. Raupach (eds) *Transfer in Language Production* (pp. 71–97). Norwood, New Jersey: Ablex.

Weinreich, U. (1953/1968) *Languages in Contact*. The Hague: Mouton.

Chapter 6
Child Second Language Acquisition and the Fossilization Puzzle

USHA LAKSHMANAN

A widely held assumption about the acquisition of a second language beyond one's native language is that children, but not adults, are typically successful with respect to ultimate attainment of the grammar of the target second language (Bley-Vroman, 1990; Johnson & Newport, 1989, 1991; Schachter, 1988). It is, therefore, not surprising that nearly all of the research investigations of the fossilization phenomenon has tended to focus on the adult second language learner/user (for review of research on fossilization see Han, 1998, 2004; Long, 2003). When Larry Selinker first proposed the Interlanguage hypothesis in 1972 it was in the context of adult second language acquisition. Likewise, the phenomenon of *fossilization* was first introduced and discussed in that same paper solely in relation to adult second language learners. The model presented there is a failure driven model, where a vast majority of adult second language learners are characterized as being permanently stuck at an intermediary stage in their grammar, which does not match the native speaker norms of the target grammar. It was only later (Selinker *et al.*, 1975) that the Interlanguage hypothesis was extended from adult second language settings to the child second language acquisition context as well. In that paper, which presents data from a Toronto French immersion program, it is proposed that child second language grammars are also potentially fossilizable. However, in contrast to adult second language acquisition, the conditions under which fossilization of errors is predicted are restricted to *'"non-simultaneous" second language acquisition contexts where the major sociolinguistic variable is the absence of native speaking peers' of the target language (TL)'* (Selinker *et al.*, 1975: 140). According to Selinker *et al.*, under these sociolinguistic conditions, child interlanguages could potentially develop as dialects in their own right.

100

Selinker *et al.* do not directly discuss child second language settings where the learners *do* have access to and interact with native speaking peers of the target language. However, we may infer from their proposals that fossilization would not be predicted in such child second language settings.

Selinker and Lakshmanan (1992) proposed the Multiple Effects Principle (MEP) as a partial explanation as to why certain linguistic structures become fossilized while others do not. According to the MEP, 'when two or more SLA factors work in tandem, there is a greater chance of stabilization of interlanguage forms leading to possible fossilization' (p. 198). Concerning various possible SLA factors, Selinker and Lakshmanan proposed that language transfer is a central SLA one, and could be either a necessary co-factor (strong form of the MEP) or a privileged co-factor (weak form of the MEP) in setting multiple effects. Selinker and Lakshmanan consider the operation of the MEP in adult L2 acquisition as well as in child L2 acquisition. Crucially, the child L2 acquisition contexts they examine do not involve ones where the sociolinguistic variable (*viz.* absence of native speaking peers of the target language) that characterized the Toronto French immersion program is operative. However, despite the absence of this sociolinguistic variable, Selinker and Lakshmanan do not rule out the possibility that interlanguage forms in children, as in the case of adults, can potentially stabilize, leading to fossilization, when the MEP is at work. However, they suggest that the results may be opposite in child L2 acquisition, in contrast to adult L2 acquisition. Specifically, they propose that stabilization of interlanguage forms in children is more likely to lead to *development* as opposed to permanent stabilization (i.e. fossilization) either because language transfer is not one of the co-factors to begin with and/or that children may be more successful than adults in their reanalysis of the target language input, thus overriding language transfer – and MEP effects. In other words, the developmental paths traversed by child L2 learners and adult L2 learners acquiring the same target language and who share a common L1 may not be the same.

In contrast, the Full Transfer/Full Access model of second language acquisition (Schwartz and Sprouse, 1996) claims that the developmental path in child L2 acquisition and adult L2 acquisition are indeed the same. In both contexts, the FT/FA model hypothesizes that the initial state of L2 acquisition is the grammar of the L1 (excluding the phonetic matrices of lexical-morphological items) and that L2 development takes place through UG constrained restructuring triggered by the learners' perception of the mismatches between the target language input and the output generated by the learners' interlanguage grammar. As a result of language transfer, in relation to those properties where the L2 initial states in child L2 and adult L2 learners differ from the initial states in child L1 acquisition, the L2 acquisition outcomes will also differ from those observed in the child L1 situation. From this perspective, both adult and child L2 acquisition, although UG constrained, need not necessarily result in convergence of the target language grammar. In other words, the FT/FA model predicts that child L2 and adult L2 grammars are both potentially fossilizable.

In what follows, I present some thoughts on how child second language acquisition data can contribute to an understanding of the fossilization puzzle. Before presenting these ideas, it is necessary to first address the definition problem: What constitutes child second language acquisition?

Defining Child Second Language Acquisition

It is generally assumed in the second language acquisition literature that exposure to and acquisition of a second language after the age of three years but before puberty constitutes child second language acquisition (McLaughlin, 1978), which encompasses early as well as late childhood. The upper age boundary stems from Lenneberg's (1967) hypothesis that puberty might represent the cut-off for a critical period for language acquisition and the findings of studies that this hypothesis generated in the second language acquisition context (see, e.g. studies by Johnson & Newport, 1989, 1991). The lower age boundary (i.e. three years) is based on the belief that acquisition of much of the grammar of the native language is completed by this age (McLaughlin, 1978). According to this criterion, exposure to a second language around age 2;0 (i.e. before the age of three years) would constitute bilingual first language acquisition (more specifically *sequential* bilingual first language acquisition) and not child second language acquisition. It is possible that the lower boundary (three years) represents an arbitrary cut-off point. Although it may be true that a major part of the grammar of the native language is acquired by the age of three years, there is also evidence that children's knowledge of certain complex aspects of the syntax and semantics of the native language matures or becomes operative at a much later age (e.g. eight years). If this is the case, then child L2 acquisition beyond the age of three years, may not, strictly speaking, represent successive L2 acquisition in relation to all aspects of the target language. On the contrary, there may be aspects of child L2 acquisition that in reality represent first language acquisition (Lakshmanan, 1995). Likewise, sequential acquisition of a second language prior to the age of three, may also be similar to child L2 acquisition in relation to certain aspects of grammatical development in the target language, and could therefore, be characterized as being both child L1 and child L2 (Foster-Cohen, 2001).

Schwartz (2003) defines child L2 learners as those whose initial exposure to the target second language occurs between the ages of four and seven; in other words, the upper boundary is not puberty but a lower cut off point. Schwartz bases her assumption in relation to the upper boundary for child L2 acquisition on findings from studies on L2 ultimate attainment (e.g. Johnson & Newport, 1989, 1991). The findings of the studies by Johnson and Newport indicated that there are no statistically significant differences between the performance of L2 speakers of English who commenced their acquisition of English no later than the age of seven and the performance of native speakers of English on language specific morphosyntactic properties and also on a principle of universal grammar (i.e. subjacency). In contrast, the performance of those L2 speakers of English who had commenced their acquisition of English after the age of seven years and beyond differed significantly from the performance of native speakers of English. However, Johnson and Newport did not address the issue of whether the *pattern* of responses of the L2 groups was also found to be different. Additionally, there are various methodological problems in the studies by Johnson and Newport. For example, their assumption that age of arrival in the U.S is the same as the age of exposure to the L2 (i.e. English) is problematic. More importantly, they do not provide evidence that those who commenced their acquisition of English by the age of seven years continued to also maintain their native language. If the group that succeeded in relation to ultimate attainment of the L2 did not in fact continue to maintain their native language, in contrast to the other groups who were found to be unsuccessful in relation to ultimate attainment of the L2, then the differences observed between these two groups could have stemmed from this other variable, namely the maintenance of the L1.

Foster-Cohen (2001) draws our attention to the 'fuzzy boundaries' used in language acquisition research to distinguish between various patterns of exposure (e.g. child L1, early child L2, late child L2, adolescent L2 and adult L2). These divisions appear to be based on established human developmental milestones, of which puberty is one obvious example. A problem, according to Foster-Cohen, is that 'we do not in practice assess whether each child has reached puberty in studies of SLA and age' (p. 337). Instead, when we observe a discontinuity in the data at age 11;0 or 12;0 or 13;0 we ascribe it *post hoc* to puberty. In other words, all that we accomplish by doing this is to give 'a name to a fuzzy boundary between late childhood and adolescence'. As Foster-Cohen has observed, global cut-offs at the boundaries typically used in language acquisition research are in the long run not very helpful given the evidence that different parts of language appear to exhibit discontinuities at different times (see, e.g. data from studies by Weber-Fox & Neville, 1999). The data from Lee and Schachter (1997) also appear to suggest that even with respect to the same linguistic module (e.g. Binding theory), the different constraints associated with it (e.g. Binding Principle A and Binding Principle B) appear to exhibit different sensitive period effects. Foster-Cohen recommends the use of a 'sliding window' in addressing questions in L1 and L2 acquisition.

> Instead of trying to divide L1 discretely from L2, and early L2 from later L2, with all the problems identified above, we need to look through the window at one or a series of ages and stages and ask, with reference to properly theoretically motivated hypotheses about the nature of language, what an infant/child/adolescent/adult knows or can do. Take, for example, two points in time, say at five years of age and at 12 years of age (and there are, of course, an infinite number of such points). We can then ask for each point where the child is in relation to a range of different developments: metalinguistic development, lexical development (of words and lexical phrases), critical period(s) for L2, theory of mind development, reasoning development, as well as all the usual linguistic structural developments... As you slide the window over the age span from zero to 20, problem-solving skills rise, native-like second language-acquisition ability falls, theory of mind capacities rise, and so do metalinguistic abilities, and so on. You do not find sharp cut-offs. You simply find different configurations of capacities and skills. If we approach the L1/L2 questions in this way, we focus on the continuities between L1 and L2 and within L2. And if you focus on the continuities, the discontinuities take care of themselves. (Foster-Cohen, 2001: 341–342)

Applying the Sliding Window: Cross-Age Comparisons

Studies on age effects in ultimate attainment of the L2, such as the ones by Johnson and Newport (1989, 1991), typically base their findings about age related differences on the observed statistical differences between the end state performance of native speakers of the target language and the end state performance of non-native speakers.[1] As

Martohardjono (1993) have shown, arguments that adult L2 acquisition is not constrained by Universal Grammar that are based solely on observed statistical differences between the performance of adult L2 speakers and native speakers on grammaticality judgment tasks are problematic. Even if statistical differences were observed in relation to the intuitional data, if the *pattern* of judgments of grammatical and ungrammatical sentences in the case of the L2 speakers and the native speakers is found to be similar, this would constitute evidence that adult L2 grammars are also constrained by UG. Additionally, what is also missing from studies on the effects of age on ultimate attainment is a comparison of the *pattern of development* across different L2 age groups in relation to the property or properties investigated (for discussion of this issue see Lakshmanan & Selinker, 1994; for a similar position see Schwartz, 1992, 2003). In order for us to be able to solve the fossilization puzzle, we need to be able to understand the internal mechanisms that underlie the fossilization process, which we can only hope to do through detailed longitudinal studies comparing the pattern of L2 development in learners exposed to the target second language at different ages.[2] Crucially, the differences in competence in the end state, in relation to a grammatical property P, between L2 learners with the same L1 (or typologically similar L1s) but with varying age of exposure to the target L2, could stem from differences in their initial hypothesis in relation to the property P in the target L2. Comparisons of L2 learners' end state performance in relation to the property P do not reveal very much about age related differences in the internal mechanisms involved, if we do not know what the initial (and intermediary) L2 hypotheses are in relation to property P. As there appear to be differences in the sensitive periods (i.e. different lower and upper boundaries) for different parts of language as well as for different universal grammatical principles, it may be predicted that the initial hypothesis of L2 learners in relation to property P could vary depending on where they were in the developmental path in relation to the lower and the upper boundaries of the sensitive period for property P, when their exposure to the target L2 began.

Cognitively speaking, children acquiring a second language (i.e. after the age of three years) are more mature than children aged below the age of 3;0, who are in the process of acquiring the language in an L1 acquisition situation. Compared to child L2 learners, adult L2 learners are, of course, cognitively more mature. One thing that both child L2 and adult L2 learners have in common, however, is prior knowledge of another language (i.e. the L1). Lakshmanan (1993/1994) and Lakshmanan and Selinker (1994) proposed that if, as has been proposed by proponents of the Maturational Hypothesis, children's knowledge of certain linguistic properties is maturationally driven (i.e. they are initially absent and mature or become operative at a later age), then at whatever age these properties mature or become available for child L1 acquisition, they should also be available at the same time for successive child L2 acquisition as well. Assuming the existence of different sensitive periods for different properties of language, then children's acquisition of universal grammatical properties instantiated in the target second language, which are shown to mature or become operative only after the age of three years (e.g. at age 5;0 or 8;0) in the child L1 acquisition context, may strictly speaking, be characterized as child L1 acquisition rather than child L2 acquisition. In other words, although both child L2 learners and adult L2 learners come to the language acquisition task with prior knowledge of an L1, child L2 learners, unlike adult L2 learners, may be more similar to child L1 learners in relation to their acquisition of certain properties of the target language which are shown to mature later in childhood.

In the remainder of this section, I will focus on two different domains (verb inflectional morphology and universal constraints) and I will explore how through the use of Susan Foster-Cohen's sliding window approach, we can understand the internal mechanisms that underlie fossilization in second language acquisition.

Verb Inflectional Morphology

One area where there has been substantial research in child L1, child L2 and adult L2 acquisition is the development of verb inflectional morphology, particularly with respect to the acquisition of English. Regardless of whether the learners are child L1 learners, child L2 learners, adolescent L2 learners or adult L2 learners of English, a phenomenon that is common to all types of language development in relation to overt verb inflectional morphology is the existence of errors of omission. At the same time, however, the pattern of development of verb inflections, in the case of child L2 learners of English differs from the pattern of development observed for child L1 learners of English.

As shown by the morpheme order studies of the 1970s (e.g. Brown, 1973; DeVilliers and deVilliers, 1973), in children acquiring English as the L1, finiteness (tense and agreement) inflectional morphemes cluster together regardless of whether the inflectional morpheme is suppletive (e.g. independent functional morphemes such as copula and auxiliary *be*) or affixal (e.g. finiteness suffixes on thematic or lexical verbs such as -*ed*, -*s*) in form (for discussion of this issue, see Rice *et al.*, 1998; Zobl & Liceras, 1994).

In the case of child L2 learners of English, on the other hand, findings from longitudinal and cross-sectional studies indicate that there is an asymmetry in the development of finiteness inflectional morphemes. Specifically, in the case of child L2 learners of English, suppletive or free functional forms (e.g. forms of the copula and auxiliary *be*), which are independent representations of finiteness, emerge earlier and are mastered prior to suffixal representations of finiteness (Haznedar, 2001; Ionin & Wexler, 2002; Kakazu & Lakshmanan, 2000; Lakshmanan, 1989, 1993/ 1994, 1994, 1998a, 1998b, 2000; Zobl & Liceras, 1994). The L1s represented in the case of these child L2 learners of English encompass a variety of languages including languages with rich affixal verb inflections (e.g. Spanish, Turkish, Japanese, Russian) as well as languages without any verb inflections (e.g. Mandarin, Cantonese). However, the asymmetry observed between the development of independent representations of finiteness and suffixal representations of finiteness in children acquiring English as the L2 in early childhood (four to six years) does not continue to persist. The evidence, particularly from longitudinal case studies, indicate that by approximately the 10th month of exposure to English, child L2 learners have mastered or are close to mastering the suffixal verb inflectional morphology as well (Kakazu & Lakshmanan, 2000; Lakshmanan, 1994).

In child L1 English, it has also been observed that there is a developmental relationship between the emergence of verb inflections and emergence of overt subjects (Guilfoyle, 1984; Jaeggli & Hyams, 1988). In contrast, longitudinal studies of child L2 English indicate that verb inflections and overt subjects are not developmentally related. Child L2 learners of English, appear to know very early on that English is not a null subject language, even though they may continue to produce uninflected lexical or thematic verbs (Haznedar & Schwartz, 1997; Lakshmanan, 1989, 1991, 1994). During the initial stage of child L1 acquisition of English when finite inflectional forms are not consistently supplied where these would be required in the target language, child L1 learners have also been observed to produce non-nominative (accusative and genitive) pronoun subjects in root clauses (Vainikka, 1993/1994). There appears to be a correlation between the occurrence of non-nominative subjects and the presence of finite verb inflection in root clauses in child L1 English. Non-nominative case marked pronoun subjects tend to occur more in root clauses where the verb is in the non-finite form than in clauses where the verb is overtly marked for finiteness (Schütze & Wexler, 1996). In contrast, non-nominative case marked subjects have not been attested in the case of child L2 learners of English. In root clauses, regardless of whether there is overt representation of finiteness or not, subject pronouns of such clauses tend to occur only in the nominative case form (Haznedar, 2001; Ito & Lakshmanan, 2001; Kakazu & Lakshmanan, 2000; Lakshmanan, 1994; Lakshmanan & Ito, 2000; Ozeki, 1995). The findings in relation to the status of overt subjects and nominative subjects in child L2 English suggest that child L2 learners do have knowledge of the abstract property of Finiteness (Tense and Agreement) associated with the Infl(ectional) node from the beginning, despite the fact that they have difficulties with the overt suppliance of suffixal verb inflections.

The asymmetry between the development of suppletive inflectional morphology and suffixal inflectional morphology attested in child L2 learners of English has also been attested in the case of adult L2 learners of English. Likewise, in relation to the case marking of subjects in root clauses, only nominative pronoun subjects (but not accusative or genitive pronoun subjects) have been attested in root clauses. As in the case of child L2 learners of English, adult L2 learners also appear to have knowledge of the abstract property of finiteness associated with the Inflectional node, despite the difficulties that they experience with the overt suppliance of suffixal verb inflections. However, in contrast to child L2 acquisition of English, the omission or the variable suppliance of suffixal inflectional morphemes may tend to persist in the long-term in adult L2 acquisition. Lardiere (1998) examined spontaneous speech samples gathered from Patty, an adult L2 speaker of English, who had been exposed to English as an adult and had lived in the U.S for approximately 19 years. The data examined by Lardiere represent Patty's end stage interlanguage grammar as they were gathered at three different sessions over a period of nine years, after Patty had been immersed in an English-speaking environment (i.e. in the U.S.) for 10 years. Lardiere reports that Patty's suppliance of tense and agreement inflection (especially suffixal inflection) is very low. However, as in the case of child L2 learners, subjects are invariably overt and nominative case marking of pronoun subjects and accusative pronoun objects is target like. Based on the evidence of Patty's suppliance of nominative case, Lardiere argued that Patty's interlanguage clausal representation in the end state does include the Inflection projection and the abstract Finiteness feature associated with it. Lardiere attributes Patty's low percentage of suppliance of past tense marking to her difficulties in morphophonological mapping (i.e. mapping from the abstract functional feature Tense to the phonetic form). Unlike pronominal case marking, which is simple and invariant in English, the mapping from feature to form in relation to tense morphology is complex and variable. According to Lardiere, the deficit in relation to Patty's interlanguage grammar is restricted to overt morpho-phonological module and not to the syntactic module, which is intact.

Typically, researchers referring to the case of Patty tend to describe her as a native speaker of Chinese. However, as Lardiere has indicated, Patty's history of acquisition of other languages prior to her exposure to English encompasses Mandarin, Indonesian and Hokkien. One aspect that is common to all three languages is that the verb forms are not inflected for tense and agreement. It is possible that Patty's difficulties with suffixal inflectional forms in her steady state grammar may be the result of the Multiple Effects principle. In addition to the complexities involved in the morphophonological mapping of abstract feature of Tense in a language such as English, a triple co-factor involved in causing permanent stabilization of her non-native-like verb inflectional morphology may be the influence exerted independently and jointly by each of her three other languages: Mandarin, Indonesian, and Hokkien (independently and jointly).[3]

The data from Patty represents her steady state/end state grammar.[4] As L2 acquisition data from the earliest stages of her exposure to English are not available, we cannot really tell whether the asymmetry observed in her end-state grammar between suppletive and suffixal inflection for the finiteness feature mirrors a stage in the earliest stages of her English interlanguage development. Lakshmanan (1998b, 2000) reports on a three-month long longitudinal study of three Chinese-speaking children (Xi-Xi, Bing-Bing and Chi-Chi aged 5;0, 5;2 and 6;1 respectively), who acquired English naturalistically in the United States. The children's exposure to English at the onset of data collection ranged from two months to four months. As in the case of other child L2 learners, the interlanguage grammars of all three Chinese-speaking children exhibit the same asymmetry in relation to concrete realizations of the finiteness feature. All three children went through an early stage where free functional morphemes (e.g. copula and auxiliary *be*) were supplied in their finite form from the moment that they are overtly produced. At the same time, lexical/thematic verbs, which also occurred at the same time, were always produced in the uninflected non-finite form. However, the three Chinese-speaking children were also observed to go through a brief initial stage prior to this period, when the free functional morphemes (i.e. copula and auxiliary *be*) were always omitted and lexical/thematic verbs, which were present during this same period, occurred only in the non-finite form. Although Spanish-speaking children and Japanese-speaking children acquiring English also have problems in supplying suffixal inflection (e.g. past tense *-ed* and *-s*), the free functional morphemes such as the copula and the auxiliary *be* have been observed to emerge very early and are rarely omitted (Lakshmanan, 1998b, 2000; Ozeki, 1995). In other words, there is no evidence that child L2 learners of English with Spanish or Japanese as the L1 go through an initial stage where all their clauses contain only non-finite verb forms. It is possible that the differences observed stem from differences between Chinese and the L1s of the Spanish and Japanese speaking children. Spanish and Japanese are languages where the finiteness feature is overtly marked in the suffixal form. In Chinese, on the other hand, verbs are always in the uninflected form and are not overtly marked for the finiteness feature.

Lakshmanan and Tezel (1998) examine spontaneous speech samples gathered from Kezeban, a 22-year-old adult L2 speaker of English with Turkish as the L1. Kezeban had lived in the United States for approximately two years when the data were gathered. Her exposure to English was primarily in informal naturalistic settings, although she had attended a few ESL classes as well. As Haznedar (2001) has reported in the case of Erdem, a Turkish-speaking child who acquired English in the United Kingdom, Kezeban's English interlanguage also exhibited an asymmetry between suppletive verb inflectional morphology and suffixal verb inflectional morphology. Kezeban's verb forms indicate that finiteness markings are consistently supplied in obligatory contexts in relation to the copula and auxiliary *be*, and also in the case of the semantically empty *do* auxiliary in negative clauses in present and past tense contexts (e.g. *I was sick yesterday; I am happy; She is housewife; He doesn't like dessert; I didn't cook for her*). Additionally, Kezeban also uses the auxiliary *did* in the unstressed form to mark past tense in root declarative non-emphatic contexts instead of supplying the past tense suffixal inflection on the verb (e.g. *Yesterday, I did cook [=Yesterday, I cooked]*). While Haznedar in relation to Erdem does not report this use of the *do* auxiliary, such uses of the *do* auxiliary have been reported in the case of other children acquiring English in the L2 as well as in the L1 acquisition context (Hollebrandese & Roeper, 1996; Lakshmanan, 2000; Ravem, 1978). As Hollebrandese and Roeper have observed, such uses of the *do* auxiliary may be a First Resort (as opposed to a Last Resort) phenomenon. In contrast to Kezeban's success with independent representations of finiteness morphology and past tense marking on irregular lexical verbs, past tense and present third person singular verb inflectional suffixes tend to be largely omitted (e.g. *She rent a video* [= she rented a video]; *he drink cigarettes* [He drinks (= smokes) cigarettes; *She like it* [= She likes it]. Despite Kezeban's difficulties with suffixal verb inflectional morphology, her suppliance of overt subjects and nominative case marking on subject pronouns is perfect. Turkish is a null subject language. But Kezeban did not have any problems in converging on the correct analysis for English in relation to the overt subject requirement. Turkish has rich suffixal verb inflections. Yet it is precisely in relation to marking of finiteness in the suffixal form that she experienced difficulties, even after two years of exposure to English. Although Kezeban's period of exposure to English is considerably less when compared to Lardiere's subject (Patty), we can predict that errors of omission in relation to suffixal verb inflections will tend to permanently stabilize in her interlanguage grammar.

In sum, the English interlanguage of both adult and child L2 learners appear to be characterized by a common developmental stage, where there is an asymmetry between suppletive and suffixal finiteness verb inflectional morphology. While this pattern of development is common to both groups, what is puzzling is why the asymmetry tends to persist in the long-term in the case of adults but not children. What does this tell us about child L2 and adult L2 differences in relation to the internal mechanisms involved for mastering target-like morphophonological mapping of the abstract finiteness feature?

Lakshmanan (1998b; 2000) proposed that the distinction that L2 learners make between free functional morphemes (e.g. the copula and auxiliary *be*) and lexical thematic verbs in relation to the overt realization of the finiteness feature does not have to do with the finite/non-finite distinction. Both the free functional morphemes bearing overt marking for finiteness (such as the copula and the auxiliary *be*) and the uninflected lexical thematic verbs are finite verb forms. But the overt morphological distinction between them reflects the strength of the verbal features of the inflectional heads of Tense and Agreement that are selected, which in turn reflects their verb raising properties. When a finite form of the copula or auxiliary is selected from the lexicon (i.e. enters the Numeration) strong Verb features of Tense and Agreement are automatically selected. When the numeration only includes a finite lexical verb in the non-finite form (bare verb or V-*ing*), the strength of the verbal features that is selected is consistent with the weak option. The copula and the auxiliary *be* in English are raising verbs; in contrast, lexical/thematic verbs cannot raise out of VP to the higher Inflectional and complementizer layers. It is possible that the asymmetry that is observed actually reflects a property of core grammar: verbs that raise have strong inflectional features associated with them whereas verbs that do not raise out of VP do not have strong Inflectional features associated with them. Under this account, the observed asymmetry in adult and child L2 English interlanguage actually reflects a UG constrained morphonological distinction between verbs that raise in the overt syntax and non-raising verbs.

A question that one can ask is why then it is that in the case of English, lexical thematic verbs, which do not raise overtly, can nevertheless take finite inflectional suffixes (e.g. past tense *-ed* and present three person singular *-s*). The concrete realization of inflectional suffixes on the thematic verb in modern day English may represent arbitrary or conventionalized use of language, that lie more at the language specific grammatical periphery as opposed to the universal core (for a similar view see Amritavalli, 2001). The fact that the asymmetry between suppletive and suffixal verb inflections typically does not persist in the long term in the case of child L2 learners suggests that they are advantaged (in comparison with adults) in relation to the successful resolution of mismatches between their developing grammar and the target grammar in the language specific grammatical periphery.

An additional question that emerges is the extent to which the observed long-term persistence of non-target-like tense marking in adult L2 learners (such as Patty) stems from a general morphphonological mapping problem per se as opposed to a more specific problem in the use of an indirect mapping procedure. In order to address this question, we would need to examine the pattern of L2 development in relation to the acquisition of morphologically uniform fusional and agglutinating languages (such as Spanish and Japanese), which express finiteness through rich suffixal inflections, by native speakers of languages with uniformly uninflected verb forms (e.g. Chinese) or verb forms that are morphologically mixed (i.e. bare forms + inflected forms), as in the case of English. In Spanish, lexical/thematic verbs bear rich inflectional suffixes and the learner will encounter positive evidence that they are raising verbs. Given the distinction outlined above between properties that relate to the grammatical core and the more conventionalized aspects of language, a prediction we can make is that the overt morphophonological mapping of the finiteness feature is not likely to pose difficulties for L2 learners of Spanish, regardless of the properties of the L1.

Universal Constraints

With respect to ultimate attainment of the L2, the end-state grammars of adult L2 learners (and perhaps child L2 learners as well) may not converge on the native speaker grammar in relation to all aspects of the target second language. At the same time, however, the growing body of evidence from UG based research on L2 acquisition suggests that L2 grammars are indeed constrained by universal grammar; in other words, simply because the end state grammar of an adult L2 learner diverges from the grammar of native speakers of the target language, it does not necessarily follow that the adult L2 grammar does not obey universal constraints (see White, 2003). What is puzzling, of course, is why the grammars of adult L2 learners tend to diverge from the grammar of native speakers in the first place. If L2 grammars are UG constrained, then the expected outcome in relation to aspects of the target language that lie at the grammatical core is convergence and not divergence.

As mentioned earlier, according to the Full Transfer/Full Access Model, in the case of both child L2 and adult L2 learners, the initial L2 hypothesis in relation to a particular property P is determined by the learners' L1. In those cases where there is a mismatch between the grammar generated by the learners' initial L2 hypothesis and the target grammar, restructuring of the learners' interlanguage grammar will need to take place. In many instances, where the learner encounters positive evidence in the input, successful restructuring is predicted and convergence is the expected outcome. However, in situations exemplifying the poverty of stimulus problem, where the property P, given the learners' initial L2 hypothesis, is underdetermined by the L2 input (i.e. no amount of positive evidence can cause a revision of the learners' current grammatical hypothesis) and is also underdetermined by the learners' L1 grammar, permanent divergence from the native speaker grammar may be predicted. Additionally, even if negative evidence were available, as it may be in a formal instructional setting, it will neither be relevant nor of the right type to trigger a change in the learners' analysis in relation to complex properties of the grammatical core.

Child L1 learners have also been known to overgeneralize causing them to generate grammars that may be larger than the target grammar. Child L1 learners, in such cases of overgeneralization, do ultimately succeed in converging on the mature grammar of native speakers, in the absence of negative evidence. Chomsky (1981: 8–9) has suggested that *indirect negative evidence*, whereby the learner somehow determines that certain structures or rules are absent in the target language, may be relevant for language acquisition. Chomsky defines indirect negative evidence as follows:

A not unreasonable acquisition system can be devised with the operating principle that if certain structures or rules fail to be exemplified in relatively simple expressions, where they would be expected to be found, then a(n) ... option selected excluding them in the grammar, so that a kind of 'negative evidence' can be available even without corrections, adverse reactions, etc.

As Pinker (1989) has stated, indirect negative evidence, is not strictly speaking, a part of the learner's linguistic environment in the same way as explicit negative evidence is. In order to count as negative data, the absence of a structure must be equated with ungrammaticality. Children's ability to retract from a larger to a smaller grammar, in the absence of negative evidence, and on the basis of limited input, may result from internal mechanisms (i.e. a learning procedure or strategy) that enable them to use *indirect negative evidence* for grammatical mapping from UG onto their developing L1 grammar.

The role of indirect negative evidence in grammar restructuring has been largely ignored in the L2 acquisition literature (but see Plough, 1995). Selinker and Lakshmanan (1992) in attempting to account for child L2–adult L2 differences in convergence suggest the possibility that children may be more successful than adults in their use of indirect negative evidence for restructuring their internalized grammar.

Universal Grammar, which is the genetic or biological blueprint for language, comprises of a finite set of principles/constraints. The constraints may be categorized into two types: constraints of form (e.g. constraints on movement of heads and phrases) and constraints of meaning (e.g. constraints on the interpretation of pronouns and reflexives). Studies on age effects on L2 ultimate attainment in relation to UG principles have tended to focus on the operation of constraints in the end state or steady state (e.g. Johnson & Newport, 1991; Lee & Schachter, 1997). To my knowledge, there are no studies that have conducted cross-age comparisons of the *pattern of development* of L2 knowledge in relation to UG constraints. Additionally, while there has been considerable research on the adult L2 acquisition of constraints of meaning (e.g. constraints relating to the interpretation of reflexives or pronouns) there is hardly any research on the status of these constraints in child L2 acquisition.

Further research, using what Susan Foster-Cohen has referred to as the *sliding window approach*, to conduct cross-age comparisons of the development of L2 competence of learners sharing the same L1 and the same target second language, but with varied ages of exposure to the L2, is crucial for an understanding of the internal mechanisms that contribute to the L2 end-state (i.e. convergence with or divergence from the native speaker grammar) in relation to the instantiation of a particular UG constraint. Such cross-age comparisons on the pattern of development of L2 learners' knowledge of UG constraints will need to address constraints of *form* as well as *meaning*. Furthermore, such comparisons should examine the acquisition of properties of the target L2 grammar that pose a potential L2 learnability problem for the learners (i.e. where the poverty of stimulus problem applies) as well as those properties that do not entail a potential learnability problem (i.e. where positive evidence is encountered for convergence on the L2 instantiated UG property). Such cross-age developmental comparisons cannot, for obvious reasons, rely on spontaneous speech alone. Instead, L2 intuitional data elicited through age appropriate tasks will also need to be used.

There are two potential outcomes of such longitudinal cross-age comparisons. Take, for example, a hypothetical study comparing the L2 developmental path over a period of two years of a five-year-old native speaker of Tamil and a 20-year-old native speaker of Tamil, both of whom are acquiring Hindi as a second language, in contexts where Hindi is the language of the community. There are two possible outcomes in relation to the pattern of development in the child and the adult L2 learner in relation to a complex property P. The pattern of development may be the *same* or *different* in the adult and child L2 learners.

In the scenario where the child L2 and the adult L2 patterns of development are the same, we can distinguish between two possibilities in relation to their initial L2 hypothesis and their success in converging on the target L2 grammar. The initial hypothesis of both learners may be based on their L1 (Tamil) or may not be based on their L1. Likewise, with respect to attainment of the target L2 grammar with respect to property P, both the child and the adult may converge or both may diverge from the target L2 grammar.

In the second scenario, where the patterns of development in the case of the adult L2 learner and the child L2 learner differ, we can distinguish between several possible outcomes. The initial hypothesis of both the child and the adult L2 learner may be the same (either L1 based or different from the L1) but their attainment type may differ (convergence in the case of the child and divergence in the case of the adult or vice versa). A second possibility under the 'different scenario' is that the child and the adult may differ in relation to their initial hypothesis (L1 based initial analysis in the case of the adult but not in the case of the child, or vice versa) but may be the same in relation to the attainment type (convergence or divergence in both). A third possibility under the 'different' scenario is that the child and the adult differ in relation to their initial hypothesis as well as in relation to convergence on the target grammar.[5]

In those L2 acquisition situations where there is a poverty of stimulus problem, and the initial hypothesis of both the child and adult stems from L1 transfer, and the child (but not the adult) converges on the target L2 grammar with respect to property P, the differences in relation to the pattern of development may stem from child–adult differences in the internal mechanisms involved in the successful use of indirect negative evidence. Specifically, the internal mechanisms of the child may enable the child to effectively use indirect negative evidence to over-ride language transfer effects and arrive at the correct generalization in relation to the instantiation of property P in the target L2. Divergence from the target L2 grammar in the case of the adult learner may result not because of the non-availability of Universal Grammar (UG) but because for some reason the adult internal mechanisms are less effective in the use of indirect negative evidence for grammatical mapping from UG to the interlanguage grammar.

What about those cases where there is no potential learnability problem, and the correct generalization can be deduced based on positive evidence in the input, and the child converges on the target grammar but the adult does not, despite the fact that their initial hypothesis is the same (either L1 based in both or not L1 based in both)? This could stem from differences between the child and adult in the internal mechanisms involved in using positive evidence in the input for grammatical mapping – i.e. from UG onto their developing L2 grammar.

It is possible, of course, that in both types of situations, the child also may not converge on the target grammar with respect to the property P. Nor might it be the case that the end state in relation to P merely reflects the status of the property in the learner's L1 grammar. The divergence may actually represent a different dialect (i.e. *idiosyncratic dialect* using Pit Corder's terminology).[6]

L2 Attrition and Reacquisition Patterns

As outlined above, one way of understanding the internal mechanisms involved in fossilization is by conducting fine-grained cross-age compara-tive studies that examine the pattern of L2 development over time in relation to a particular property. A necessary condition that must be met for such comparisons is that there is sustained or continuous exposure to the target L2 during the time that the learners are observed.

Another approach to studying fossilization would be to compare the patterns of L2 attrition and patterns of L2 reacquisition in the case of an individual with different periods of exposure to the target L2 environment that are separated by periods during which the individual is removed from the target second language environment.[7]

In what follows, I examine the patterns of L2 acquisition, attrition and reacquisition of two child native speakers of English (Rebecca and Eric) who were exposed to Hindi/Urdu in naturalistic contexts in Pakistan and India. These Hindi interlanguage data, which were originally gathered and reported on in Hansen (1980, 1983), were reanalyzed by Lakshmanan (1999) from the perspective of the Minimalist program.

As Hansen has reported, there were three periods during which Rebecca, the older child, was exposed to Hindi/Urdu: R-I, (age: 3;9–3;11) R-II (age: 4;7–5;3) and R-III (age: 6;6–7;6). There were two periods of exposure to Hindi/Urdu in the case of Rebecca's brother Eric: E-I (2;1–2;9); E-II (4;0–5;0). The duration of stay in the Hindi–Urdu speaking environment in relation to the three periods of exposure was as follows: R-I: [1-3-1974 to 3-24-1974]; R-II and E-I: [11-20-1974 to 7-26-1975]; R-III and E-II: [10-23-1976 to 10-18-1977]. With the exception of the time spent in Pakistan and India during the different periods of exposure to Hindi/Urdu, the two children's experience was limited to an English-speaking environment in the United States. The data consisted of primarily audio-tape recordings of spontaneous speech samples gathered once every month. Supplementary data consisted of diary notes. During their final period of exposure in India (R-III and E-II) and for approximately one year and a half following their final return to the United States, Hindi negative sentences were elicited experimentally through a picture cued production task.

In her analysis of the data, Hansen focused on the development of Hindi–Urdu negation across the different periods of exposure to the target L2. Hindi–Urdu is an SOV language. The canonical word order of a negative sentence (i.e. sentential negation) is Subject–Object–Negative–Verb), where the direct object has scrambled past the negative from its underlying position within the VP (e.g. *ram seeb nahiiN khaayeegaa* = Ram apple NEG eatFUT3SM). Other word orders that are possible in Hindi–Urdu include OSNegV (where the object has scrambled past the Subject) and ONegVS, where the subject has moved rightward, and the subject gets extra emphasis. Occasionally, one also finds SNegVO order, where the object, which has moved rightward is more like an afterthought, and SOVNeg, where the negative receives extra emphasis. However, despite the variation in the word order, in a negative transitive sentence, the following orders are not possible: *SNegOV, *NegSOV, and *SVNegO.

In her analysis, Hansen focused on the position of the negative in relation to the verb, which she characterizes as being of the *Prepredicate type* in Hindi. However, Lakshmanan (1999) reanalyzed the SONegV order as one resulting from Object shift. Specifically, she proposed that the direct object moves leftward, from its underlying position within VP (SNegOV), past the negative to a position above the functional projection NegP, resulting in the surface order SONegV. Thus, in Hindi, unlike in English, there is overt object shift, which is visible in negative sentences.

Let us now turn to the results pertaining to the object shift rule in Rebecca's and Eric's Hindi–Urdu interlanguage grammar, based on the spontaneous speech samples. Hansen reports that in R-I (3;9–3;11), there are no occurrences of the grammatical SONegV order in the spontaneous speech samples gathered during the first month of RI. The dominant word order during the entire three-month period of R-I is *SNegOV. The percentage of occurrence of SNegOV is 56% in month 1, and 33% in months 2 and 3. As mentioned earlier, the SNegOV order is not permitted in Hindi–Urdu. The second-most dominant order in R-I is SOVNeg or Xneg (33% in RI, month 1, 28% in RI, month 2 and 19% in month 3). Interestingly, the SNegVO order, which would be similar to the word order in English, does not occur at all in the spontaneous speech samples gathered during this period, which is not what would be predicted by the Full Transfer/Full Access hypothesis. The canonical (and grammatical) word order of SONegV, where the object has scrambled leftward past Neg, emerges during the second month and is also present during the third month of R-I. However, the percentage of suppliance of SONegV is very low (17–19%).

In R-II (4;7–5;3), which represents Rebecca's second period of exposure to Hindi–Urdu after being separated from a Hindi–Urdu speaking environment for approximately eight months, Hansen reports that initially the dominant word order is once again the ungrammatical SNegOV (42% in month 1 of R-II) and decreases over the following four months in this same exposure period (38% → 42% → 30% → 8%). Although the SONegV order had already emerged in R-I, this word order is not attested at all for the first month of RII and is supplied at an extremely low percentage from months 2 to 3 (5% and 10% respectively) of R-II. However, from month 4 until the final data collection session of R-II (i.e. month 8), the percentage of negative utterances with the canonical SONegV order increases from 20% in month 4 to 57% in month 8 during this period of exposure. The second most dominant word order throughout R-II is X-Neg/SOV-Neg.

The ungrammatical word order (*SNegOV) does not occur at all in months 6 and 7 of RII. In the final session of RII (month 8) the ungrammatical word order occurs but is present only in 3% of the negative utterances. The data suggest that at least by month 5 of R-II, Rebecca has figured out that SNegOV order, where the object has not scrambled past the negative, is not allowed in Hindi–Urdu.

Approximately one year and five months after the end of the second period of her exposure to Hindi–Urdu, 29% of Rebecca's negative utterances during the first month of her third period of exposure (R-III) are in the ungrammatical *SNegOV order. After the first month of R-III, and except for a very low percentage of occurrence (3%) during months 5 and 8, the *SNegOV order is not attested in the remaining samples. The SOVNeg order predominates in the first sample during this period (approximately 34%) and is also the second most predominant order for the remainder of R-III. The grammatical SONegV order, where the object has scrambled past NegP is also present in 20% of her negative utterances in the first sample of R-III. Subsequent to the first sample, during the remaining eight months of R-III, it is the SONegV order that predominates (range 41–53%). It is also interesting to note that it is only in R-III that the OSNegV order, where the object has scrambled further upward past the subject to a Topic position, is attested for the first time. However, it is exceedingly rare and only shows up in the latter half of R-III.

The data from Rebecca suggest that she did not have a problem with figuring out that Hindi–Urdu VPs are head final. However, the data also suggest that she had difficulties in figuring out that Hindi–Urdu does not permit the SNegOV order, where the direct object remains underlyingly inside of VP, and that in Hindi–Urdu direct objects must scramble out of VP to a higher position.

What is further interesting is that the SNegOV order, which appeared to have disappeared from the latter part of R-II (suggesting that Rebecca had figured out that the object must move past Neg in Hindi–Urdu), reemerges (albeit briefly) during the initial part of R-III. Recall that the grammatical SONegV order occurred during the last two months of R-I. Recall further that it was not initially present during R-II, but was the dominant word order for the remainder of this period. In R-III, in contrast, the SONegV order is present from the very beginning and is the dominant order in all except for the first two months of R-III.

The persistence of the *SNegOV order across three different periods of exposure, despite the emergence of the grammatical SONegV order needs to be explained. Interestingly, the *SNegOV order has not been attested in child L1 learners of Hindi. The dominant word order of negative transitive utterances in the initial stage of child L1 Hindi is Xneg/SOV Neg.

But Hindi speaking children do not go through a stage where they produce utterances with the ungrammatical SNegOV order (Sharma, 1974; Varma, 1973). Although the dominant word order is SOV-Neg, they also do not have problems figuring out that in Hindi–Urdu the direct object cannot stay within VP but must scramble upward out of VP and past the negative. The fact that SNegOV is attested in Rebecca, a child L2 learner of Hindi–Urdu but not in children acquiring Hindi–Urdu as a first language, suggests that the SNegOV order may stem from L1 transfer: Rebecca's initial hypothesis appears to be that Hindi–Urdu, like her English L1, does not have the object shift rule. Even though SONegV is present in all three periods of her exposure and is the predominant word order for most of R-II and nearly all of R-III, as the SNegOV order persists for about half of RII and during the first month of R-III, Rebecca appears to have problems in figuring our that the SNegOV order is ungrammatical in Hindi–Urdu. The co-occurrence of the both the *SNegOV order and the SONegV order during the same period also suggests that the Object Shift rule is an optional rule in Rebecca's interlanguage grammar (i.e. R-I, part of R-II, and possibly the first month of RIII).[8]

There appear to be at least two factors involved in the persistence of the SNegOV order in the course of acquisition and reacquisition. One factor is that of L1 transfer, as English does not instantiate the overt object shift rule. Another important co-factor from a Minimalist perspective is the UG Principle of Procrastinate (Chomsky, 1995), according to which, the most economical derivation in computational terms is one where movement occurs as late as possible. In other words, covert movement (at the level of Logical Form) is preferred to Overt Movement (i.e. in the syntax, prior to Spell-Out). In other words, the Multiple Effects Principle (MEP) appears to be operative here as well. In order to override L1 transfer and MEP effects, the absence of structures in the input with the SNegOV order will have to be noticed.

Let us now turn to the spontaneous speech data gathered from Rebecca's brother Eric. Eric was exposed to Hindi–Urdu for the first time, when he was just 2;1. So his acquisition (i.e. during EI) could be termed as *sequential* bilingual first language acquisition rather than child L2 acquisition. In Eric I (2;1–2;9), 60% of Eric's utterances in the first month are in the ungrammatical (S)NegO(V) order and 40% of the utterances in the same month are in the X-Neg/SOVNeg order.[9] After the second month of Eric I, the *SNegOV order is exceedingly rare (3%) or completely absent from the months following the first two months of E-I. Over 90% of the negative utterances in months 3–8 of E-I are in the X-Neg/SOV-Neg order, which is similar to what has been attested for child L1 learners of Hindi. As in the case of Rebecca, the canonical SONegV order is initially absent in E-I. During two months in the latter half of Eric I, a few utterances with the SONegV order do occur, but they are exceedingly rare (approximately 5%).

In contrast to Eric I (2;1–2;9), in E-II (4;0–5;0), which may be termed as child L2 acquisition rather than child sequential bilingual first language acquisition, the dominant word order is the ungrammatical SNegOV order. It is only with the emergence of the canonical SONegV order in the latter half of Eric II that the SNegOV order decreases until it is exceedingly rare in occurrence (2% in the last sample of E-II). As in the case of Rebecca, the OSNegV order emerges very late, and only after the SONegV order has become more productive.

Ignoring the first month of Eric I, when the predominant word order was (S)NegO(V), a key difference between Eric I and Eric II is that in the case of the former, the predominant word order is X-Neg/SOVNeg), which is similar to child L1 Hindi. It is only in Eric's second period of exposure, which commenced more than a year later when he was four years old, that the pattern of development is similar to that of Rebecca I. The predominant word order during Eric II is the ungrammatical SNegOV order and not the SOVNeg order as was the case in E-I. Even though we have an acquisition–reacquisition situation involving the same individual during different periods of exposure, we notice clear differences in the pattern of development depending on the age when the exposure to the target language occurred. Specifically, it is only in Eric II (which represents child second language acquisition) but not in Eric I (which represents sequential bilingual first language acquisition) that we see clear effects of transfer of properties of Eric's L1 (i.e. English) to his Hindi–Urdu.[10] As in the case of Rebecca, Eric (in E-II) experienced difficulties in figuring out that the *SNegOV order, where the direct object has not scrambled leftward past the negative, is ungrammatical, and that scrambling of the object, past the negative, is not an optional but an obligatory rule in Hindi–Urdu.

Recall that during their final stay in India (R-III and E-II) and for approximately a year and a half following their final return to the United States, Hindi negative utterances were elicited experimentally through a picture-cued production task. Table 6.1 presents Hansen's results of the negative elicitation task. The patterns above the horizontal dotted line in the middle represent the predominant word orders observed in the negative utterances experimentally elicited from the children during their final stay in India. The word order patterns shown

Table 6.1 Negative elicitation test sentence patterns (Rebecca and Eric) (based on Hansen, 1980)

Date	Rebecca III	Eric II
Re-acquisition patterns (during final stay in a Hindi–Urdu speech milieu		
11-76	S NEG V O	S NEG V O
3-77	S O NEG V	S NEG OV
5-77	S O NEG V	S NEG O V
8-77	S O NEG V	S NEG O V
10-77	S O NEG V	S O NEG V
Attrition patterns (after return to the U.S.)		
11-77	S O NEG V	S O NEG V
1-78	S O NEG V	S O NEG V
3-78	S O NEG V	S O NEG V
6-78	S O NEG V	S NEG O V
9-78	S O NEG V	S NEG O V
11-78	S NEG V O	S NEG O V
2-79	S NEG V O	S NEG O V
5-79	S NEG V O	S NEG V O

below the horizontal line represent the predominant word orders attested in the children's experimentally elicited negative utterances after their return to the United States (i.e. when they were no longer exposed to Hindi–Urdu).

Both Rebecca and Eric preferred the SNegVO order during the first time that the elicitation test was administered, which was two weeks after they returned to a Hindi–Urdu speech milieu for the last time. Recall, however, that this was not an order that initially occurred in the spontaneous speech data. Hansen proposes that this is a result of an L1 relexification strategy that the subjects resorted to in order to complete the task. What is interesting is that in the case of Rebecca, the ungrammatical SNegOV order does not occur in the negative utterances that were experimentally elicited from her during her final stay in a Hindi–Urdu speech milieu. Recall that in the case of the spontaneous speech data gathered from her during this same period (R-III), the SNegOV order was very brief and only lasted for the first month. In contrast, the SONegV order was the predominant word order in the remainder of the spontaneous speech samples in R-III. In the case of Eric, the SNegOV order was the dominant word order in the spontaneous speech data gathered from him during the first five months of his second exposure period. In the case of the elicitation test, Eric also exhibited a strong preference for the SNegOV order. It was only in the case of the final administration of the elicitation test before his return to the United States that his experimentally elicited utterances began to be consistent with the SONegV order.

When we examine the attrition patterns for Rebecca and Eric, we notice interesting differences between the two learners. In the case of Rebecca, the SNegOV order does not show up at all in the data. Instead, the grammatical SONegV order, where the object has shifted past the Negative, persists for nine months after her removal from a Hindi–Urdu speech milieu. Recall that the ungrammatical SNegOV order was not attested at all in the data experimentally elicited from her during her final stay in the United States. Recall also that in R-III, the SNegOV order is fleeting (i.e. in the spontaneous speech data) and not captured in the elicitation data during acquisition. As mentioned earlier, it is in R-III that Rebecca appears to have figured out that the object shift rule in Hindi–Urdu is an obligatory and not an optional rule. Once having determined that SNegOV order is not permitted in Hindi–Urdu, which could only have been done by noticing the absence of this structure in the input (i.e. through the use of indirect negative evidence), the correct SONegV order continues to persist in the elicited data for a *whole year* after leaving the Hindi–Urdu speech milieu, indicating that with respect to the object shift rule she has successfully overridden language transfer and MEP effects. Subsequently, as Table 6.1 indicates, Rebecca resorts to an L1 relexification strategy.

In the E-II speech record, the ungrammatical SNegOV order is a tenacious early stage. In the elicitation data, the SNegOV order is the predominant order. Although the SONegV order is attested in the spontaneous speech samples and the elicited utterances in E-II, unlike in the case of Rebecca, there is no strong evidence that Eric has figured out that the object must scramble leftward past the negative in Hindi–Urdu, unlike in English. The language attrition patterns for Eric indicate that the SNegOV order is reverted to over many months in the elicitation data in the course of language loss as well. The persistence of this non-target-like structure in Eric's attrition data suggests that unlike in the case of Rebecca, Eric has not overridden L1 transfer effects in relation to the object shift rule in the course of his acquisition of Hindi–Urdu during his second and final exposure period.[11] Thus, the SNegOV order also persists in the course of language loss as well.

Conclusion

Second language acquisition research on the fossilization phenomenon has tended to focus on adult L2 learners. What I have attempted to do here is to suggest ways in which child second language acquisition data (as well as child L2 attrition and reacquisition data) can contribute to our understanding of the internal mechanisms involved in fossilization. Crucially, as I have argued above, what is needed are detailed longitudinal studies, using what Susan Foster-Cohen has termed as a sliding window approach, to compare the pattern of L2 development in learners sharing the same L1 and the same target second language, but with varied ages of exposure to the L2. Such cross-age comparisons of the pattern of development of interlanguage grammars should be more revealing about the internal mechanisms involved in second language acquisition and fossilization, in contrast to studies that focus solely on cross-age comparisons of the end state alone (for a similar position see Schwartz, 2003).

Using Susan Foster Cohen's sliding window approach in the domain of verb inflectional morphology in L2 English, I argued that the pattern of development in both child L2 learners and adult L2 learners is strikingly similar (but different from child L1 English). In the case of both child L2 learners and adult L2 learners of English, there is an asymmetry between the development of suppletive inflectional morphology and suffixal inflectional morphology (i.e. on the thematic verb). However, while this pattern is common to both L2 groups, the available evidence suggests that the asymmetry tends to persist in the long-term in the case of adults but not in the case of child L2 learners of English. As discussed above, the concrete realization of inflectional suffixes on thematic verbs in modern-day English, which are not raising verbs, represent arbitrary or conventionalized use of language, that lie more at the language specific periphery as opposed to the universal core. In fact, as discussed above, the observed asymmetry in adult and child English interlanguage may actually reflect a UG constrained morphological distinction between verbs that raise in the overt syntax and verbs that do not raise. The fact that the asymmetry between suppletive and suffixal verb inflections typically does not persist in the long term in the case of child L2 learners suggests that they are more advantaged with respect to the successful resolution of the mismatches between their developing grammar and the target grammar in the language specific grammatical periphery. Additionally, the long-term persistence of the asymmetrical pattern in the case of adults, suggests that they adhere more strictly (compared to children) to what may well be a UG constrained morphophonological distinction between raising and non-raising verbs.

In addition to verb inflectional morphology, I explored ways in which longitudinal cross-age comparisons of the pattern of L2 development, using the sliding window approach, can tell us more about the internal mechanisms that underlie fossilization of L2 knowledge in relation to constraints of Universal Grammar. I emphasized the need for such cross-age comparisons to address UG constraints of not only *form* but also *meaning*. Additionally, I stressed the importance of conducting such comparisons in situations entailing a potential learnability problem (i.e. where the poverty of stimulus applies) and situations where there is no potential learnability problem (i.e. where positive evidence is available for the convergence on the L2 grammar). Theoretically speaking, it is indeed possible that in the case of the former situation (i.e. a Poverty of Stimulus situation), both adult and child L2 learners may fail to converge on the target L2 grammar. I suggested, however, that although both children and adults may initially overgeneralize based on, for example, their L1, children might be able to retract from their overgeneralizations and restructure their interlanguage grammar in line with the target L2 more easily than adults. I suggested that this may be because of their superior ability in applying the learning/operating procedures that are involved in using indirect negative evidence (i.e. noticing the absence of a structure/rule and equating it with ungrammaticality) for grammatical mapping from UG onto their developing L2 grammar. The role of indirect negative evidence in grammar restructuring has been largely ignored. More attention needs to be paid to this issue in cross-age comparison studies – using the sliding window approach.

In addition to longitudinal cross-age comparisons of the pattern of L2 development over time, I suggested that another way of learning about the internal mechanisms involved in fossilization would be to use the sliding window approach to examine the patterns of L2 acquisition, reacquisition and attrition (i.e. in an individual learner with different periods of exposure to the target L2 separated by periods during which the individual is removed from the target second language environment). Specifically, I examined the patterns of L2 acquisition, reacquisition and attrition in relation to word order in Hindi/Urdu negatives of two English-speaking children. The acquisition and reacquisition data suggested that although the children did not have any problems in figuring out that Hindi–Urdu VPs are head final, they had considerable difficulties in figuring out that in Hindi–Urdu, the direct object moves overtly out of VP to a higher position. The learnability problem that they faced is evidenced by the persistence of the ungrammatical SNegOV order, where the object has failed to scramble overtly out of the VP to a position to the left of the negative. As stated above, the fact that the SNegOV order persists despite the emergence of the correct SONegV order, suggests that the children had difficulties in realizing that the object shift rule is an obligatory rule rather than an optional one in Hindi–Urdu.

I argued that the persistence of the ungrammatical SNegOV order in the course of acquisition and reacquisition stems from the Multiple Effects Principle. Specifically, I suggested that the learnability problem is a result of the conspiracy of at least two factors. One factor is that of language transfer (the L1 does not instantiate the overt object shift rule). Another co-factor is the fact that UG option instantiated in the L1 is consistent with the most economical derivation from a computational perspective; that is, a derivation where the movement occurs as late as possible (i.e. covertly) is preferred to one where the movement occurs in the overt syntax. Based on a comparison of the first phase of Eric's acquisition of Hindi–Urdu (which represents bilingual sequential first language acquisition) with phase two of his acquisition (which represents successive child L2 acquisition), I suggested that the language transfer (in relation to the object shift rule) sets in only in the latter phase, after Eric has reached a threshold of proficiency in relation to his L1. In other words, in relation to word order in negatives and the object shift rule, bilingual sequential acquisition of Hindi–Urdu prior to the age of three years is more similar to what has been reported for monolingual child L1 learners of Hindi–Urdu, for whom the ungrammatical SNegOV order, observed in E-II and R-I, has not been attested. As in the case of the monolingual child L1 learners of Hindi–Urdu, the predominant word order of negative transitive sentences in phase one of Eric's acquisition of Hindi–Urdu was X-Neg/SOV Neg (in contrast to E-II and RI).

I suggested that another co-factor responsible for the learnability problem is the fact that in order to realize that the object shift rule is an obligatory one in Hindi–Urdu, the absence of utterances with the ungrammatical SNegOV order in the input will have to be noticed by the learner. In other words, indirect negative evidence is needed to trigger the correct generalization. The pattern of development during phase three of Rebecca's exposure to Hindi–Urdu, along with the patterns of her attrition data beyond phase three, indicates that she was successful in using indirect negative data to correctly restructure her grammar in line with the target L2 in relation to the obligatory nature of the object shift rule. The pattern of development in phase two of Eric's exposure to Hindi–Urdu, along with his subsequent attrition patterns (i.e. his reversion to the ungrammatical SNegOV order over many months), suggests that unlike his older sibling, Rebecca, Eric was unable to figure out that the object shift rule is an obligatory rule in Hindi–Urdu. Recall that Rebecca's total exposure to a Hindi–Urdu speech milieu spanned a longer period of time than her younger sibling Eric's exposure to Hindi–Urdu. It is conceivable that more time and further exposure to Hindi–Urdu is needed in order for the learner to successfully use indirect negative evidence to expunge the optionality in relation to the object shift rule, thereby overriding language transfer and Multiple Effects.

I conclude with some thoughts on the monolingual native speaker bias that characterizes studies of the L2 end-state in particular and second language acquisition research in general (for discussion of the monolingual bias in second language acquisition research, see Cook, 1997). Criteria for determining whether interlanguage grammars have converged on the target grammar are typically based on monolingual native speaker norms. As Susan Foster-Cohen (2001) has stated, monolingual native speakers of the same dialect of a particular language may not necessarily pattern exactly alike in relation to their intuitions about grammaticality and ungrammaticality. Additionally, as Grosjean (1998) has stated, comparing bilinguals with monolingual speakers is like comparing apples and oranges. A bilingual individual is not the same as two monolingual speakers in the same person. This suggests that in order to make strides in our understanding of the phenomenon of fossilization, there needs to be a change in the criteria used for determining whether the learner has converged on the target grammar or not. Instead of using monolingual native speaker norms, where feasible, we need to establish criteria based on analysis of competence of people who have acquired the two languages simultaneously from birth and who have continued to maintain both languages. For example, in the case of the acquisition of property P in Hindi by native speakers of Tamil, for determining whether or not there has been convergence on the target grammar, we would need to determine what the competence of individuals who have acquired both Tamil and Hindi simultaneously from birth is in relation to the same property P.

Notes

1. One reviewer pointed out that even characterizing the performance of the non-native speakers in the Johnson and Newport study as 'end state performance' is suspect.
2. To my knowledge, Cancino *et al.* (1978) were the first to undertake such a longitudinal study comparing the development of negation and auxiliaries in the English interlanguage grammars of six native speakers of Spanish (two children, two adolescents, and two adults). However, the child L2–adult L2

developmental differences they observed may be attributed (at least partially) to the fact that the adult L2 subjects of the study may not have been appropriately matched with the younger subjects in relation to one of the necessary factors for L2 acquisition: i.e. exposure to input in the target language. For example, Alberto, one of the adult L2 learners who was observed to have fossilized at the No-V stage/unanalyzed *don't* V stage, was exposed to highly restrictive input in English, which probably contributed to the cessation in his L2 development at the No-V/unanalyzed *don't* V stage. It is important therefore that longitudinal studies comparing the pattern of L2 development across different ages take steps to ensure that the learners match in relation to the input factor.

3. See Lakshmanan and Selinker (2001) for discussion on how the use of obligatory contexts for past tense marking, established from the perspective of the target grammar, could result in the underestimation of the learner's knowledge.

4. One reviewer observed that although no-one has questioned Lardiere's characterization of Patty's interlanguage grammar as representing her steady state-end state competence, it is doubtful whether the data do indeed represent her end state grammar. According to the reviewer, the data from Patty reported in Lardiere (1998) were spoken data and not written data and may have been contaminated by processing factors.

5. These hypothetical scenarios differ from the ones depicted in White (2000) in that they, unlike the latter, crucially involve a comparison of child L2 and adult L2 with respect to their pattern of development from an initial state, through intermediary stages to an end state, and are not merely models of the L2 initial state in general

6. A reviewer questioned the use of the term dialect/idiosyncratic dialect, as opposed to the term Interlanguage. Interlanguages can indeed evolve into new dialects of their own. However, a problem with the term interlanguage, unlike the term dialect/idiosyncratic dialect, is that it does not necessarily imply the creation of a new/different dialect of the target second language. Instead, the term implies that the grammar is in the process of development in the direction of the target second language dialect, although of course, the grammar may permanently stabilize at any point in the Interlanguage continuum. Additionally, the term interlanguage has a negative connotation as it implies that a person who acquires a second language (i.e. non-natively) remains a second language learner on a permanent basis.

7. One of the reviewers wondered whether the second approach contradicts the first approach. This is, however, not the case. The second approach crucially involves the *comparison* of patterns of acquisition and reacquisition during periods of sustained exposure to/immersion in the target L2 that are separated by periods of removal from the L2 speech milieu.

8. One reviewer pointed out that while it is possible that the Object shift rule is an optional one in Rebecca's interlanguage grammar (i.e. R-1, part of R-II and possibly the first month of RIII), another possibility is that both constructions (SNegOV and SONegV) were acquired by Rebecca as unanalyzed chunks. It is unlikely that utterances with the SNegOV and SONegV order are unanalyzed chunks. First, the SNegOV order is ungrammatical in Hindi and is not likely to have been present in the Hindi/Urdu input that she was exposed to. Secondly, if they are unanalyzed chunks we would expect their occurrence to be

restricted to one or two lexical items (e.g. verbs). However, this is not the case and the two orders are productive and occur with different verbs and objects. The reviewer suggests that another possibility is that Rebecca may have adopted an instance-based approach, as opposed to a rule-based approach to acquiring SONegV and because of this got some instances right and some wrong. However, a major problem with this scenario is that it would not really explain what would trigger the disappearance of the SNegOV order in R-II (i.e. the second half) and in R-III (i.e. beyond the first month).

9. The utterances categorized by Hansen as (S)NegO(V), include utterances where the subject and the verb are omitted and utterances where there the subject and the verb are overtly present. In those cases (i.e. Eric's two word utterances) where only the Neg and the object are present and the Neg precedes the object, we cannot really tell what the relation of the object is to the implicit verb (i.e. in such utterances, the implicit verb could actually be located immediately following the negative element). Alternatively, such two-word utterances may be Pivot-Open constructions. Although Hansen does not provide separate counts for Neg-O word order, it is possible that most or many of the utterances in the (S)NegO(V) category are actually of the NegO type. If this is the case, it would indicate that E-I, which represents sequential bilingual first language acquisition of English and Hindi/Urdu is not similar to R-I, which represents successive child second language acquisition of Hindi/Urdu by a native speaker of English.

10. One reviewer wondered at what stage/phase in his acquisition of Hindi L1 transfer (i.e. from Eric's English to his Hindi–Urdu) might have set in, and what the counterpart negative structure during Eric first and second phase of acquisition of Hindi–Urdu. Hansen reports that at the beginning of Eric's first phase of aquisition of Hindi–Urdu (2;1), he was at the threshold of the one-word stage in English, although shortly thereafter, he began to produce utterances consisting of more than one word. Within a couple of weeks of entry in the new speech mileu, and in less than four months the lexicon of the South Asian language was clearly predominant. As Hansen observes, shortly after Eric's arrival in Pakistan, the negative element in his English negative utterances, which was realized as *no*, occurred in either utterance initial or utterance final position. Later, during this first phase, the English negative was realized as *nope* in the utterance/sentence final position. Hansen reports that it was only after several months of being removed from a Hindi–Urdu speech milieu that his English negative utterances were more adult-like with respect to the word order. When Eric commenced the second phase of his acquisition of Hindi–Urdu, his English negative utterances corresponded to that of adult native speakers of English. The status of Eric's negative utterances in his L1 (English) during his first phase of acquisition of Hindi–Urdu is additional evidence that transfer from his L1 (English) to his L2 (Hindi–Urdu) in relation to the object shift rule had probably not set in at this stage. Instead, what we appear to have is an instance of influence of the head final word order properties of his Hindi–Urdu on his English.

11. As explained earlier, L1 transfer from Eric's English to his Hindi–Urdu in relation to the object shift rule probably did not set in until phase two of his exposure to Hindi–Urdu.

References

Amritavalli, R. (2001) Morphological inaccuracy in second language performance: fossilization or fluidity? Paper presented at the International Congress, World Languages in Multilingual Contexts, Central Institute of English & Foreign Languages, Hyderabad, January 2001.

Bley-Vroman, R. (1990) The logical problem of foreign language learning. *Linguistic Analysis* 20, 3–49.

Brown, R. (1973) *A First Language: The Early Stages.* Cambridge, Massachusetts: Harvard University Press.

Cancino, H., Rosansky, E. and Schumann, J. (1978) The acquisition of English negatives and interrogatives by native Spanish speakers. In E. Hatch (ed.) *Second Language Acquisition: A Book of Readings* (pp. 207–230). Rowley, Massachusetts: Newbury House.

Chomsky, N. (1981) *Lectures on Government and Binding.* Dordrecht: Foris.

Chomsky, N. (1995) *The Minimalist Program.* Cambridge, Massachusetts: MIT Press.

Cook, V. (1997) Monolingual bias in second language acquisition research, *Revista Canaria de Estudios Ingleses*, 34, 35–50.

DeVilliers, J. and deVilliers, P. (1973) A cross-sectional study of the acquisition of grammatical morphemes in child speech. *Journal of Psycholinguistic Research* 2, 267–278.

Foster-Cohen, S. (2001) First language acquisition . . . second language acquisition: What's Hecuba to him or he to Hecuba? *Second Language Research* 17, 329–344.

Grosjean, F. (1998) Studying bilinguals: Methodological and conceptual issues. *Bilingualism: Language and Cognition* 1, 131–149.

Guilfoyle, E. (1984) The acquisition of tense and the emergence of thematic subjects in child grammars of English. *The McGill Working Papers in Linguistics* 2, 20–30.

Han, Z.-H. (1998) Fossilization: An investigation into advanced L2 learning of a typologically distant language. Doctoral Dissertation, University of London.

Han, Z.-H. (2004) *Fossilization in Adult Second Language Acquisition.* Clevedon: Multilingual Matters.

Hansen, L. (1980) Learning and forgetting a second language: the acquisition, loss and reacquisition of Hindi-Urdu negated structures by English-speaking children. PhD dissertation, University of California, Berkeley.

Hansen, L. (1983) The acquisition and forgetting of Hindi-Urdu negation by English-speaking children. In K. Bailey, M. Long and S. Peck (eds) *Second Language Acquisition Studies* (pp. 93–103). Rowley, Massachusetts: Newbury House.

Haznedar, B. (2001) The acquisition of the IP system in child L2 English. *Studies in Second Language Acquisition* 23, 1–39.

Haznedar, B. and Schwartz, B. (1997) Are there optional infinitives in child L2 acquisition? In E. Hughes, M. Hughes and A. Greenhill (eds) *Proceedings of the 21st Annual Boston University Conference on Language Development* (pp. 257–268). Somerville, Massachusetts: Cascadilla Press.

Hollebrandese, B. and Roeper, T. (1996) The concept of Do-insertion and the theory of INFL in acquisition. In C. Koster and F. Wijnen (eds) *Proceedings of the Conference on Generative Approaches to Language Acquisition.* Groningen, The Netherlands: Center for Language and Cognition.

Ionin, T. and Wexler, K. (2002) Why is 'is' easier than '-s'?: Acquisition of tense and agreement morphology by child second language learners of English. *Second Language Research* 18, 95–136.

Ito, Y. and Lakshmanan, U. (2001) Root infinitives and non-nominative subjects in the bilingual first language acquisition of Japanese and English. Paper presented at the International Congress, World Languages in Multilingual Contexts, Central Institute of English & Foreign Languages, Hyderabad, January 2001.

Jaeggli, O. and Hyams, N. (1988) Morphological uniformity and the setting of the null subject parameter. *Proceedings of NELS 18* (238-53). GLSA, University of Massachusetts, Amherst.

Johnson, J. and Newport, E. (1989) Critical period effects in second language learning: the influence of maturational state on the acquisition of English as a second language. *Cognitive Psychology* 21, 60–99.

Johnson, J. and Newport, E. (1991) Critical period effects on universal properties of language: The status of subjacency in the acquisition of a second language. *Cognition* 39, 215–258.

Kakazu, Y. and Lakshmanan, U. (2000) The status of IP and CP in Child L2 acquisition. In B. Swierzbin, F. Morris, M. Anderson, C. Klee and E. Tarone (eds) *Social and Cognitive Factors in Second Language Acquisition: Selected Proceedings of the 1999 Second Language Research Forum* (pp. 201–221). Somerville, Massachusetts: Cascadilla Press.

Lakshmanan, U. (1989) Accessibility to Universal Grammar in child second language acquisition. Doctoral Dissertation, University of Michigan, Ann Arbor.

Lakshmanan, U. (1991) Morphological uniformity and null subjects in child second language acquisition. In L. Eubank (ed.) *Point and Conterpont: Universal Grammar in the Second Language* (pp. 389–411). Amsterdam: John Benjamins.

Lakshmanan, U. (1993/1994) The boy for the cookie: Some evidence of the non-violation of the Case Filter principle in child second language acquisition. *Language Acquisition* 3, 55–91.

Lakshmanan, U. (1994) *Universal Grammar in Child Second Language Acquisition.* Amsterdam: John Benjamins.

Lakshmanan, U. (1995) Child second language acquisition of syntax. *Studies in Second Language Acquisition* 17, 301–329.

Lakshmanan, U. (1998a) Functional categories and related mechanisms in child second language acquisition. In S. Flynn, G. Martohardjono and W. O'Neil (eds) *The Generative Study of Second Language Acquisition* (pp. 3–16). Mahwah, NJ: Lawrence Erlbaum.

Lakshmanan, U. (1998b) Clause structure in child second language grammars. Plenary talk, Generative Approaches to Second Language Acquisition, University of Pittsburgh and Carnegie Melon University.

Lakshmanan, U. (1999) Object shift and the position of NegP in the child L2 grammars of Hindi-Urdu. In P. Robinson (ed.) *Representation and Process: Proceedings of the 3rd PacSLRF, Vol. 1.* Aoyama Gakuin University.

Lakshmanan, U. (2000) *Clause Structure in Child Second Language Grammars.* In A. Juffs, T. Talpas, G. Mizera and B. Burtt (eds) *Proceedings of 1998 GASLA IV,* (pp. 15–40). University of Pittsburgh.

Lakshmanan, U. and Selinker, L. (1994) The status of CP and the tensed complementizer *that* in the developing L2 grammars of English. *Second Language Research* 10, 25–48.

Lakshmanan, U. and Ito, Y. (2000) Root infinitives and non-nominative subjects in the bilingual first language acquisition of Japanese and English. Paper presented at the GASLA conference, MIT, March 2000.

Lakshmanan, U. and Selinker, L. (2001) Analysing interlanguage: How do we know what learners know? *Second Language Research* 17.4, 393–420.

Lakshmanan, U. and Tezel, Z. (1998) The acquisition of English syntax by an adult native speaker of Turkish. Unpublished raw data.

Lardiere, D. (1998) Case and Tense in the fossilized steady state. *Second Language Research* 14.1, 1–26.

Lee, D. and Schachter, J. (1997) Sensitive period effects in binding theory. *Language Acquisition* 6, 333–362.

Lenneberg, E. (1967) *Biological Foundations of Language*. New York: Wiley.

Long, M. (2003) Stabilization and fossilization in interlanguage development. In C. Doughty and M. Long (eds) *Handbook of Second Language Acquisition*. Oxford: Blackwell.

Martohardjono, G. (1993) *Wh-Movement in the Acquisition of a Second Language: A Cross-Linguistics Study of 3 Languages With and Without Overt Movement*. Unpublished Dostoral Dissertation, Cornell University, Ithaca, New York.

McLaughlin, B. (1978) *Second Language Acquisition in Childhood*. Hillsdale, NJ: Erlbaum.

Ozeki, M. (1995) *Functional Categories in the Acquisition of Japanese and English by a Two-Year-Old Child*. Unpublished M.A. Research Paper, Southern Illinois, University at Carbondale.

Pinker, S. (1989) *Learnability and Cognition: The Acquisition of Argument Structure*. Cambridge, Massachusetts: MIT Press.

Plough, I. (1995) Indirect negative evidence, inductive inferencing and second language acquisition. In L. Eubank, L. Selinker and M. Sharwood Smith (eds) *The Current State of Interlanguage: Studies in Honor of William E. Rutherford* (pp. 89–106). Amsterdam: John Benjamins.

Ravem, R. (1978) Two Norwegian children's acquisition of English syntax. In E. Hatch (ed.) *Second Language Acquisition: A Book of Readings* (pp. 148–154). Rowley, Massachusetts: Newbury House.

Rice, M., Wexler, K. and Hershberger, S. (1998) Tense over time: the longitudinal course of tense acquisition in children with specific language impairment. *Journal of Speech and Hearing Research* 41, 1412–1431.

Schachter, J. (1988) Second language acquisition and its relationship to universal grammar. *Applied Linguistics* 9, 219–235.

Schütze, C. and Wexler, C. (1996) Subject case licensing and English root infinitives. In A. Stringfellow, D. Cahana-Amitay, E. Hughes and A. Zukowski (eds) *Proceedings of the 20th Annual Boston University Conference on Language Development* (pp. 670–681). Somerville, Massachusetts: Cascadilla Press.

Schwartz, B. (1992) Testing between UG-based and problem-solving models of L2A: Developmental sequence data. *Language Acquisition* 2, 1–19.

Schwartz, B. (2003) Why child L2 acquisition? *Proceedings of the 2003 Generative Approaches to Language Acquisition*, Utrecht, Netherlands.

Schwartz, B. and Sprouse, R. (1996) L2 cognitive states and the Full Transfer/ Full Access model. *Second Language Research* 12, 40–72.

Selinker, L. (1972) Interlanguage. *IRAL* 10, 209–231.

Selinker, L. and Lakshmanan, U. (1992) Language transfer and fossilization: The "Multiple Effects Principle". In S. Gass and L. Selinker (eds) *Language Transfer in Language Learning* (pp. 197–216). Amsterdam: Benjamins.

Selinker, L., Swain, M. and Dumas, G. (1975) The Interlanguage hypothesis extended to children. *Language Learning* 25, 139–152.

Sharma, V. (1974) A linguistic study of speech development in early childhood. Unpublished PhD dissertation, University of Agra.

Vainikka, A. (1993/1994) Case in the development of English syntax. *Language Acquisition* 3, 257–325.

Varma, T. (1973) Some aspects of the early speech of a Hindi speaking child. Unpublished Mlitt thesis, University of Delhi.

Weber-Fox, C.M. and Neville, H.J. (1999) Functional neural subsystems are differentially affected by delays in second language immersion: ERP and behavioral evidence in bilinguals. In D. Birdsong (ed.) *Second Language Acquisition and the Critical Period Hypothesis* (pp. 23–38). Mahwah, New Jersey: Lawrence Erlbaum.

White, L. (2003) *Second Language Acquisition and Universal Grammar.* Cambridge University Press.

Zobl, H. and Liceras, J. (1994) Review Article: Functional categories and acquisition orders. *Language Learning* 44 (1), 159–180.

Chapter 7
Emergent Fossilization

BRIAN MACWHINNEY

Aging is an inescapable fact of human life. In most areas of our lives, aging leads to an unremarkable, gradual decline in physical ability. For example, no one questions why a 40-year-old runner can no longer compete in the Olympics. As the body ages, metabolism slows, joints wear out, and energy is diminished. Aging also has a uniform natural effect on the learning of new skills. As a result, we are not surprised to find that someone who tries to learn soccer at age 30 makes less progress than someone who begins learning at 12. We approach these gradual age-related physical declines and losses in learning ability with equanimity, since few of these skills are crucial for everyday functioning. No one would suggest that these declines represent the sudden expiration of an innate ability linked to a specific biological time fuse.

However, when we look at the decline in language learning abilities that comes with age, we assume a somewhat different position. We are distressed to find that a 35-year-old Romanian immigrant to the United States is unable to lose her Romanian accent, saying that this may limit her ability to adjust to the new society. We may wonder whether the observed fossilization represents the final expiration of some special gift for language learning. Or we may worry that a 28-year-old graduate student from Japan has trouble learning to use English articles. If these error patterns continue year after year, we say that the language spoken by these immigrants has 'fossilized' (Selinker, 1972).

Fossilization can also affect the young. For example, American university students in Japan in their twenties often make good progress in learning for two or three years and then level off before attaining native speaker competence. This pattern of acquisitions is seldom reported for students visiting other countries, leading one to wonder what features of Japanese language and culture may be inducing these problems. We should distinguish this type of immigrant fossilization from cases of incomplete learning or forgetting when students go abroad to study a language and then later show fossilized or diminished abilities when they return home and cease regular practice of the language.

In truth, fossilization is not an across-the-board phenomenon (Birdsong, this volume: chap. 9; Han, 2003, 2004; Han & Odlin, this volume: chap. 1). Rather, we find continual growth in some areas and relative stability of error in others. For example, older 'fossilized' Hungarian learners of English may continue to pick up new verbs, constructions, and phrases, while continuing to pronounce English _water_ as _vater_. Somehow, we tend to focus our attention more on these ongoing errors than the continuing new acquisitions. However, for those particular areas that show little change, it is accurate enough to think about localized fossilization.

Critical Periods

One traditional approach treats fossilization as a consequence of the expiration of a critical period for language acquisition. Customarily, this idea has been referred to as the Critical Period Hypothesis (CPH). For biologists, the concept of a critical period is grounded on studies of the maturation of tissues in the embryo. For example, Sperry (1956) showed how eye cells in the frog embryo could be transplanted at an early period and still form the correct pattern of connectivity with the brain. This happens because the cells are induced into appropriate connectivity by the surrounding tissue. However, if the eyes are transplanted after the critical period, then they will have committed to their previous position and will wire up incorrectly to the brain.

These embryological characterizations of critical periods depend on an understanding of the unfolding of the epigenetic landscape (Waddington, 1957) during the embryogenesis. By extension, similar processes are thought to occur in infant animals during the first days of life. For example, greylag geese will imprint on the first face they see after hatching, whether it be that of their mother or Konrad Lorenz (1958). Salmon hatchlings will imprint on the location of their home pond for later breeding.

A fundamental difference between prenatal and postnatal critical periods is that the latter require specific external stimuli as input. Because of this, we have to speak about experience-dependent or experience-expectant processes during the postnatal period. Eventually, as the critical period widens and the shape of the triggers broadens, we begin to talk about sensitive periods rather than critical periods. As we move away from the traditional embryological critical period to the postnatal sensitive period, the biochemical basis of the period often becomes increasingly complex. This is not to say that epigenesis is necessarily limited to the embryo and the infant. Stages such as puberty and menopause could well form the backdrop for critical period events later in life. For example, the rapid increase in members of the opposite sex that we find in teenagers could be analogized to the critical period for the greylag geese. However, hopefully young boys or girls will not immediately and irrevocably imprint on their true love on the first day of puberty.

A further problem with the notion of a critical period is that, without further definition and analysis, it would apply equally across all linguistic levels and systems. However, all of us – linguists, psychologists, and educators alike – would agree that language involves control of a diverse set of systems for articulation, audition, lexicon, grammar, and meaning. It is difficult to imagine how a single biological mechanism could have a uniform impact across all of these systems.

We can avoid all of these conceptual and empirical problems by speaking about the effects of the Age of Arrival (AoA) variable, rather than the expiration of critical period. The AoA variable measures the age at which an immigrant arrives in a new country and begins serious exposure to L2. It is AoA, rather than length of residence, that most strongly predicts the extent of achievement of nativelike proficiency in L2 (Birdsong, 2005). By focusing our attention on accounting for AoA effects, rather than critical period effects, we create a level playing field for the equal consideration of neurological, psychological, physiological, and sociological determinants of localized fossilization.

Possible Accounts

We would like to be able to construct and test models that account for the observed AoA and fossilization patterns using clearly stated mechanisms for processing and learning. Fortunately, the last decade has seen a proliferation of possible accounts. We can now distinguish at least these 10 concrete proposals.

(1) The lateralization hypothesis (Lenneberg, 1967).
(2) The neural commitment hypothesis (Lenneberg, 1967).
(3) The parameter-setting hypothesis (Flynn, 1996).
(4) The metabolic hypothesis (Pinker, 1994).
(5) The reproductive fitness hypothesis (Hurford & Kirby, 1999).
(6) The aging hypothesis (Barkow *et al.*, 1992).

(7)   The fragile rate hypothesis (Birdsong, in press).

(8)   The starting small hypothesis (Elman, 1993).

(9)   The entrenchment hypothesis (Marchman, 1992).

(10) The entrenchment and balance hypothesis (MacWhinney, 2005).

My goal in this chapter is to evaluate each of these 10 proposals against the whole range of age-related effects in language learning, including not only fossilization, but also earlier changes throughout the lifespan.

We could classify the first seven of these accounts as supporting a nativist view of language learning and the last three (or perhaps four) as tending toward empiricism or emergentism. However, little is to be gained from this characterization, since each of the views makes reference both to biological and psychological processes (MacWhinney, 2002). Thus, rather than trying to extract a set of binary features for evaluating these models (Newell, 1973), let us take a detailed look at each proposal in turn.

The Lateralization Hypothesis

The idea that AoA effects arise from maturational changes in the brain related to lateralization of function was first developed systematically by Lenneberg (1967). Lenneberg viewed the two cerebral hemispheres as equipotential at birth for the acquisition of language. However, over time, the left hemisphere assumed dominance for language functions. Lenneberg viewed this process of gradual lateralization as providing biological limits on first and second language acquisition. He placed great emphasis on evidence from children undergoing hemispherectomy to correct epileptic seizures which showed that, up until age 13, language could be relearned after removal of the left hemisphere (Basser, 1962). The idea here is that the massive changes that occur at puberty serve to terminate the language learning abilities of the child by finalizing the process of lateralization. Johnson and Newport (1989) and others have pointed to the onset of puberty as the defining moment in terms of the loss of an ability to acquire nativelike L2 skills. However, it is not clear why a growth in lateralization should, by itself, lead to a decline in the ability to acquire a first or second language. One model, suggested in the 1970s (Hardyck *et al.*, 1978) was that the first language would be organized to the left hemisphere and that the second language would be represented in the right hemisphere. According to this account, continued plasticity of the right hemisphere was required for nativelike learning of L2. Once this plasticity disappeared, nativelike L2 learning would become impossible. However, this account has not received consistent empirical support. Moreover, recent evidence (Muter *et al.*, 1997; Vargha Khadem *et al.*, 1994) has called into question the extent to which equipotentiality vanishes, even by puberty.

Research on language development during the first three years has demonstrated a variety of lateralization-related effects. There is abundant evidence suggesting that the left hemisphere is the preferred locus for speech from birth (Dennis & Whitaker, 1976; Kinsbourne & Hiscock, 1983; Molfese *et al.*, 1975; Molfese & Betz, 1987; Molfese & Hess, 1978; Wada *et al.*, 1975; Witelson, 1977; Witelson & Pallie, 1973; Woods & Teuber, 1977). However, dominance may shift to the right, if there are insufficient resources in the left hemisphere to allow it to perform its usual function (Zangwill, 1960). Children may experience brain damage at various points during development. Because the brain is experiencing ongoing and progressive (Luria, 1973) language organization during the first years of life (Satz *et al.*, 1990), brain damage will have very different effects at different points during development.

Together these studies point to important changes in lateralization for language during the first years of life. However, there is little in this literature suggesting that changes in lateralization are major determinants of age-related effects after the first three years. One exception is an fMRI study from our group (Booth *et al.*, 2001), showing somewhat stronger lateralization for adults compared to 10-year-olds for the processing of difficult embedded relative clauses. However, this effect may be due to late learning of these structures, rather than overall changes in lateralization.

The Commitment Hypothesis

A second proposed mechanism for AoA effects involves a progressive maturational commitment of language areas to linguistic functioning. Recent advances in the study of neural plasticity and commitment make accounts of this type increasingly attractive. This hypothesis would claim that some specific brain region or set of regions is undergoing commitment in parallel with the period during which AoA effects are demonstrated for learners. Data reviewed by Flege *et al.* (1999) show a decline in the ability to acquire nativelike articulatory competency, beginning at age five. The commitment hypothesis could account for these results if we could show that some area of the brain involved in the acquisition of phonology undergoes progressive commitment during this period.

To demonstrate this effect, we could conceivably use functional magnetic resonance imaging (fMRI) to track activation of brain areas across the age range of four to 20. Ideally, these fMRI studies would focus on the control of articulation. However, because articulation produces movement artifacts in the scanner, this study is not currently possible. Alternatively, the stimuli could be auditory sounds or words. We would expect that regions activated for these stimuli would become progressively narrower across this age range (Booth *et al.*, 2001; Haier, 2001).

It is likely that we will eventually be able to demonstrate some commitment effects during the relevant period. We already know that there are increases in myelinization (Lecours, 1975) and white matter commitment (McArdle *et al.*, 1987) up to age seven. These changes might well coincide with data on AoA effects for articulation (Flege *et al.*, 1999), but they may not match up as well for earlier effects in audition (Werker, 1995) and later effects in lexical learning (Snow & Hoefnagel-Hohle, 1978).

The Parameter Setting Hypothesis

Generative linguists (Flynn, 1996) have proposed a very different approach to AoA effects. This account suggests that first language learning depends on a process of parameter setting (Chomsky, 1981) specified by universal grammar (UG). For example, languages like English require that each verb have a subject, whereas languages like Italian allow dropping of pronominal subjects. Generative grammar holds that children use a set of syntactic triggers to determine the correct setting of parameters for their language. Once all of these settings are made for some small set of parameters, the language is fully identified. Years later, when the learner tries to learn a second language, these same parameters could perhaps be reset and be used to identify that second language.

The problem with this first version of L2 parameter setting is that it fails to predict any AoA effects, since resetting for L2 would not be influenced by transfer from L1 or any loss in ability to access UG. To deal with this, some UG researchers have favored a second model that holds that the parameters of UG that were available to the child are no longer available to the older second language learner. This account does not propose any specific biological mechanism for this maturational phenomenon, although one could invoke either commitment or lateralization as possible mechanisms.

The major problem with this second account, as currently articulated, is that there are no independent theoretical grounds for understanding why a given parameter would become either available or unavailable for the L2 learner. Lacking any independent biological or psychological grounding, this theory must rely on linguistic constraints to determine these predictions. If the constraints are set on the basis of evidence derived from L2 learning and fossilization, then this second version becomes circular and vacuous.

Both versions of the UG parameter-setting analysis suffer from another problem. This is the fact that UG only determines certain core features of a grammar, such as branching direction or binding, leaving other features such as agreement or case to the periphery. However, both core UG features and peripheral non-UG features are subject to AoA effects (Johnson & Newport, 1991; McDonald, 2000). Thus, we would have to supplement any UG theory of AoA and fossilization with a parallel external theory, perhaps following different principles.

The Metabolic Hypothesis

Pinker (1994) has proposed an innovative account of AoA effects based on notions from cognitive neuroscience and evolution. He suggests (p. 293) that 'a decline in metabolic rate and the number of neurons during early school-age years' is a probable cause of the loss of language-learning ability. However, Pinker's analysis places the neurological cart before the neurological horse. It is certainly true that subjects show greater metabolic activity for problems that are being learned (Haier, 2001; Merzenich, 2001) and less for ones that are fully controlled. However, this difference is not one that is shut down after early childhood. Rather, whenever learners – even older adults – are confronted with new tasks they show widespread metabolic activity during learning and narrower regions of activation for automated tasks (Raichle *et al.*, 1994). Thus, there is no evidence for any overall loss in metabolic activity of the type Pinker is suggesting.

The Reproductive Fitness Hypothesis

Hurford and Kirby (1999) present an account of AoA effects in both first and second language learning based on an analysis of evolutionary considerations. They reason that, over the course of human evolution, the attainment of complete fluency in a first language was a major determinant of reproductive fitness. If a child had not successfully acquired language by the age of sexual maturity, they would not be as attractive to a sexual partner and would therefore be less likely to produce offspring. Conversely, those who had acquired a high level of language ability would be highly attractive and would reproduce. Hurford and Kirby simulate this effect by imagining that a given target L1 has a fixed size expressed as a number of units. Children with a given amount of language learning ability acquire a fraction of these total units on each learning cycle. Because there is no advantage to completing learning before puberty, the simulation settles in with a pattern in which most learners acquire the full language just before puberty.

Initially, it would seem that assumptions and claims of this model are strikingly at odds with established wisdom from the field of child language. Child language researchers often consider that the core of a language is learned by age four (Brown, 1973). In fact, some generativists (Poeppel & Wexler, 1993; Wexler, 1998) believe that full competence is acquired even by the time of the first productive syntactic combinations. However, Hurford and Kirby's analysis can also be given an interpretation that escapes from these problems. This is not an interpretation that they themselves present, but it does seem consistent with their account. According to this extended co-evolutionary account, full control of a language involves acquisition of a variety of non-core language-related skills such as oratory, poetry, song, reading, and verbal memory. To the degree that progressive advances in social structure over the last 10,000 years have led to an increased evolutionary pressure for attainment of these extended linguistic abilities, we should indeed expect to see a continuing movement toward consolidation of these skills just before puberty.

Unlike Pinker, Hurford and Kirby are interested in determining the age by which language must be learned, rather than the age after which a second language cannot be learned. There is little in their analysis that would suggest that the ability to learn language should decline after puberty, only that first language learning must be completed by puberty. In fact, evolutionary considerations suggest that there should be strong pressures in some groups for ongoing maintenance of language learning abilities. For example, many tribal groups in Australia, Southeast Asia, and South America practice a form of alternating bride exchange between villages. In such cases, husband and wife will often speak different dialects or even different languages. Cases of this type show that there is continuing co-evolutionary pressure toward maintenance of language learning abilities into adulthood. Moreover, the fact that dominant males continue to procreate up to age 60 and beyond suggests that there should be evolutionary pressure away from a decline in language learning loss during adulthood.

These pressures for reproductive diversity and exogamy are in direct competition with another set of pressures forcing group loyalty and cohesion (MacWhinney, 2004). These pressures tend to favor mates from a related lineage, preferring endogamy to exogamy. The clearest way of establishing in-group membership is to lock in on a phonological accent, perhaps during early childhood. In this sense, a phonological accent functions in human communities much like dialect variation in song birds (Marler, 1991). However, if reproductive fitness were only conditioned on conservative maintenance of a local dialect, it would be difficult to account for the fact that reproductively attractive adolescent males often drive processes of phonological change (Labov, 1994).

Because of the diversity of these various pressures and the complexity of written languages with rich literatures, it is difficult to imagine that any single evolutionary mechanism would determine all aspects of adult linguistic ability. However, the wide range of individual differences in successful mastery of a second language after early children does indeed suggest that a variety of fairly recent evolutionary pressures have been operating to produce the observed population diversity.

The Aging Hypothesis

The most uncontroversial account of AoA and fossilization effects is one that emphasizes the physiological and neurological changes that occur with aging. As they age, most people begin to experience a marked slowdown in metabolic activity, energy, and flexibility. Hormonal processes slow down; arteries become blocked by platelets leading to strokes; Parkinsonism produces a loss of motor control; hearing acuity diminishes; and rheumatism and osteoporosis can lead to physical collapse. Core cognitive functions such as the storage of new memories and the retrieval of old memories can be disrupted by degeneration in the hippocampus and temporal lobe (Scheibel, 1996).

Although we typically think of these effects as impacting people over age 65, many of these effects begin even by age 45. However, even if we allow for an early onset of some of this decline, it seems difficult to attribute all AoA effects to aging. On the one hand, there is a clear and progressive decrement in language attainment that occurs well before 45. On the other hand, there are clear cases of partially successful language learning after age 65. I can relate a case I observed my Romanian relative from the city of Arad who began learning English when he retired at age 65. Married to a Hungarian woman in this bilingual community, he had spoken fluent Romanian and Hungarian all his life, and had some knowledge of German. With no input from native speakers, he began learning English from textbooks and dictionaries at 65. At first his speaking and writing was extremely difficult to follow. However, after 10 years of practice, particularly through letters mailed to relatives in the United States, his speaking and writing became increasingly comprehensible. In fact, he continued to progress in his language learning until his death at age

76 with no evidence of fossilization. Cases of this show that, although biological wear and tear undoubtedly leads to loss of language learning ability in some speakers, not all elderly people are equally impacted.

This illustrates an important principle. Many researchers in SLA would like to identify a single hypothesis that could account single-handedly for all of the observed age-related effects in language learning. Aging is certainly not going to account for all age-related effects, since it tells us nothing about changes before 45. However, it is clearly a contributory factor to some fossilization. Therefore a plausible account will have to show how aging combines with other factors. In general, our goal must be to provide independent support for each factor that we believe contributes to fossilization and to see how fossilization patterns emerge from these combinations.

The Fragile Rote Hypothesis

Birdsong (2005) suggests that, with increasing age, learners may have more problems acquiring irregular forms as opposed to regular forms. He suggests that irregular forms may include not only words with irregular inflections, but also irregular use of particles and prepositions in phrasal verbs. Birdsong seeks to ground the decline in learning of irregulars on neuroanatomical changes in the parts of the brain subserving the declarative memory system.

Currently, there is little data available to evaluate this hypothesis. Even in first language learners, irregulars can pose problems. However, it does seem reasonable to believe that these problems may increase in adult learning. On the other hand, the declarative memory loss that Birdsong invokes only plays a major role after age 50. Therefore, this account leaves unexplained the declines in language learning with AoA that we see before that time as well as changes in attainment of nativelike fluency that occur during childhood. If this hypothesis could be grounded on a mechanism that may change earlier in life, such as auditory memory, it might be able to do a better job accounting for observed patterns in age-related effects on language learning.

The Starting Small Hypothesis

Having now considered seven hypotheses that emphasize biological determinants of AoA effects, we can now turn to a consideration of three hypotheses that go beyond Biology to consider the role of psychological processing mechanisms. The first hypothesis we will examine in this area is the 'starting small' hypothesis of Newport (1990). Newport argued that 'language learning declines over maturation precisely because cognitive abilities increase.' The idea is that children have a smaller short-term memory span and that this shorter span makes it more difficult for them to store large chunks of utterances as formulaic items. As a result, children are forced to analyze language into its pieces.

Before turning to an analysis of the predictions of this model, it is worth noting that the idea that there is a growth in working memory during childhood is well accepted and documented by developmental psychologists (Halford *et al.*, 1995; MacWhinney *et al.*, 2000). Although a basic growth in working memory capacity is not disputed, it is not at all clear how this growth in memory capacity translates into changes in processing of sentences. In particular, children appear to have an auditory memory roughly equivalent to that of adults (Aslin *et al.*, 1999). On the other hand, their ability to pick up new lexical items is more limited (Gupta & MacWhinney, 1997; Snow & Hoefnagel-Hohle, 1978). It is unclear whether adults differ from children in terms of ability to piece together syntactic strings. How these discrepant abilities on these different levels interact with the growth of short-term memory capacity is also unclear.

Whatever its claims about these interactions, the starting small hypothesis makes at least four clear predictions. The first is that young children will not acquire complex multimorphemic words, preferring instead to pick up monosyllables. This claim is difficult to evaluate in languages like English or Chinese where the majority of words are only one or two syllables long. However, in languages like Hungarian (MacWhinney, 1974), Inuktitut (Crago & Allen, 1998), or Navajo, children seldom reduce four or five syllable words to single syllable components. Moreover, we often find the opposite effects in which young children learning English pick up formulaic utterances and clusters of words (Clark, 1974; Peters, 1983). Thus, it seems clear that this first basic prediction is at least partially incorrect.

A second prediction of this model is that the size of formulaic chunks will increase with age. This prediction seems to be supported in studies of school-age immigrant children learning English as a second language (Wong-Fillmore, 1976). These children do indeed pick up a variety of phrasal formulas such as 'why don't you__' or 'I wish I could just__.' However, the eight- and 10-year-old children who show these patterns are likely to end up learning their new language quite well, with non-native features being more evident in phonology than in sentence construction. Thus, although this prediction is generally supported, it fails to match up well to the overall course of age-related effects in second language learning.

A third prediction of the starting small hypothesis is that adults should be particularly good at acquiring larger phrasal chunks. For example, learners of German should be successful in picking up phrases such as *ins Mittelalter* or *des meine Mannes,* rather than learning these phrases as combinations of *in, das, Mittelalter, meine,* and *Mannes.* However, if adult learners were really using their memory to analyze these phrases as chunks, they would be able to use this database of adjectives and prepositions with nouns to acquire accurate use of German gender-number-case marking. In fact, adult learners have terrible trouble learning German gender, because they pick up each new noun as a separate analyzed unit, rather than as a part of a richer phrase. It is children who pick up the longer phrases and succeed thereby in acquiring correct use of gender. Thus, this third prediction of the model also seems to be wrong.

A fourth prediction of the model is that children with a smaller working memory should actually learn language better than those with a larger memory. It has often been shown that children with Specific Language Impairment have a smaller working memory capacity. This limitation should actually be a strength, but there is no evidence that learning works this way.

Given the empirical problems facing this model, one might wonder why it has received so much attention. In part, this may be a result of the fact that there have been several successful attempts to model this process (Elman, 1993; Goldowsky & Newport, 1993; Kareev, 1995) and also some failures to replicate the successes (Rohde & Plaut, 1999). However, these models all present a rather limited view of the acquisitional process, focusing on the learning of abstract syntactic patterns from 'predigested' input. For such abstract patterns, it may well be the case that a memory filter furthers attention to certain covariation patterns. Certainly, adults will do better at the extraction of lexical forms and rules if they are not overloaded with too much input (Cochran *et al.,* 1999; Kersten & Earles, 2001). However, the assistance that this filtering provides may be counterproductive in the long run, blocking the acquisition of larger chunks as in the case of the German example given above.

Overall, we can say that filters could be useful in terms of forcing attention to covariation patterns. However, a more powerful approach to language learning combines filtering with an opposed ability to pick up large unanalyzed chunks. More work is needed to see how these abilities change across the lifespan.

The Entrenchment Hypothesis

The most intuitive account for fossilization focuses on the notion of entrenchment. When we practice a given skill thousands of times, we soon find that it has become automated or entrenched. The more we continue to practice that skill, the deeper the entrenchment and the more difficult it becomes to vary or block the use of the skill. Entrenchment occurs in neural networks when a high frequency pattern is presented continuously in the input training data. For example, Marchman (1992) shows how irregular morphological forms such as *went* can become entrenched in a network learning English morphology. The entrenchment of a form such as *went* can serve to block overregularizations such as *goed*.

Entrenchment can be observed in many areas of our lives. Consider the case of a Hungarian peasant who has learned the dance forms of the Hungarian plain or Alföld with its csárdás steps and emphasis on straight posture in couple dances. For that dancer, the more flowery, style of Transylvania with its leaps and twists will be a bigger challenge. If the dancer only begins to learn the Transylvanian style after age 30, having danced the Alföld style for 20 years, there will be an unmistakable Alföld dance accent (Sándor Timár, folk ethnographer, personal communication) and we may even see fossilization in the learning of Transylvanian dance style. If the dancer learns both styles during adolescence, then there will be no clear fossilization and the dancer will be a 'balanced bilingual' in dance styles. However, if that same bilingual now turns to learning Thai dance at age 30, we can expect that the entrenchment of Hungarian dance styles and postures will produce strong fossilization during the learning of Thai patterns. If the learner waits until 40 to learn Thai dancing, this effect will be even stronger, since there will then be effects from both entrenchment and the decrease in joint and muscle flexibility that comes with aging.

Within a single system, entrenchment can work smoothly to block overregularizations and speed responses. However, when there is a radical shift in the input to an entrenchment system, neural network systems can suffer from 'catastrophic interference.' For example, Janice Johnson and I taught a neural network to assign grammatical roles to 178 different English sentence patterns. Once the network had learned these patterns, we shifted training to Dutch. However, the shift to a second language led to a catastrophic decline in the network's ability to process English, even though there were units in the training corpora that clearly identified the language of each sentence.

Not all neural networks are subject to catastrophic interference. Architectures that use local organization, such as self-organizing maps (SOM), can pick up new words as variants of old forms. Consider a feature map that has already encoded the word *table* on both a phonological map and a separate semantic map (Li *et al.*, 2004) along with an association between the two maps. When this system begins to learn the Spanish word *mesa*, it will enter first into the phonological map as just a new word (although possibly with English rather than Spanish phonology). This form will then be associated to the preexisting pattern for *table* in the semantic map. In this form of learning, *mesa* becomes parasitic on the meaning of *table*, because it is acquired simply as another way of saying *table*.

However, if we turn to syntactic learning, the problem is more serious. In that area, most models rely on back propagation. For example, in order to avoid catastrophic interference, Johnson and MacWhinney had to interleave training of Dutch and English from the beginning. This will work for some purposes, but it is clearly not a general solution to the problem, since many cases of real second language learning involve major shifts in language environment. To deal with these problems, neural network models of syntactic learning will need to shift to a lexicalist focus, as discussed in MacWhinney (2000). This focus emphasizes the extent to which syntax can be controlled through item-based patterns. For example, when learning the Spanish adjective *grande*, the system will not only encode the new word as a variant of English *big*, but will also encode its position as following the noun as in *una mesa grande*. This item-based positional pattern is encoded directly as a property of *grande* that does not interfere with related patterns for English. Eventually, a set of item-based patterns of this type will yield a general construction that places Spanish adjectives after their nouns, but this construction will be dependent on the collection of new Spanish word forms and will not interfere with the existing English system for placing the adjective before the noun. I should note that we have not yet implemented this system, but the nature of activation patterns in self-organizing maps indicate that it should operate in this way.

The Entrenchment and Balance Hypothesis

We see then that catastrophic interference can be solved by systems that emphasize the lexical and item-based nature of second language learning. Moreover, these lexically-grounded systems can also illustrate another important aspect of second language learning. This is the parasitic nature of L2 learning when L1 is already well consolidated.

Parasitism occurs because the L1 form is already well consolidated and entrenched by the time the learner tries to add the L2 form to the map. But what happens when both L1 and L2 are acquired simultaneously during childhood (Cenoz & Genesee, 2001). In this case, the LX and the LY forms should compete for nearby territory in the semantic space. In some cases, the LX form might be parasitic on the LY form. In other cases, the LY forms may be parasitic on the LX form. In still other cases, the learner may enter the two forms in related areas of the map along with additional features that distinguish particular properties of the words. For example, the Spanish noun *vaso* will be encoded as referring only to a container from which we drink, whereas the English noun *glass* will refer both to the container and the material used in bottles and windows. In this way, simultaneous bilingual acquisition tends to minimize the misleading effects of transfer and parasitism.

A Preliminary Assessment

We have now examined ten proposed accounts of fossilization and AoA effects in second language learning. The majority of these accounts generate predictions that are inconsistent with the observed patterns. For example, the lateralization hypothesis targets effects occurring at puberty despite the fact that the major changes in lateralization occur during the first three years. The parameter setting hypothesis, when coupled with the idea that UG becomes inaccessible at a discrete moment, would predict a rapid drop in L2 learning that is not observed in the data. The metabolic decline hypothesis does not align well with evidence from neuroscience that decreased metabolic activity actually represents increased learning and increased automaticity. The reproductive fitness hypothesis is in sharp disagreement with basic facts regarding early child language learning. A further problem with each of these first four hypotheses is that they treat language ability as a single undifferentiated whole, failing to distinguish different age-related patterns for phonology, lexicon, syntax, morphology, and pragmatics.

The fragile rote hypothesis is linked to the decline in memory abilities that occurs after age 50. As such, it may account for some fossilization effects, but not for AoA and other age-related effects at younger ages. The same can be said with the aging hypothesis with which it is closely related. The starting small hypothesis succeeds in accounting for some adult experimental data, but makes a series of incorrect predictions regarding child language learning.

Of the first eight models we have examined, the one that seems most nearly in accord with observed AoA and fossilization effects is the neuronal commitment hypothesis. However, there are two reasons why we should be careful in evaluating this apparent success. First, within specific evidence about how specific neuronal areas lose their plasticity at particular ages, we can simply invoke this hypothesis to explain any observed pattern. Second, it is different to draw a sharp conceptual difference between neuronal commitment and entrenchment. Rather, entrenchment seems to be the psychological result of processes of neuronal commitment operating on the cellular level. Given this, it is perhaps best to focus on an evaluation of entrenchment. We have already seen that an entrenchment account, by itself, will not provide a full account of basic AoA and fossilization effects. Instead, we clearly need to view entrenchment as working in the context of the additional mechanism of parasitism.

Thus it seems that the best currently available account of AoA and fossilization effects is one that combines the concepts of entrenchment and parasitic transfer. This is also the account most in accord with the Unified Competition Model (MacWhinney, 2005) – a model that emphasizes the role of transfer in second language learning, the use of item-based patterns to avoid catastrophic interference, and chunking and item learning as methods for automatization and entrenchment.

The entrenchment-and-transfer account predicts a gradual decline of L2 attainment beginning as early as age five and extending through adulthood. It predicts no sharp drop, but rather a slow, gradual decline. These predictions are in good accord with the basic shape of observed AoA patterns. Moreover, the specific predictions of the model are further differentiated across linguistic areas or arenas.

The Unified Competition Model holds that transfer should be particularly strong on the level of phonology, since new phonological words are initially learned as combinations (Gupta & MacWhinney, 1997) of old L1 segments and syllables. For lexical learning, there is also massive initial transfer of old meanings. Syntax shows some item-based transfer effects, but less than the other areas, since these patterns are dependent on new lexical items. Moreover, even when there is a match between languages (Pienemann *et al.*, 2005), transfer does not operate in terms of whole sentence patterns, but only individual word combinations such as adjective + noun (MacWhinney, 2005). Finally, in the area of morphological marking, we only expect transfer of grammatical function, if these functions have a close match, not transfer of specific grammatical forms or patterns. Entrenchment also operates differentially across linguistic areas, with the strongest entrenchment occurring in output phonology and the least entrenchment in the area of lexicon, where new learning continues to occur in L1 in any case.

The Social Stratification Hypothesis

Although an account based on transfer and entrenchment captures the overall shape of fossilization phenomena, it fails to predict the observed diversity of outcomes among adult learners. It also fails to predict the extent to which some adult learners achieve nearly complete mastery, whereas others seldom advance beyond the lowest levels. To account for these additional patterns in adult learners, I believe that we need to invoke two further processes. The first involves the social positioning of the older learner and the shape of the input that this positioning will provide. The second process involves the strategic mechanisms that adults need to employ to overcome the effects of entrenchment and parasitism. I will refer to these two additional processes as the social stratification hypothesis and the compensatory strategies hypothesis.

It is difficult to overestimate the potential impact of social structures on language acquisition by both older children and adults. In most modern cultures, children acquire a first language within the context of a nuclear family group. Although there are strong variations between and within cultural and socioeconomic groups, virtually all children benefit from rich and consistent input from their parents, the extended family, co-wives, or older children. Whatever the exact configuration of the input social group, children are always treated as apprentices who need to be guided through the language learning process. Their silly mistakes and inarticulate productions are considered cute and lovable and they are never made to feel embarrassed or inadequate. Age-matched peers are also engaged in language learning and are in no position to make fun of errors from their playmates.

By the time children enter school at age five, the situation has begun to change. An immigrant child arriving in a new country at this age will immediately seem strange and out of place. At school, they cannot express themselves and at home their parents may provide little in terms of L2 input. During the early school years, the child's best approach is to be withdrawn and silent at first, only entering into social groups after picking up a few basic phrases. By the time the child reaches adolescence, the pressure of the L1 community on the immigrant child can be truly massive and sometimes even vicious. In order to become exposed to adequate peer group input, the adolescent must be willing to suffer a major degradation in status and rights. However, even this will not guarantee full acceptance. Although the rewards of improved L2 competence are great, the barriers to attainment of that competence also increase greatly.

Acculturation during adulthood involves a far greater diversity of situations. In some cases, immigrants may marry into the L1 community, thereby guaranteeing basic acceptance and access to input. However, even in these cases, they will not be treated in as supportive a manner as a parent treats a child. When they are overtly corrected, they will feel a certain loss of prestige that can strain social relations. Outside of marriage, L2 acculturation may succeed through work groups and casual social groups. However, in many other contexts the immigrant withdraws at least partially from the dominant language and remains tightly within the L1-speaking immigrant community. Because of the growing importance of English as an international language, L1 speakers may place pressure on English-speaking immigrants to converse in English, thereby further blocking potential L2 acquisition. This effect can be further exacerbated by modern communication systems such as email, phone, television, and the Internet that allow travelers to remain within an English language capsule from the beginning to the end of even month-long stays abroad.

The Compensatory Strategies Hypothesis

The variance we find in adult L2 attainment must certainly be explained in large part by variation in the social contexts facing immigrants and the ways in which they deal with these contexts socially. However, even in unfavorable social situations, learners can make use of compensatory learning strategies. These strategies are designed to directly combat the effects of increased L1 entrenchment, as well as the effects of biological aging. There are at least three major strategies: input maximization, recoding, and resonance.

Input maximization involves a whole series of strategies designed to obtain good learning input. The learner may try to use dictionaries, work through grammars, take classes, watch movies, listen to lectures, talk to friends, or just go shopping. The goal here is to simply practice use of the language.

Recoding involves the construction of alternative images of new words and phrases. Because of the likely decline in raw auditory memory with age and the possible further decline in declarative storage, older learners need to construct methods of keeping new words and phrases in memory while they are being learned. The easiest way to do this is to represent the new word orthographically. Orthographic learning has two important roles for older learners. First, it provides a solid recoding of transient auditory input. Second, it opens access to input from books, signs, and product labels. This second effect is relatively weaker in the learning of languages such as Navajo or Inuktitut. Although these languages have an ample written literature, there is relatively less use of signage and written instructions in these rural cultures than in more urban communities.

When both L1 and L2 use the Roman alphabet, it is relatively easy to recode L2 into L1, although there may be some glitches in this recoding, as in the recoding of French, using English grapheme-phoneme correspondences. However, these glitches can be readily repaired. Even the mapping from Roman onto phonetic alphabets such as Cyrillic for Russian, Hangul for Korean, or Kana for Japanese is within reach of older learners. However, acquisition of a non-phonemic script such as Chinese Hanzi characters is a major challenge for older learners. Because younger learners rely relatively less on recoding, they will be able to pick up Chinese more directly. Thus older learners attempting to overcome entrenchment through reliance on orthographic recoding are at a particular disadvantage until they have mastered the new writing system. As a result, older learners must either acquire the new orthography or rely relatively more on alternative compensatory strategies.

Because learning through resonant connections is highly strategic, L2 learners will vary markedly in the constructions they can control or which are missing or incorrectly transferred (Birdsong, this volume: chap. 9). In addition to the basic forces of entrenchment, transfer, and strategic resonant learning, older learners will be affected by problems with restricted social contacts, commitments to ongoing L1 interactions, and declining cognitive abilities. None of these changes predict a sharp drop at a certain age in L2 learning abilities. Instead, they predict a gradual decline across the life span.

A final important strategy available to adult learners is resonance. Resonance involves the establishment of a series of associative relations between words and meanings that can allow the learner to maintain a vivid image of the word until the relations are consolidated. In this sense, resonance is really the general case of recoding. Examples of resonance include the use of the keyword mnemonic or imagery method for learning new words (Atkinson, 1975). For example, Italian *pomodoro* 'tomato' can be encoded as 'Dora sitting under a palm tree eating a tomato.' Or the learner might recognize *pomodoro* as a *golden* (doro) *apple* (pomme). Or the learner may create some idiosyncratic relation between the sound of *pomodoro* and the action of slicing a tomato with its sounds and smells. It does not matter if these connections are real or fanciful. All that matters is that they help to maintain a resonant trace of the word's sound and meaning until the new item can be consolidated. Similar methods can be used to acquire longer phrases that encode for properties such as gender, tone, or particle usage.

Conclusions

In this chapter, we have examined a set of twelve hypotheses regarding the etiology of age of acquisition (AoA) and fossilization effects. Of the various candidate hypotheses, the one that matches most clearly with the basic data on a gradual decline in learning ability is the hypothesis that combines the effects of ongoing L1 entrenchment with the notion that L2 develops at first as parasitic or dependent on L1. Although this account correctly predicts the overall gradual decline in L2 learning, it fails to predict the diversity of fossilization patterns we see among older learners. To account for these additional effects, we need to look at both the effects of social stratification on older immigrants and the extent to which they can use compensatory strategies to combat the effects of entrenchment.

References

Aslin, R.N., Saffran, J.R. and Newport, E.L. (1999) Statistical learning in linguistic and nonlinguistic domains. In B. MacWhinney (ed.) *The Emergence of Language* (pp. 359–380). Mahwah, NJ: Lawrence Erlbaum Associates.

Atkinson, R. (1975) Mnemotechnics in second-language learning. *American Psychologist* 30, 821–828.

Barkow, J., Cosmides, L. and Tooby, J. (eds) (1992) *The Adapted Mind: Evolutionary Psychology and the Generation of Culture.* New York: Oxford University Press.

Basser, L.S. (1962) Hemiplegia of early onset and the faculty of speech with special reference to the effects of hemispherectomy. *Brain* 85, 427–460.

Birdsong, D. (2005) Interpreting age effects in second language acquisition. In J.F. Kroll and A.M.B. deGroot (eds) *Handbook of Bilingualism: Psycholinguistic Approaches* (pp. 109–127). New York: Oxford University Press.

Booth, J.R., MacWhinney, B., Thulborn, K.R., Sacco, K., Voyvodic, J.T. and Feldman, H.M. (2001) Developmental and lesion effects during brain activation for sentence comprehension and mental rotation. *Developmental Neuropsychology* 18, 139–169.

Brown, R. (1973) *A First Language: The Early Stages.* Cambridge, MA: Harvard.

Cenoz, J. and Genesee, F. (2001) *Trends in Bilingual Acquisition.* Amsterdam: John Benjamins.

Chomsky, N. (1981) *Lectures on Government and Binding.* Cinnaminson, NJ: Foris.

Clark, R. (1974) Performing without competence. *Journal of Child Language* 1, 1–10.

Cochran, B.P., McDonald, J.L. and Parault, S.J. (1999) Too smart for their own good: The disadvantage of superior processing capacity for adult language learners. *Journal of Memory and Language* 41, 30–58.

Crago, M.B. and Allen, S.E.M. (1998) Acquiring Inukitut. In O. Taylor and L. Leonard (eds) *Language Acquisition Across North America: Cross-Cultural and Cross-Linguistic Perspectives* (pp. 245–279). San Diego, CA: Singular Publishing Group.

Dennis, M. and Whitaker, H. (1976) Linguistic superiority of the left over the right hemisphere. *Brain and Language* 3, 404–433.

Elman, J. (1993) Incremental learning, or the importance of starting small. *Cognition* 48, 71–99.

Flege, J.E., Yeni-Komshian, G.H. and Liu, S. (1999) Age constraints on second-language acquisition. *Journal of Memory and Language* 41, 78–104.

Flynn, S. (1996) A parameter-setting approach to second language acquisition. In W.C. Ritchie and T.K. Bhatia (eds) *Handbook of Second Language Acquisition* (pp. 121–158). San Diego: Academic Press.

Goldowsky, B.N. and Newport, E. (1993) Modeling the effects of processing limitations on the acquisition of morphology: The less is more hypothesis. In E. Clark (ed.) *Proceedings of the 24th Annual Child Language Research Forum* (pp. 124–138). Stanford: CSLI.

Gupta, P. and MacWhinney, B. (1997) Vocabulary acquisition and verbal short-term memory: Computational and neural bases. *Brain and Language* 59, 267–333.

Haier, R. (2001) PET studies of learning and individual differences. In J. McClelland and R. Siegler (eds) *Mechanisms of Cognitive Development* (pp. 123–148). Mahwah, NJ: Lawrence Erlbaum Associates.

Halford, G.S., Smith, S.B., Dickson, J.C., Mayberry, M.T., Kelly, M.E., Bain, J.D. *et al.* (1995) Modeling the development of reasoning strategies: The roles of analogy, knowledge, and capacity. In T. Simon and G. Halford (eds) *Developing Cognitive Competence: New Approaches to Process Modeling* (pp. 156–182). Hillsdale, NJ: Lawrence Erlbaum Associates.

Han, Z.-H. (2003, March) Fossilization: Facts, fancies, fallacies, and methodological problems. Paper presented at the AAAL 2003 Conference, Arlington, Virginia.

Han, Z.-H. (2004) *Fossilization in Adult Second Language Acquisition.* Clevedon: Multilingual Matters.

Hardyck, C., Tzeng, O. and Wang, W. (1978) Cerebral lateralization of function and bilingual decision processes: Is thinking lateralized? *Brain and Language* 5, 56–71.

Hurford, J. and Kirby, S. (1999). Co-evolution of language size and the criticial period. In D. Birdsong (ed.) *Second Language Acquisition and the Critical Period Hypothesis* (pp. 39–63). Mahwah, NJ: Lawrence Erlbaum Associates.

Johnson, J. and Newport, E. (1989) Critical period effects in second language learning: The influence of maturational state on the acquisition of English as a second language. *Cognitive Psychology* 21, 60–99.

Johnson, J. and Newport, E.L. (1991) Critical period effects on universal properties of language: The status of subjacency in the acquisition of a second language. *Cognition* 39, 215–258.

Kareev, Y. (1995) Through a narrow window: Working memory capacity and the detection of covariation. *Cognition* 56, 263–269.

Kersten, A.W. and Earles, J.L. (2001) Less really is more for adults learning a miniature artificial language. *Journal of Memory and Language* 44, 250–273.

Kinsbourne, M. and Hiscock, M. (1983) The normal and deviant development of functional lateralization of the brain. In P. Mussen, M. Haith and J. Campos (eds) *Handbook of Child Psychology*. New York: Wiley.

Labov, W. (1994) *Principles of Linguistic Change: Internal Factors*. Oxford: Blackwell.

Lecours, A.R. (1975) Myelogenetic correlates of the development of speech and language. In E.H. Lenneberg and E. Lenneberg (eds) *Foundations of Language Development: A Multidisciplinary Approach* (Vol. 1, pp. 121–136). New York: Academic Press.

Lenneberg, E.H. (1967) *Biological Foundations of Language*. New York: Wiley.
Li, P., Farkas, I. and MacWhinney, B. (2004) Early lexical development in a self-organizing neural network. *Neural Networks*, 17, 1345–1362.
Lorenz, K.Z. (1958) The evolution of behavior. *Scientific American* 199, 95–104.
Luria, A.R. (1973) *The Working Brain*. New York: Basic Books.
MacWhinney, B. (1974) *How Hungarian Children Learn to Speak*. University of California, Berkeley.
MacWhinney, B. (2000) Lexicalist connectionism. In P. Broeder and J. Murre (eds) *Models of Language Acquisition: Inductive and Deductive Approaches* (pp. 9–32). Cambridge, MA: MIT Press.
MacWhinney, B. (2002) Language emergence. In P. Burmeister, T. Piske and A. Rohde (eds) *An Integrated View of Language Development–Papers in Honor of Henning Wode* (pp. 17–42). Trier: Wissenschaftlicher Verlag Trier.
MacWhinney, B. (2004) Language evolution and human development. In D. Bjorklund and A. Pellegrini (eds) *Child Development and Evolutionary Psychology*. New York: Cambridge University Press.
MacWhinney, B. (2005) A unified model of language acquisition. In J.F. Kroll and A.M.B. deGroot (eds) *Handbook of Bilingualism: Psycholinguistic Approaches* (pp. 49–67). New York: Oxford University Press.
MacWhinney, B., Feldman, H.M., Sacco, K. and Valdes-Perez, R. (2000) Online measures of basic language skills in children with early focal brain lesions. *Brain and Language* 71, 400–431.
Marchman, V. (1992) Constraint on plasticity in a connectionist model of the English past tense. *Journal of Cognitive Neuroscience* 4, 215–234.
Marler, P. (1991) Song-learning behavior: The interface with neuroethology. *Trends in Neuroscience* 14, 199–206.
McArdle, C.B., Richardson, C.J., Nicholas, D.A., Mirfakhraee, M., Hayden, C.K. and Amparo, E.G. (1987) Developmental features of the neonatal brain: MR imaging – Part 1. Gray white matter: Differentiation and myelination. *Radiology* 162, 162–223.
McDonald, J. (2000) Grammaticality judgments in a second language: Influences of age of acquisition and native language. *Applied Psycholinguistics* 21, 395–423.
Merzenich, M. (2001) Cortical plasticity contributing to child development. In J. McClelland and R. Siegler (eds) *Mechanisms of Cognitive Development* (pp. 67–96). Mahwah, NJ: Lawrence Erlbaum Associates.
Molfese, D., Freeman, R.D. and Palermo, D.S. (1975) The ontogeny of brain lateralization for speech and nonspeech stimuli. *Brain and Language* 2, 356–368.
Molfese, D. and Hess, T. (1978) Hemispheric specialization for VOT perception in the preschool child. *Journal of Experimental Child Psychology* 26, 71–84.
Molfese, V. and Betz, J. (1987) Language and motor development in infancy: Three views with neuropsychological implications. *Developmental Neuropsychology* 3, 255–274.
Muter, V., Taylor, S. and Vargha-Khadem, F. (1997) A longitudinal study of early intellectual development in hemiplegic children. *Neuropsychologia* 35, 289–298.
Newell, A. (1973) You can't play 20 questions with nature and win: Projective comments on the papers of this symposium. In W. Chase (ed.) *Visual Information Processing*. New York: Academic Press.
Newport, E. (1990) Maturational constraints on language learning. *Cognitive Science* 14, 11–28.

Peters, A. (1983) *The Units of Language Acquisition*. New York: Cambridge University Press.

Pienemann, M., Di Biase, B., Kawaguchi, S. and Håkansson, G. (2005) Processing constraints on L1 transfer. In J.F. Kroll and A.M.B. deGroot (eds) *Handbook of Bilingualism: Psycholinguistic Approaches* (pp. 128–153). New York: Oxford University Press.

Pinker, S. (1994) *The Language Instinct*. New York: William Morrow.

Poeppel, D. and Wexler, K. (1993) The full competence hypothesis of clause structure in early German. *Language* 69, 1–33.

Raichle, M.E., Fiez, J.A., Videen, T.O., Macleod, A.K., Pardo, J.V., T., F.P. *et al.* (1994) Practice-related changes in human brain functional anatomy during non-motor learning. *Cerebral Cortex* 4, 8–26.

Rohde, D. and Plaut, D. (1999) Language acquisition in the absence of explicit negative evidence: How important is starting small? *Cognition* 72, 67–109.

Satz, P., Strauss, E. and Whitaker, H. (1990) The ontogeny of hemispheric specialization: Some old hypotheses revisited. *Brain and Language* 38, 596–614.

Scheibel, A.B. (1996) Structural and functional changes in the aging brain. In J.E. Birren and K.W. Schaie (eds) *Handbook of the Psychology of Aging, Fourth Edition* (pp. 105–128). San Diego: Academic Press.

Selinker, L. (1972) Interlanguage. *International Review of Applied Linguistics* 10, 209–231.

Snow, C. and Hoefnagel-Hohle, M. (1978) The critical period for language acquisition: Evidence from second language learning. *Child Development* 49, 1114–1128.

Sperry, R. (1956) The eye and the brain. *Scientific American* 194, 48–52.

Vargha Khadem, F., Isaacs, E. and Muter, V. (1994) A review of cognitive outcome after unilateral lesions sustained during childhood. *Journal of Child Neurology* 9, 2s67–62s73.

Wada, J.A., Clarke, R. and Hamm, A. (1975) Cerebral hemispheric asymmetry in humans. *Archives of Neurology* 32, 239–246.

Waddington, C.H. (1957) *The Strategy of the Genes*. New York: MacMillan.

Werker, J.F. (1995) Exploring developmental changes in cross-language speech perception. In L. Gleitman and M. Liberman (eds) *An Invitation to Cognitive Science. Language Volume 1* (pp. 87–106). Cambridge, MA: MIT Press.

Wexler, K. (1998) Very early parameter setting and the unique checking constraint: A new explanation of the optional infinitive stage. *Lingua* 106, 23–79.

Witelson, S. (1977) Early hemisphere specialization and interhemisphere plasticity: An empirical and theoretical review. In S. Segalowitz and F. Gruber (eds) *Language Development and Neurological Theory*. New York: Academic Press.

Witelson, S. and Pallie, W. (1973) Left hemisphere specialization for language in the newborn. *Brain* 96, 641–646.

Wong-Fillmore, L. (1976) *The Second Time Around: Cognitive and Social Strategies in Second Language Acquisition*. Stanford: Stanford University Press.

Woods, B. and Teuber, H. (1977) Changing patterns of childhood aphasia. *Annals of Neurology* 3, 273–280.

Zangwill, O.L. (1960) *Cerebral Dominance and Its Relation to Psychological Function*. Ediburgh: Oliver and Boyd.

Chapter 8
Fossilization, Social Context and Language Play

ELAINE TARONE

The passage of time causes the human organism, and all its functions, to age. As each function ages and changes, it affects each other function as well. In other words, the passage of time makes the human organism increasingly complex: an increasingly messy web of interrelated functions affected by an increasing number of events. Suppose, for example, that we wish to identify the cause of persistent abdominal pain in an aging woman. The passage of time has given her a hiatal hernia, arterial blockage, a deteriorating reproductive system that has borne three children, exposure to allergens she reacts to, and anxiety. The woman's social network disappears as husband, family, and friends die and children move away; she becomes depressed, her contact with the outside world becomes minimal, and she stubbornly refuses to eat healthy foods. Her attempts to self-medicate impair her physical and cognitive functioning, affecting in turn some or all of the original causes. It is easy to see how the passage of time makes it increasingly likely that some or all of these factors interact, and less and less likely that there is only one cause of the continuing original symptom: persistent abdominal pain. My point here is this: the aging process does not lend itself well to any research design in which one holds all variables constant except the one variable one wishes to identify as THE cause of one particular outcome.

Complex Social and Psychological Context of Fossilization

Consider then the dilemma faced by the second language acquisition scholar who wishes to understand the phenomenon of fossilization. Fossilization will be defined here as *the cessation of the continued development of interlanguage over time.* (Whether this fossilization occurs at a steady rate over time, or in fits and starts, is an empirical question, and not assumed in our definition.) As in our example of the aging woman, the aging second language learner – moving through the ages of 15, 25, 35, or 45 – is affected by an increasingly complex web of experiential, maturational, and social factors that must surely have an increasingly complex and cumulatively negative impact on the language learning process (Treat, 2001). A possibly extreme example of this is the 40-year-old Somali immigrant woman who is learning English as a second language in Minnesota. To achieve success in her second language acquisition, she faces a daunting set of factors that her six-year-old son does not: the need to spend 40 hours/week in a custodial job where she speaks to almost no one; to maintain a household in a high-rise apartment complex; to feed, transport, clothe and nurture a child; to deal with cognitive impairment resulting from earlier trauma in refugee camps as well as cognitive barriers caused by her total lack of schooling (including lack of native language literacy) in her native land; to square her identity as a home-bound rural Somali woman with pressure to assume a new identity as a woman in an urban Minnesota society; and last but not least for a woman reliant on the Minnesota public transit system, to get to English classes in sub-zero temperatures for three months of the year (compare with Curiel, 2003). Her son faces none of these barriers in his second language acquisition process.

The study of the impact of the passage of time on second language acquisition outcomes does not lend itself to the experimental paradigm, or easy answers. The young and the older second language learner live in very different worlds, in bodies with very different functions: we would expect their learning outcomes to be different. And while the 20-year-old college student does not face all the barriers the 40-year-old Somali immigrant does, he must still deal with a more complex social and experiential world than he did at age six. Are the complex factors in the lives of older language learners irrelevant? Is the cognitive process of second language acquisition totally unaffected by the increasingly complex experiential and social factors in the lives of older learners? I do not think so.

Two Ways Cognitive Processing in SLA Can be Affected by Social Factors

This chapter will argue that fossilization can be explained, at least in part, as a result of social and socio-psychological forces that affect cognitive processing and so impede acquisition on the part of some learners.

These forces result in a socio-psychological barrier that prevents L2 input from affecting cognitive processes that might alter the structure of the interlanguage. If we consider interlanguage to be the product of balancing complex forces of stability and creativity, the fossilized interlanguage is one in which the forces of stability predominate. Factors that stimulate creativity in language use may counteract those forces of stability and lead to renewed development of the interlanguage (within the increasingly complex and interlocking systemic forces navigated over time by the learner).

First, how do social and socio-psychological forces affect cognitive processing synchronically, and through this, affect second language acquisition over time? Tarone (2000a, 2003) has previously presented evidence that such forces can alter learners' processing of the second language. I will briefly summarize that evidence here.

Socio-psychological influences on noticing

One central cognitive process in SLA is now taken to be learners' 'noticing' of key forms in the L2 input provided by others. Scholarly work on input processing (VanPatten, 1996) and focus on form (Long & Robinson, 1998) suggests that acquisition benefits most when second-language learners focus, not on linguistic form alone, or on communicative meaning alone, but on both form and meaning when they use the L2. Focus on form (FonF), for example, has been most frequently operationalized as a brief shift of a learner's attention from meaningful content to linguistic code features.

It has long been argued that attention to either language form or language meaning is an important cognitive mechanism that influences learners' variable attempts to be accurate when speaking in the L2. However, Bell (1984), in discussing native speakers' processing of language made the crucial point that attention, or noticing, is a construct that bridges the cognitive (attention is a cognitive process) and the social (attention is differentially directed by social factors). It is not a root cause; rather, it is the speaker's responsiveness to the social relationships among speakers that causes attention to shift from meaning to form to meaning. Bell's Style Axiom, applied to a second language acquisition situation, allows us to posit that what second language learners notice is influenced in a major way by social contextual factors, factors such as the social group membership of the learner and the learner's interlocutors.

There are research findings in several areas of SLA that support our application of Bell's Style Axiom to the domain of second-language acquisition. For example, Kormos (1999) points to several such findings in her review of studies exploring Levelt's perceptual loop theory of monitoring in SLA. These studies suggest that error detection depends not just on psycholinguistic factors, like availability of attention but also on factors of social context such as the 'accuracy demand of the situation' and 'various listener-based discourse constraints' (p. 324). In another example, as they review the body of research on learner awareness of negative feedback provided to them, Nicholas *et al.* (2001) point out that learner awareness seems to be affected differently by different social contexts:

> there are differences between the findings of laboratory and classroom studies, differences between primarily structure-focused and primarily content-focused classrooms, and differences between observational studies of naturally occurring feedback patterns in classrooms and experimental studies that focus on specific linguistic features and feedback types. (Nicholas *et al.*, 2001: 751)

If it is true, as Schmidt (1993) claims, that learners must notice the difference between their own and new language forms in order to acquire the new form, then failure to notice means failure to acquire – and failure to acquire, over the long haul, means fossilization.

Krashen (1981) has used the metaphor of the 'affective filter' to refer to learners' socio-psychological barriers that prevent new L2 input from being considered in the process of second-language acquisition. (Krashen's description of S., a middle-aged Chinese woman whose English has fossilized, is instructive here: she says that she has decided that the 'little words' such as 'is,' 'to,' 'of,' 'the,' 'a,' really do not matter, so she is not going to pay any attention to them. She says she does not care whether her English is grammatical, or sounds American.)

Socio-psychological influences on orientation to new L2 norms

Socio-psychological factors can affect more than the noticing of negative feedback. At a more global level, these factors can prevent L2 learners from identifying with certain interlocutors and adopting new linguistic norms used by those interlocutors. Learners in this situation may resist linguistic change, preferring their own stable IL norms.

Beebe and Giles (1984) explain learners' second-language acquisition processes in terms of Speech Accommodation Theory (SAT). This theory predicts that L2 learners will adjust their production of L2 forms to the forms that are used by their interlocutors. L2 learners may choose to converge, to sound more like interlocutors they wish to identify with, or to diverge from the speech patterns of interlocutors they do not wish to identify with. Beebe (1977, 1980) demonstrates that as L2 learners move from one conversation to another at a single point in time, certain interlanguage forms they produce will converge, become more similar, to those of interlocutors from whom they desire approval or with whom they wish to express social identity. Beebe documents such short-term shifts, lasting only for the duration of the conversation. Similarly, SAT predicts that L2 learners' interlanguage forms will diverge, or become dissimilar from, those of interlocutors with whom they differ socially. Rampton (1995) documents the sort of divergence predicted by SAT, where L2 speakers emphasize speech and nonverbal differences between themselves and their interlocutors. He describes Pakistani students in London who deliberately use a 'Me no + verb' construction with their teacher, when they are perfectly capable of saying 'I don't + verb' with other interlocutors. Both convergence and divergence constitute strategies of short-term identification with the communicative norms of some reference group, either present or absent at the time of speaking. But can such short-term divergence result in long-term fossilization?

There is some evidence in the research literature that this can occur. Schumann (1978) explained his subject, Alberto's, fossilization in his acquisition of English L2 as the result of a failure to acculturate: a long-term failure to converge with the norms of American society or with the English speakers who belong to it. The Acculturation Model predicts that learners like Alberto who do not acculturate will fail to acquire the L2; indeed, their interlanguage may even pidginize, fossilizing at a very early stage of development.

Lybeck's (2002) longitudinal study of Americans in Norway provides empirical evidence in support of Schumann's model; her study shows that learners' progress or fossilization in the process of acquiring L2 phonological forms is directly related to those learners' learner's acculturation and formation of a new socio-cultural identity. American women sojourning over several years in Norway were interviewed twice during one year, once in the Fall and again in the Spring. Their production of several Norwegian phonological features was judged for nativeness by native phonologists at Time 1 and Time 2. Their social networks (compare with Milroy, 1980), comprised of both Norwegians and other American ex-patriots, were mapped at Time 1 and Time 2, based on interviews with the researcher. Most of these women established good social networks with Norwegians and showed progress over time, improving their production of target L2 Norwegian variants.

However, one learner who began with very native-like Norwegian phonology became alienated from the target culture during the study, dramatically altering her social network; as a result she exhibited back-sliding, and after six months, produced a fossilized phonology with more NL variants than she'd had at the beginning of the year. Her negative experiences with her Norwegian in-laws as well as other Norwegians in a range of social situations had led her to believe that Norwegians were not likely to provide her with the kinds of supportive relationships she needed. Interviews suggested a negative change in her self-described socio-cultural identity and attitude toward the target culture. Over the same period of time, this learner's interlanguage phonology showed a dramatic drop in native-like accuracy; she began using a more American variant of R, and global ratings of her phonology nativeness also dropped substantially.

While it is clear that more longitudinal research is needed to trace the long-term impact of socio-psychological factors on IL fossilization, there already exist several studies which, taken together, suggest that this would be a very profitable line of research.

Chaos Theory and Fossilization

The studies I have cited seem to suggest that learners' social inter-actions in a range of different social situations may result in their for-mation of a socio-psychological barrier that prevents them from noticing negative feedback, or from using L2 input provided in certain situations to alter the structure of the interlanguage. An interlanguage shielded behind these socio-psychological barriers is one in which the forces of stability rule. When these barriers have formed before the IL reached proximity to TL norms, then we may say the IL has fossilized.

The problem faced by second-language educators and second-language learners alike, then, is this: how can forces of creativity be introduced into this kind of interlanguage system to counterbalance the forces of stability, and once again de-stabilize the system? To put it another way: how can these strong socio-psychological barriers be breached? If socio-psychological barriers were formed to any degree by social interactions in social contexts, then perhaps one way to counteract them is also by means of social interactions in social contexts.

In the remainder of this chapter, I will suggest that one powerful socio-psychological tool that can help counter forces of fossilization is language play. Language play may help to counterbalance forces of stability and lead to renewed development of the interlanguage.

IL as a dynamic, complex, non-linear system

A productive model of second-language acquisition for our purposes is one in which interlanguage is viewed as a dynamic, complex non-linear system (Larsen-Freeman, 1997) or as a system existing in tension between centralizing and individualizing forces (Bakhtin, 1981). In such a model there is a recognition of, and a vital role played by, the inherent instability and unpredictability characteristic of language in use. Language play can be seen as the realm of such unpredictable elements (Cook, personal communication, Feb. 1999). In such a model, language play has a role as a manifestation of the force of creativity that is essential to the process of language acquisition and language change. Work is needed to develop a comprehensive theory that might show how such forces for individual creativity in language use interact with more conservative forces for system maintenance, though one could argue that all study of language change, including historical linguistics and sociolinguistics as disciplines, focuses on the tension between innovation and conservatism in language use.

In the first half of the twentieth century, Bakhtin (1981) situated his discussion of the balance between creativity and stability within a socio-cultural theory of language, one that acknowledges the impact that social factors have on human cognition. Bakhtin stressed that in an individual's language use, centripetal (or centralizing, normalizing) forces are typically in tension with the centrifugal forces of individual creativity, which introduce innovation and diversity. In Bakhtin's view, these forces operate at all linguistic levels, though he was most interested in creativity at the semantic and discourse level, manifested in adult language play such as 'double voicing' (speaking in the 'voice' of someone else), irony and parody.

Bakhtin said that linguistic scholars had paid little attention to the:

> great and diverse world of verbal forms that ridicule the straightforward, serious word in all its generic guises. This world is very rich, considerably richer than we are accustomed to believe. The nature and methods available for ridiculing something are highly varied, and not exhausted by parodying and travestying in a strict sense. These methods for making fun of the straightforward word have as yet received little scholarly attention. (Bakhtin, 1981: 52)

Defining language play

Cook (1997, 2000) identifies two kinds of language play: (1) play with language form, e.g. the sounds of language, rhyme, rhythm, song, alliteration, puns, grammatical parallelism, and (2) semantic play, 'play with units of meaning, combining them in ways which create worlds which do not exist: fictions' (1997, p. 228).

Play with language form, especially sound play, has long been attested as prominent in the speech of young children (compare with Weir, 1962). Peck (1977) describes children's language play as language use that is non-literal, intrinsically motivating, and deliberately flouts the regular patterns of language use, both linguistic and social. She comments that a distinguishing characteristic of child–child discourse is that it can be both social and 'non-referential,' that is, it does not refer to the 'real' world of reference (p. 33). Children's language play creates a world of reference that is separate from the prosaic, everyday world of reference and is often socially constructed, with a separate world of meaning being jointly constructed for mutual entertainment.

Language play occurs in interlanguage discourse

Broner and Tarone (2001) document many instances of language play in the discourse of Spanish immersion fifth graders. In the following excerpt, notice how 11-year-old Leonard deliberately violates a pronunciation norm and when criticized, proclaims his allegiance to the forces of creativity in his IL use:

Leonard (singing): (a) *Ricola. Tricola.*
Dave: (b) *No es tricola. Es ri [cola.]* (It's not tricola.
           It's ri[cola.])
Leonard: (c) [I know] but I can say whatever I want to.

(Broner & Tarone, 2001: 363)

In the following conversation Leonard plays with the sounds of 'doce' and 'dieciocho' in his second language, varying the intonation and rhythm, and even singing. He knows these words very well; he is not practicing them. Rather, his playful repetition of these words is motivated by his desire to entertain himself:

Leonard: doce. (p) doce! doce!
          (with different voices, apparently trying to get the
          teacher's attention.)
          doce (to himself) doce. do:ce. doce. doce (sings it)

Child:	dieciocho!
Child:	dieciocho!
Leonard:	dieciocho, dieciocho. (singing to the same tune) dieciocho!
Child:	no sabemos.
Leonard:	doce!
Child:	no sabemos, diciocho, dieciocho, dieciocho (singing to the same tune as Leonard)
Leonard:	es doce, doce, doce, doce, doce, doce, doce (all really fast to the tune). (Broner & Tarone, 2001)

And consider the interaction documented by Peck (1978) between Joe (a native speaker of English) and Angel, a Spanish speaker who is learning English as a second language; in this interaction, Joe makes fun of Angel's apparent failure to aspirate the initial voiceless stop in the word 'camera'. He does this by playing with the word as Angel pronounces it: singing it, announcing it like a circus barker, in a way that initially angers Angel, but in the end engages Angel himself in joint play with the word 'gamera':

J:	//And – a//
A:	Camera – /l/– is camera
J:	(mocking his accent:)/gæmera/!
A:	Camera.
J:	/gæmera/.
A:	Like – tha' – you have camera?//I like –//
J:	(to the tune of "Camelot") Ca//mera!// Camera! Camera!
A:	CAmera
J:	(circus barker's voice) Announcing the mighty gamera! (laugh)
A:	(louder)/kæ/ – /me/ – /ra/
J:	(sing-song) GAmera.
A:	(irritated, shouting:) Camerá.
J:	(laughing, loud) GAmera. (softer:) /gamera/
A:	(soft, laughing) /gamera/

(Peck, 1978: 395)

This is surely a fairly explicit kind of 'focus on form' (see also Doughty & Williams, 1998). Bigelow (personal communication, 2003) suggests that it is input enhancement (as with Van Patten's work), input flood and contains a sort of recast of Angel's production, one which Angel certainly notices and takes up. Interestingly, the use of different 'voices' (compare with Bakhtin, 1981) in making fun of Angel's pronunciation of a word (variation of the pitch and volume, using the intonation contour of a circus barker), is something that seems to be a consistent 'marker' of language play in the discourse of older children, adolescents and adults. It is a kind of sound play that involves the variable repetition of a phonological sequence, which is now being embedded in other kinds of play: parody, ridicule, and 'double-voicing.'

Note how Joe and Angel, in the following example, continue their uses of different voices, sound play ('crazy daisy') and play with syntax in discourse that ridicules Joe this time. Angel varies his L2 syntax, moving from 'No, like a crazy boy,' to 'a crazy,' then to 'no, a crazy you,' and finally to 'you are crazy.' The meaning does not change here, and there is no negotiation of meaning; Angel just varies the form of the syntax as he encodes the same meaning several ways. What we notice here is that these friends are deliberately violating normal language usage through their play, and so may be said to be destabilizing their linguistic systems through their creativity:

(14) **Joe:** That's like on – Ernie and Bert – (roar)
Angel: No, like a crazy boy! (laugh)
Joe: (laugh) That's more like it. (high pitch:) What?
Angel: (chuckling) Like a crazy boy!
Joe: (even higher) What?
Angel: (softer) Like a crazy boy.
Joe: Like a mazy – like a – a –
Angel: (loudly) Crazy!
Joe: I – I mean – li' li' (pretending to stutter) I mean – I – I – I mean – I mean – I mean – I mean – I mean – (normal voice) I mean a crazy?
Angel: A crazy.
Joe: A crazy what, a crazy daisy?
Angel: No, a crazy you.
Joe: Oh! Oh! Oh!
Angel: You are crazy.
Joe: Oh! Oh! (10×)

(Peck, 1977: 78)

Finally, Tarone (2000b) shows that it is not just children who engage in language play with their interlanguages. Teenagers in foreign language classrooms also have been recorded using their L2 in instances of language play. Cross-language puns seemed to be particularly popular with a group of Hungarian teenagers learning English L2 in a task-based instruction project. For example, two teenage girls joked and laughed several times in a conversation in English about getting 'soaked'; in Hungarian, 'elazni,' 'to get soaked' also means 'to get drunk' in teen vernacular.[1]

It seems clear, then, that second-language learners may produce many forms of language play, and that they do so quite spontaneously in their interlanguage discourse. They play with language forms in rhyme, rhythm, songs and puns, and they play with semantics, creating fictions, 'make-believe,' irony and 'double-voicing.' But does this language play facilitate or hinder the second-language acquisition process? Or is it simply irrelevant to that process?

Language play exploits and encourages variability in interlanguage systems

We have seen that current research on SLA is examining the role of noticing and focus on form as a fundamental cognitive process fueling SLA. It is interesting therefore to discover that a large part of the language play that occurs naturally in the L2 discourse of both young and older language learners *is* in fact play with L2 forms, and this at *all* linguistic levels, as Tarone (2000b) shows. Surely this kind of play is only possible if learners have *noticed* the forms being played with.

But it would be simplistic to view language play with L2 forms as simply a 'noticing' of L2 forms that need to be acquired. There is something important about the *way* in which learners play with L2 forms in our data. Language play with form involves not just noticing correct L2 forms in order to weed out incorrect productions and acquire the correct ones. Quite the contrary; play with second-language forms introduces *more* variation into the IL system, not *less* – for example, using a whole series of different ways to (mis)pronounce a word, or producing several variations of the stress pattern of a word, not just the 'correct' one. Play with second-language forms is highly creative, not aimed at achieving accuracy, but rather, devoted to the production of whole sets of unpredictable and often incorrect forms. This is clearly not the sort of focus on form that Long and Robinson (1998) refer to; for them, 'focus on form' means drawing 'learners' attention to mismatches between input and output' (p. 23), with the clear implication that learners will want to get rid of that mismatch by adjusting their output to conform to the more correct input. The sort of focus on form that occurs in language play does not result in convergence on a single accurate form, as the Long and Robinson model of FonF implies, but rather in an unpredictable generation of a whole set of loosely-related formal possibilities, most of which are not correct in the target language.

This increased IL variation can be accounted for and explained as a part of the process of SLA if (following Larsen-Freeman, 1997) we view the interlanguage system as a whole as a complex dynamical system in which forces that foster stability must be balanced with forces of creativity. The IL system could not develop unless the more conservative forces for stability were at times overruled by more creative forces demanding innovation, in Bakhtin's (1981) terms. Using a chaos theory model that views IL as a complex dynamical system thus encourages us to try to identify, not just the forces that stabilize the IL, but also the creative forces in SLA. In a view of SLA that is motivated by chaos theory, IL is a system built and modified as a result of a constant tension between the forces of individual creativity and the forces maintaining system norms, forces which may ultimately result in fossilization. In other words, viewing IL as a complex dynamic system may help us to explain the inherently unstable and variable yet systematic nature of interlanguage (compare with Tarone, 1983; Preston, 2000), and to seek to identify and study the impact of creativity as an important force that shapes IL. In complex dynamic systems, there is always persistent instability deriving from the interplay of creativity and the self-organizing properties of all nonlinear systems, so that 'an unstable system is not a contradiction in terms' (Larsen-Freeman, 1997: 156).

In discussing individuals' language use, Bakhtin (1981) stressed that the force of conformity to any language norm is necessarily centripetal and restricts the creative freedom of the individual. Yet, Bakhtin said, in real language use, those centripetal forces are typically in tension with the *centrifugal* forces of innovation and creativity. The identification of centrifugal, or creative forces, in the interlanguage system leads us to explore the impact of language play upon IL development and fossilization. Following Bakhtin, it can be argued that the L2 learner who plays with the form of IL utterances is a learner who is asserting creative freedom – declaring a measure of independence from conformity to the IL superordinate norm in order to be able to experiment with new language varieties and to create novel constructions or use novel voices. Play with L2 forms involves creative use of the interlanguage, which in turn may allow the development of the permeable parts of the learner's interlanguage, stretching the learner's rule system beyond the limits of its current norm. Language play with L2 forms may thus be one manifestation of a destabilizing force in IL – a sociolinguistic force like Preston's (1989) 'change from below' being another – which provides a productive counterweight to the stable force of adherence to interlanguage norms. What is unique about language play with L2 forms is that in it, a speaker's production may deviate from all norms – NL, TL or IL – in its expression of individual creativity.

Does language play prevent formation of fossilized forms?

Is there evidence that language play does prevent formation of fossilized forms? At present there is suggestive but not definitive evidence that this dynamic does occur. (Of course, it is only recently that researchers have even begun to recognize the possible importance of language play in shaping IL.) Suggestive evidence is provided by descriptions of interactions among second language learners in studies by Broner and Tarone (2001), Belz (2002), and Bell (2002, 2005).

In Broner and Tarone (2001), Leonard plays with two possible IL variants for 'head': 'cerebro' and 'celebro,' an alternation that produces hilarity on the part of his friends. Leonard begins his play episode with the correct 'cerebro,' but as he plays with the possible alternative 'celebro' and his friends join in, he appears to shift to the inaccurate variant 'celebro,' and in fact uses 'celebro' some days later in his final presentation. This suggests a movement over time from use of one form to another, a movement apparently facilitated by an episode of language play.

Belz (2002) studies German L2 learners' play in a writing assignment requiring that they produce a multilingual text using German and another language. She finds that the learners themselves, in reflecting on their, and their classmates', creative use of two languages in a single essay, state that it helped them change aspects of their IL that were previously problematic – areas where they had felt stuck. For example, one learner said that another learner's play helped him deal with separable prefixes in German:

'I liked the playful parts [of the multilingual essays] where people were very obviously experimenting: I mean LIN ... because it really takes a certain amount of force to push words into an alternate grammar, at least for me it's really hard. You have to think about it ... LIN really made me think about separable prefixes...'

Finally, Bell (2002) identifies Playful Language Related Episodes (PLREs) in the discourse of advanced learners of English as a second language. She shows that such events can have the effect of drawing learners' attention to IL items they had previously thought were incorrect, causing them to reevaluate their previous judgments of acceptability. She provides an example of a lexical item ('clone') which a Russian learner of English believed was wrongly used by a native speaker of English in a language play episode. The native speaker's play with that word leads that learner into an extended PLRE focused upon that item. During the course of the PLRE, the learner becomes increasingly convinced that her previous judgment may have been wrong.

Of course, all these examples are simply suggestive. What is missing in these examples, and in the rest of the research literature, if we are trying to find support for the position that language play prevents fossilization, is evidence that exposure to language play with a structure or item creates change in a learner's IL with regard to that item or structure, which previously had appeared to be a candidate for fossilization. Definitive evidence must await a longitudinal study that is designed specifically to identify and trace the effects of what Bell calls PLREs upon later language development. Bell suggests a methodology based on that used by Williams (2001), in which individualized post-tests could be constructed based on items that were the subject of playful discussion during taped discourse, to see if the use of those items in language play destabilized rules or lexical items that had previously appeared to be candidates for fossilization. Specifically, one would determine whether new items used in play later replaced older items in the IL system that had appeared to be fossilized.

Conclusion

I have argued that fossilization can be explained, at least in part, as a result of a complex web of social and socio-psychological forces that increases in complexity with the increasing age of second language learners. If we consider interlanguage to be the product of balancing forces of stability and creativity, the fossilized interlanguage is one in which the forces of stability have come to predominate. These forces can produce a socio-psychological barrier that prevents the learner from noticing L2 input or from converging toward an L2 speaker's language norms. The consequence is a failure to acquire the L2, and even fossilization. A socio-cultural or socio-psychological model of second-language acquisition based on chaos theory leads us to search for creative forces such as language play that might have the potential to counteract forces of stability to some degree, and lead to opportunities for the development of the interlanguage.

With the increasing age of the second language learner, it will become less and less likely that we will be able to identify single causes of fossilization, and more and more likely that those causes will be multiple and interlocking in nature. The model of second language acquisition provided by chaos/complexity theory (Larsen-Freeman, 1997), with its notion of counterbalanced complex forces of stability vs. creativity, provides a promising model for second language researchers interested in further study of the impact of the passage of time on the human's ability to acquire second languages.

Note

1. Thanks to Beata Loch (personal communication) for pointing this out to me.

References

Bakhtin, M. (1981) *The Dialogic Imagination: Four Essays by M.M. Bakhtin*. In Michael Holquist (ed.) Caryl Emerson & Michael Holquist (translators). Austin: University of Texas Press.

Beebe, L. (1977) The influence of the listener on code-switching. *Language Learning* 27 (2), 331–339.

Beebe, L. (1980) Sociolinguistic variation and style-shifting in second language acquisition. *Language Learning*, 30 (2), 433–447.

Beebe, L. and Giles, H. (1984) Speech accommodation theories: A discussion in terms of second language acquisition. *International Journal of the Sociology of Language* 46, 5–32.

Bell, A. (1984) Language style as audience design. *Language in Society* 13, 145–204.

Bell, N. (2002) Using and understanding humor in a second language: A case study. Doctoral dissertation, University of Pennsylvania.

Bell, N. (2005) Exploring L2 language play as an aid to SLL: A case study of humour in NS–NNS interaction. *Applied Linguistics* 26 (2), 192–218.

Belz, J. (2002) Second language play as a representation of the multicompetent self in foreign language study. *Journal of Language, Identity, and Education* 1, 13–39.

Broner, M. and Tarone, E. (2001) Is it fun? Language play in a fifth grade Spanish immersion classroom. *Modern Language Journal* 85 (3), 363–379.

Cook, G. (1997) Language play, language learning. *ELT Journal* 51 (3), 224–231.

Cook, G. (2000) *Language Play, Language Learning*. Oxford: Oxford University Press.

Curiel, J. (2003) 'Go slowly with these people': Somali female refugees learning English. MA qualifying paper, University of Minnesota.

Doughty, C. and Williams, J. (eds) (1998) *Focus on Form in Classroom Second Language Acquisition*. Cambridge: Cambridge University Press.

Kormos, J. (1999) Monitoring and self-repair in a second language. *Language Learning* 49, 303–342.

Krashen, S. (1981) *Second Language Acquisition and Learning*. Oxford: Pergamon Press.

Larsen-Freeman, D. (1997) Chaos/complexity science and second language acquisition. *Applied Linguistics* 18 (2), 141–165.

Long, M. and Robinson, P. (1998) Focus on form: Theory, research and practice. In C. Doughty and J. Williams (eds) *Focus on Form in Classroom Second Language Acquisition* (pp. 15–41). Cambridge: Cambridge University Press.

Lybeck, K. (2002) The role of acculturation and social networks in the acquisition of second language pronunciation. PhD thesis, University of Minnesota.

Milroy, L. (1980) *Language and Social Networks*. Oxford: Basil Blackwell.

Nicholas, H., Lightbown, P. and Spada, N. (2001) Recasts as feedback to language learners. *Language Learning* 51 (4), 719–758.

Peck, S. (1977) Play in child second language acquisition. PhD thesis, UCLA.

Peck, S. (1978) Child-child discourse in second language acquisition. In E. Hatch (ed.) *Second Language Acquisition: A Book of Readings* (pp. 383–400). Rowley, MA: Newbury House.

Preston, D. (1989) *Sociolinguistics and Second Language Acquisition*. Oxford: Basil Blackwell.

Preston, D. (2000) Three kinds of sociolinguistics and SLA: A psycholinguistic perspective. In B. Swierzbin, F. Morris, M. Anderson, C. Klee and E. Tarone (eds) *Social and Cognitive Factors in Second Language Acquisition: Selected Proceedings of the 1999 Second Language Research Forum* (pp. 3–30). Somerville, MA: Cascadilla Press.

Rampton, B. (1995) *Crossing: Language and Ethnicity Among Adolescents*. London: Longman.

Schmidt, R. (1993) Awareness and second language acquisition. *Annual Review of Applied Linguistics* 13, 206–226.

Schumann, J. (1978) *The Pidginization Process: A Model for Second Language Acquisition*. Rowley, MA: Newbury House Publishers.

Tarone, E. (1983) On the variability of interlanguage systems. *Applied Linguistics* 4 (2), 143–163.

Tarone, E. (2000a) Still wrestling with 'context' in interlanguage theory. *Annual Review of Applied Linguistics* 20, 182–198.

Tarone, E. (2000b) Getting serious about language play: Language play, interlanguage variation and second language acquisition. In B. Swierzbin, F. Morris, M. Anderson, C. Klee and E. Tarone (eds) *Social and Cognitive Factors in SLA: Proceedings of the 1999 Second Language Research Forum* (pp. 31–54). Somerville, MA: Cascadilla Press.

Tarone, E. (2003) Social context does affect second language acquisition: Recent evidence on how it works. APPLE Lecture, Departments of Applied Linguistics and TESOL, Teachers College Columbia University, New York City, March 7, 2003.

Treat, S. (2001) Older adults and second language acquisition: A review of the literature. MA qualifying paper, University of Minnesota.

VanPatten, B. (1996) *Input Processing and Grammar Instruction: Theory and Research*. Norwood, NJ: Ablex.

Weir, R. (1962) *Language in the Crib*. The Hague: Mouton.

Williams, J. (2001) The effectiveness of spontaneous attention to form. *System* 29, 325–340.

Chapter 9
Why Not Fossilization

DAVID BIRDSONG

The absence of a question mark in the title is meant to suggest that this chapter will consider reasons to treat with due diligence the term fossilization, and likewise reasons to deal cautiously with constructs linked to it. The title is also intended to suggest that there are other ways of looking at learner failures to acquire nativelike grammars than through the lens of fossilization. The chapter addresses the possibility that the study of L2 learner shortcomings – which are the core, classical focus of fossilization research – might be constructively complemented by approaches that seek to determine the upper limits of attainment, i.e. the potential of the learner.

I hasten to add a disclaimer: I am honored to contribute to the present volume, and this chapter constitutes no disrespect to the research and researchers associated with fossilization. As will become apparent, I make a relatively tame case for my reluctance to embrace the topic of fossilization (and the term itself) and a somewhat stronger case for looking at research paths that should properly coexist alongside fossilization research.

From diverse perspectives, this contribution is a foray into the ontological linchpin of fossilization, non-nativelikeness. We explore the nature of non-nativelikeness (and nativelikeness) in L2 acquisition, along with various approaches to the description and understanding of nativelikeness. The chapter has a bit of a historical flavor to it, with occasional recollections of major themes in the fossilization tradition.

In sum, in this chapter I suggest that the study of fossilization is not without peril, and that the study of nativelikeness – an area considered by many to be quite perilous itself – is perhaps less so than fossilization and potentially quite rewarding. In addition, the approach I espouse inverts the perspective from learner 'failures' associated with fossilization (philosophically and phenomenologically) in favor of an examination of learner potential. Such an examination is, I believe, underrepresented in L2A research and may be of considerable heuristic value.

Just What is Fossilization?

As Han (2003) and Selinker and Han (2001) have superbly demonstrated in their analytic papers, fossilization is a notion that has defied ready characterization. Birdsong (2004: 86–87) describes the state of affairs as follows:

> Since the term was popularized in the L2A context by Selinker (1972), 'fossilization' has been understood in various ways, among them, as a process, as a cognitive mechanism, and as a result of learning. Selinker and Han (2001) catalogue various learner behaviors that researchers have associated with fossilization. These include backsliding, low proficiency, errors that are impervious to negative evidence, and persistent non-targetlike performance. They also list a host of proposed explanations for these behaviors, such as simplification, avoidance, end of sensitivity to language data, and lack of understanding, acculturation, input, or corrective feedback.
>
> Unquestionably, the study of various representational and acquisitional facts that might fall under the umbrella of fossilization has advanced our knowledge of L2A. But among researchers there is disagreement at the most basic level, for example, on whether fossilization is an *explanans* or an *explanandum*, whether it is a process or a product, whether its domain extends to L1A, and on whether it refers to invariant non-native forms or variable non-native forms. (Birdsong, 2004)

From a meta-analytic perspective on L2 acquisition research, particularly studies of learners presumed to be at the L2 acquisition end state, fossilization comes across as 'a protean, catch-all term' (Birdsong, 2004: 87) that begs for a unitary construct to refer to (see also Long, 2003; MacWhinney, this volume: chap. 7). In this respect, fossilization is a label in search of a referent. Sometimes the quest goes in the other direction – a referent looking for a proper label – as researchers try to decide whether such-and-such linguistic behavior qualifies as an instance of fossilization. In both cases, the prospect of ensnarlment in the textured lexical semantics of fossilization is daunting indeed. The inherent confusion around the f-word and its debatable utility in L2 acquisition research is further discussed by Long (2003), and in the following section.

(Dis)connecting Fossilization and Nativelikeness: Examples From the Study of Instability

From its origins, the idea of fossilization has been associated with observed non-nativelikeness. There is something of a tautology in this linkage, for if all L2 learners attained nativelike proficiency, it is unlikely that the term fossilization would ever have been appropriated for the L2 acquisition context. As a routine matter in applied linguistics, the diagnosis of fossilization is predicated on evidence of learner departures from nativelikeness. Practically as well as theoretically, the keystone in the fossilization vault – and the common thread uniting most of the various uses and applications of the term – is non-nativelikeness. See Long (2003: 487–488, 519–520, Note 1) for elaboration on this connection.

But what is and is not nativelike? It is not always clear that we know what natives do and do not do. A case in point comes from research relating to the question of instability in L2 grammatical representations. In a study of Sinophone late ESL learners presumed to be at the L2 acquisition end state, Johnson *et al.* (1996) found inconsistent judgments of grammaticality in a Time 1–Time 2 comparison for about 35% of the items tested. Subjects were asked to provide binary (Yes – grammatical; No – ungrammatical) judgments for items such as *Can Annie ride a bicycle/*Can ride Annie a bicycle? Last night the books fell off the shelf/*Last night the books falled off the shelf. Josh lets his kids watch TV/*Josh lets his kids to watch TV. Ryan called Krissy up for a date/*Ryan called Krissy for a date up.* The learners' failure to replicate judgments across the two-week interval between Time 1 and Time 2 testing was seen by the authors as evidence of a non-deterministic grammar.

Johnson *et al.* (1996) claim that the behaviors they observed in late learners are non-nativelike, because the native controls in the study did not demonstrate comparable inconsistency. The researchers go on to assert that, in adult L2A, the grammar underlying unstable judgments 'is not the same kind of formal object as that formed by child (L1) learners' (p. 335). On tasks involving judgments of grammaticality, Johnson *et al.* state that 'native speakers tend to give highly consistent judgments, which suggest that the underlying system is itself rule governed. This consistency does not appear to be a characteristic of adult learners' (p. 337).

Note that the (in)consistency in question is observed at the level of performance, i.e. the judgments rendered by the experimental subjects. As many scholars have pointed out (for an overview, see Birdsong, 1989; Sorace, 1996), the relationship between the decisions made in grammaticality judgments and the underlying grammar is modulated by a variety of non-linguistic factors. One must therefore recognize that any inference of indeterminate grammars from unstable judgments is perforce indirect.

Mindful of the limitations of the grammaticality judgment methodology, the question remains: Are indeterminate grammars exclusively proprietary to learners, and not to natives, as the assertions and evidence of Johnson *et al.* would lead us to believe? Some studies suggest that Johnson *et al.* might have it backwards. For example, Gass (1989) found highly consistent judgments among learners, while Nagata (1988), Carroll *et al.* (1981) and Birdsong (1989) have evidence for inconsistent judgments among natives.

But these studies did not systematically compare natives and non-natives in terms of consistency of judgments. One of the few studies besides Johnson *et al.* that rigorously makes such a comparison is Adams and Ross-Feldman (2003). Adams and Ross-Feldman tested early learners of L2 English, late L2 English learners, and native speakers of English. All non-native subjects had a minimum length of residence of 10 years in the United States. The instrument included items used by Johnson *et al.* (1996), along with sentences such as *Danny wanted Becky and I to go to the game with him, I am a better baseball player than her, He was one of those lucky people who loved their job*, and *Which [of the actors] do you wanna film?* By design, the latter types of sentences differ in many respects from those used by Johnson *et al.* Typical ungrammaticalities in Johnson *et al.* included violations of surface morphology and word order that are conspicuous by their absence in written and spoken English. In the Adams and Ross-Feldman instrument, the items not appropriated from Johnson *et al.* included violations in case assignment that are often subject to sociolinguistic variation (*Danny wanted Becky and I to go to the game with him, I am a better baseball player than her*); person-number agreement that is unspecified in the grammar and therefore rather idiosyncratically determined (*He was one of those lucky people who loved their job*); and *want-to* contraction that is licensed if the preceding argument is the object of *want-to* INFIN (*Which of the actors do you wanna film?*) but is ungrammatical if the argument is the subject of *want-to* INFIN (**Which of the cameramen do you wanna film?*). Unlike the Johnson *et al.* ungrammatical sentences, the first two of the item types developed by Adams and Ross-Feldman are often attested in the input (and are subject to a high degree of inter-speaker variability among natives), and all three represent rather subtle features of the grammar.

Adams and Ross-Feldman found that all groups, natives included, give inconsistent judgments across the seven-to-ten-day Time 1–Time 2 testing interval. Judgments were rendered on a 7-point scale, yet the magnitude of the inconsistencies was in many cases quite dramatic. Instability was observed not only among all three groups of participants but for all types of items, including those used by Johnson *et al.* (1996). Interestingly, across all items, late bilinguals displayed the most, not the least, judgment consistency.

The contrast of the Adams and Ross-Feldman results with those of Johnson *et al.* could hardly be more striking. Adams and Ross-Feldman show that both natives and non-natives have inconsistent judgments, and that late L2 acquisition is not the only recipe for unstable grammars. Sorace (1996: 385–386) concurs, noting that in fact indeterminacy may correlate with increases in sophistication of linguistic L2 knowledge. In sum – and recalling the importance of knowing what is and what is not nativelike – instability appears not to be a feature of non-nativelikeness. The Adams and Ross-Feldman evidence suggests that indeterminacy characterizes both native and learner grammars. Thus, in this respect, and contrary to the claim of Johnson *et al.*, the L1 and the L2 are not different formal objects.

The Adams and Ross-Feldman study does reveal an important difference between natives and learners, in terms of which grammatical features the respondents judge inconsistently. Native judgments are most unstable for items not tested by Johnson *et al.* (see above), that is, for items exemplifying case assignment, person/number agreement, and *want-to* contraction. Again, this is consistent with the observation of Sorace (1996: 385–386): native judgments are likely to be indeterminate when the structures in question 'are highly marked or very subtle syntactic properties.' Compared to natives, late L2 learners tend to exhibit relatively greater stability in these 'squishy' areas of English, on which the grammar of English is fluid, and where judgments often take into consideration presumed norms, prescriptivism, hyper-correctness, stylistic register, and other variables that are not strictly grammatical in nature.

On the basis of these results, we must conclude that (in)determinacy is not a general characteristic of grammars, but a local phenomenon in both L1 and L2 grammars. Observed instability varies by sentence type (and often by sentence token; see Birdsong, 1989). Nativelikeness is not determined by fiat or by assumption; as an empirical matter we must ascertain the loci of indeterminacy in the L1 and compare these with the loci of indeterminacy in the L2.

This first example from the study of instability illustrates the need for methodological finesse in identifying what is and is not nativelike. Observed instability in L2 acquisition can also be used to bring into focus the inherent imprecision of the term fossilization. Let us imagine that an end-state L2 learner manifests instability at a locus that is not congruent with any loci of instability observed among natives. This is clearly a non-nativelike outcome of L2 acquisition. But, since this product of acquisition is not rigid and invariant, dare we deem it an instance of fossilization?

In his case study of Ayako, a Japanese woman who moved to the United States at age 22 and has continuously resided there for more than 50 years, Long (2003) points out that certain features of this learner's grammar are nomadic, forever wandering unpredictably hither and yon. Unsystematic variability is readily observed in surface morphological features, such as regular plural marking on nouns and past tense inflections on verbs. On the basis of her output, Ayako's grammar could be characterized, somewhat oxymoronically, as 'permanently unstable.' The permanence of this non-nativelike grammar meshes well with an intuitive notion of fossilization: for the structures in question, the grammar is 'stuck' and will remain non-nativelike. What is more difficult to accommodate intuitively is the observed instability. The grammar may indeed be permanently non-nativelike, yet it appears to be in flux, not rigid and invariant as one might expect of an entity that has fossilized.

Han (2003) argues persuasively that stability and fossilization are logically and phenomenologically separable. It is not clear, however, that L2A researchers systematically observe this distinction, as it is often the case that 'anything non-nativelike' is labeled as fossilization. In the interest of granularity and precision, a compelling argument can be made for not considering all non-nativelike outcomes to be instances of fossilization. Rather, the many varieties of non-nativelike outcomes (e.g. incompleteness, divergence, non-UG compliance, non-native optionality, non-native instability, etc.) should be individually identified, described, labeled, and accounted for.

Nativelikeness for Its Own Sake

The preceding sections presented arguments for rejecting the one-size-fits-all imprecision associated with fossilization. It was also suggested that a potentially informative approach would be to better understand the phenomenon that is the basis for conceptualizing fossilization in the first place, namely non-nativelikeness. Amid terminological and conceptual uncertainty, this is what many L2 acquisition researchers have done. For example, Sorace (1993) provides L2 end-state evidence for distinguishing incompleteness from divergence, properly analyzing the two as ontologically distinct varieties of non-nativelike grammars.

However, in addition to the challenging empirical matter of knowing what is and is not nativelike, there are knotty theoretical problems associated with examining end-state L2 learners in terms of attained nativelikeness or non-nativelikeness. Bley-Vroman (1983) warned of the comparative fallacy in interlanguage research, decrying the practice of assuming that native grammars are represented as algorithmic sentence-level well-formedness generators, and that interlanguage grammars should be compared to native grammars under this assumption; i.e. as observed learner deviations from not just nominally licit forms, but from those that are required in so-called obligatory contexts. More recently, Cook (1997), Flege (2002), and Grosjean (1998), from varying points of departure, admonished researchers not to expect monolingual-like representations of L2 grammars – or, indeed, to observe nativelike grammars – as the two (or more) systems inevitably have reciprocal influences on one another.

At the same time, there are sound reasons for studying learner performance in terms of meeting or falling short of nativelike performance measures. A fundamental justification is that the experimental method calls for control groups. Native speakers' behavior on an experimental task establishes a central tendency and associated range of performance against which comparisons of learner performance can be meaningfully made. In most cases of group comparisons, late L2 learners and native controls are significantly different. At the level of the individual subject, however, numerous studies have shown that significant numbers of learners perform within the range of native controls. Even with use of criteria stricter than the nominal range of native performance, the numbers of nativelike attainers are not negligible (see Birdsong, 2004).

The documentation of native behaviors has the added benefit of bypassing *presumptions* of native norms. Presumed norms have been shown repeatedly not to line up perfectly with performance, either in the experimental or the naturalistic context (e.g. Frei, 1929; Harmer, 1979). Naturally, any inference from experimental behaviors to underlying competence is done with methodological sophistication and proper caveats. Such a method of determining nativelikeness in L2A is well established in the literature and is not particularly controversial.

Another good reason to conduct research on nativelikeness is that the potential of the learner is meaningfully measured by the benchmark of the native speaker. Recent research, samples of which are outlined below, is oriented toward establishing empirically what the upper limits of L2A are. From this perspective, the standard of nativelikeness is commonsensically appealing. Nativelike attainment is not a small accomplishment. For theorists, teachers, policy makers, and learners themselves, observations of nativelike attainment in late L2A testify to the tremendous potential of the individual (see Mack, 1997).

The Upper Limits of L2 Attainment

Often the question of learner potential is ignored. This is because historically, and particularly within the fossilization tradition, most L2 acquisition research studies have been undertaken with the goal of trying to find out what goes wrong and why. A complementary (but not mutually exclusive) orientation emphasizes not learner deficits but learner potential. The perspective is thus inverted from what often goes wrong to what sometimes goes right.

Among late L2 learners, nativelike performance on experimental tasks has been observed in many studies (see review in Birdsong, 1999). Some researchers have dismissed such demonstrations of attained nativelikeness, contending that the tasks required of subjects are not sufficiently challenging and are not sufficiently varied (Hyltenstam & Abrahamsson, 2003; Long, 1990). These objections are countered in recent studies by Birdsong (2003) and Marinova-Todd (2003). The methodology in both studies involves examining individual subjects' performances on each of several challenging experimental language tasks. These tasks tap knowledge of an array of linguistic subdomains – pronunciation, comprehension, morphosyntax, pragmatics, etc.

The multi-task methodology is reminiscent of that employed by Ioup *et al.* (1994); however, in that study only two individuals were examined. Otherwise, for groups of learners, this style of investigation has been rare in L2 end-state research. Some group studies do break out results of individual subjects, but in these investigations a subject's performance across all items is collapsed into a single quantitative measurement (e.g. Birdsong, 1992; Coppieters, 1987).

In Birdsong (2003) and Marinova-Todd (2003), for each task and each subject, comparisons with performance of native controls are carried out. The results reveal if there are individuals who appear nativelike across multiple varieties of performance. In this way researchers may be in a position to determine if observed nativelikeness is necessarily limited to narrow performance domains. Another advantage of this method is that it can reveal if there are some areas of language performance that simply cannot be mastered by any learner. Conversely, if there is no task where nativelike performance proves to be out of reach for at least one or more learners, then it can be argued that the upper limits of L2 attainment are not, in principle, inferior to benchmarks set by native L1 acquirers.

Marinova-Todd (2003) investigated the L2 English ultimate attainment of 30 individuals who had lived in an Anglophone environment for at least five years (mean = 11 years). None of the participants had been immersed in English before age 16 (mean = 22), though incidental exposure or minimal instruction had occurred in some cases as early as 10 years of age (mean = 13). All were college educated, as were the 30 native English controls. Prior to testing, subjects had been identified informally as 'highly proficient' in spoken English by native speakers.

Subjects performed nine tasks. Two of the tasks tested English pronunciation (reading aloud a paragraph from a novel; telling aloud the 'Frog Story'); two probed lexical knowledge (lexical diversity in telling the 'Frog Story'; Revised Peabody Picture Vocabulary Test); three tasks measured accuracy in morphosyntax (error analysis of 'Frog Story' telling; the grammaticality judgment task from White & Genesee, 1996; the sentence comprehension test from Dabrowska, 1997); and two tasks relating to language use (a test of narrative coherence in English; the Discourse Completion Test adapted from Blum-Kulka *et al.*, 1989). See Marinova-Todd (2003) for details.

Three of Marinova-Todd's subjects performed within the range of native controls across all nine tasks. In some cases, these subjects performed above native means. In addition, six other subjects performed like natives on seven of the nine tasks.

Birdsong (2003) tested 22 adult Anglophones immersed in French after age 18 (mean = 24.5 years), all living in the Paris area for at least five years (mean = 11 years). Some had had incidental exposure to French, but none before the age of 12. No screening for French proficiency was carried out. The control group consisted of 17 adult French native controls. Both groups of subjects were college-educated and were of comparable chronological age at the time of testing.

Seven discrete experimental performances provided measurements of accent, lexical and syntactic knowledge, and knowledge of parameterized features of French syntax. Participants read aloud lists of French phrases and sentences, producing quantitative data for three dimensions of pronunciation: Voice Onset Time (VOT) for word-initial obstruents, word-final vowel duration, and syntactically-conditioned *liaisons interdites* (non-permissible liaisons). These measures were subjected to acoustic analysis. A fourth task involved reading aloud prose paragraphs from a literary text. These elicited global pronunciations were evaluated by three trained native-speaker judges. To test for knowledge of French morphosyntax, participants provided grammaticality judgments for three problematic areas of French grammar: (1) Null object (V-Governed Expletive pro): ex. *L'armée (*le) trouve difficile de prévoir les nouvelles attaques de l'ennemi.* The army finds (it) difficult to predict new attacks by the enemy. (2) Exceptional Case Marking: ex. *Mes profs trouvent ces vers (*être) indignes de Shakespeare.* My profs find these lines (to be) unworthy of Shakespeare. (3) Distribution of *se* in unaccusatives: ex. *Ces chênes *se verdoient au printemps.* These oak trees turn green in the spring. *Le ciel s'empourpre juste avant l'orage.* The sky turns purple just before the storm. Previous L2A research had identified these areas as problematic for Anglophones, and had suggested that few if any late learners of French perform like natives in these areas (Birdsong, 1997; Flege & Hillenbrand, 1984; Hawkins, 1994; Mack *et al.*, 1995).

Three of the 22 non-natives performed like native controls on six of the seven measures. This result, along with those of Marinova-Todd (2003) suggests that nativelikeness is not confined to narrow performance domains (compare with Hyltenstam & Abrahamsson, 2003). Since subjects had not been selected for meeting French proficiency criteria, the present results show that nativelikeness is not limited to samples of 'the cream of the crop'; in this respect the Birdsong (2003) study is a methodological departure from Marinova-Todd (2003), Montrul and Slabakova (2003), and White and Genesee (1996).

Further, as was the case with Marinova-Todd (2003), in Birdsong (2004), there is no domain of performance in which all learners fell short of nativelikeness. This finding, though by no means derived from an exhaustive survey of linguistic performances, points to the possibility that the acquisition potential in late L2A is not inferior to that of L1A. We are therefore in a position to formulate, for the case of post-pubertal L2 learners, a falsifiable hypothesis: no feature of an L2 is unlearnable. In experimental terms, this would mean that there is no task which all sampled subjects fail to perform at native levels. Note that the subjects in question must be judged to be at end state (for discussion on operationalizing the end state, see Birdsong, 2004), and should have been exposed to the L2 under benign conditions, in particular having consistently had high quantities of input and interaction with native speakers (Birdsong, 1999: 14–15). In this way, we can minimize the likelihood that the subjects tested are not at asymptote; that is, we are reasonably confident that they have realized their full attainment potential.

As stated, the hypothesis (which, for lack of a better name, we will call the Universal Learnability Hypothesis), makes vague reference to 'features' of the L2. The vagueness is deliberate for, at present, it is desirable to state the hypothesis in atheoretical terms. The Universal Learnability Hypothesis (ULH) is meant to be an initial, provisional heuristic for guiding the development of tasks that challenge the learner, with the underlying goal of finding out what can and cannot be done to nativelike levels. In the same spirit, the ULH could guide re-interpretation of results of existing experimental group studies – which notoriously are characterized by variability in the range of individual subjects' performances – from the perspective of inherent learnability at the L2 acquisition end state: Can any learners perform like natives? This does not mean that the choice of tasks should not itself be guided by theory, particularly if the theory specifically addresses the end state of L2A. However, in my reading of the literature, most L2 acquisition theory is not explicitly oriented toward establishing what the upper limits of L2 learning are. Much theoretical research is derived from principled distinctions such as $+/-$ UG, lexical versus functional categories, open versus closed class items, words versus rules, etc. The relevant evidence is in the form of asymmetries, i.e. statistically significant differences relating to the factors that have been identified as independent variables. Such data reveal much about relative difficulty, but little about learner potential. Theories based on the position of 'no access to UG' and the Fundamental Difference Hypothesis speak indirectly to learner potential, by virtue of the fact that they predict non-nativelike outcomes of L2 acquisition. But with the exception of studies that seek to determine if it is possible to learn a non-natural (UG non-compliant) grammar (e.g. Smith & Tsimpli, 1995), the upper limits of learnability are not specifically probed.

Thus, on the short term at least, it makes sense to assemble and examine an inventory of late L2 learner performances to determine which linguistic features are and are not acquired (by at least some subjects) to nativelike levels. We would thereby be in an empirically-grounded position to subsequently identify linguistic features that should be specifically targeted by theory as being $+/-$ learnable.

The heuristic exercise just described will undoubtedly require many conceptual and methodological refinements along the way. For example, representing rather conspicuous counterpoints to the premise of universal learnability are studies that show that, with respect to certain language *processing* tasks (e.g. lexical retrieval; parsing strategies; structural ambiguity resolution; detection of fine acoustic distinctions inherent in syllable stress, consonant voicing, and vowel duration), nativelike performance is not observed among high-proficiency late L2 learners (e.g. Dussias, 2004; Dupoux & Peperkamp, 2002; Papadopoulou & Clahsen, 2004). Such results suggest, in contradistinction to universal learnability, a hypothesis that posits selective processability effects. Grossly, the hypothesis would state that not all on-line language processing tasks can be performed to nativelike levels. As with the ULH, however, it would be important to understand the susceptibility of L2 learners to intervention such as focused instruction and (qualitatively and quantitatively) enhanced input. For example, recent studies have revealed that perceptual/processing deficiencies may not be permanent if learners are provided with proper perceptual training (e.g. McClelland *et al.*, 2002).

Another factor to be considered is the sense in which *learning* is understood under the Universal Learnability Hypothesis. Anyone familiar with language acquisition research recognizes that conceptualizing and operationalizing this basic notion is fraught with controversy. For example, L2 acquisition theory grapples with a knotty levels-of-analysis problem: for nativelikeness to have been attained, does it suffice to have congruence at abstract levels of grammatical representation (e.g. functional categories) or do surface realizations have to converge with natives' production as well? (For discussion, see, e.g. Epstein *et al.*, 1996 and accompanying commentary; Lardiere, 1998a, 1998b; White, 2003). As mentioned earlier, we know too that L1 knowledge and L2 knowledge are not segregated entities, neither epistemologically nor neurofunctionally; consequently, one cannot isolate the grammars of a bilingual and expect them to be identical to those of two monolinguals (Grosjean, 1998). As for the means by which learning is achieved, in terms of cognitive maturity and in terms of procedures for going about learning, late L2 acquisition is not the same as L1 acquisition. Yet L2 end-state research has shown that, despite ostensibly different processes in L1 acquisition and L2 acquisition, similar if not identical products (end state grammars) can be reached (Birdsong, 1999, 2004); moreover, the linguistic performances associated with these grammars are indistinguishable from that of natives. Thus, at least at the present point in the development of this heuristic exercise, attainment under the ULH is understood in terms of functional equivalence with natives, that is, the (experimental) performance of late learners as compared with that of native controls (for examples of nativelikeness in naturalistic contexts, see Piller, 2002). Any inferences of underlying competence or extrapolations to performance in other contexts are to be made only with proper interpretive caveats.

Conclusion

The preceding section considered ways to approach the question of the upper limits of L2 acquisition. This perspective, in stressing the potential of the learner, is complementary to the orientation toward learner deficiencies that has historically been adopted by researchers interested in fossilization. The two perspectives should not be thought of as mutually exclusive, however, as both are needed to produce a complete picture of the L2 learner.

Recent developments in the medical sciences represent an instructive parallel. Modern researchers in geriatrics are not only looking at pathology and illness, but also at wellness and fitness, along with the biological and environmental factors that are associated with longevity (see, e.g. Benson & Stuart, 1993; Cotman, 2000).

The 21st-century study of human potential has demonstrated that, in many dimensions of human performance, there are both logical and scientific bases for distinguishing between what people inevitably *can't do* and what we typically *don't do*. Moreover, this type of research does not ignore what, under favorable conditions, we *can do*.[1] It is my hope that L2 acquisition researchers will likewise respect these distinctions, and by so doing better understand both the shortcomings and the upper bounds of L2 learning.

Note

1. For discussion of exogenous factors such as perceptual training, L2 input/ interaction, pronunciation instruction, and lifestyle variables that are associated with enhanced L2 attainment, see Birdsong (2003) and Doughty (2003). In addition, the upper limits of L2 attainment are conditioned in part by endogenous factors such as aptitude, motivation, and learning style and strategies (see e.g. Dörnyei & Skehan, 2003).

References

Adams, R. and Ross-Feldman, L. (2003) An investigation of determinacy in the grammar of NS and end-state NNS. Conference paper presented at Georgetown University Roundtable on Languages and Linguistics (GURT).

Benson, H. and Stuart, E.M. (1993) *The Wellness Book*. New York: Scribners.

Birdsong, D. (1989) *Metalinguistic Performance and Interlinguistic Competence*. New York and Berlin: Springer.

Birdsong, D. (1992) Ultimate attainment in second language acquisition. *Language* 68, 706–755.

Birdsong, D. (1997) Intransitivity and SE in French: Aspects of late learnability. 22nd Boston University Conference on Language Development.

Birdsong, D. (1999) Introduction: Whys and why nots of the Critical Period Hypothesis for second language acquisition. In D. Birdsong (ed.) *Second*

Language Acquisition and the Critical Period Hypothesis (pp. 1–22). Mahwah, NJ: Erlbaum.

Birdsong, D. (2003) The end state of L2 acquisition. Language and Mind Conference III. University of Southern California, May 2003.

Birdsong, D. (2004) Second language acquisition and ultimate attainment. In A. Davies and C. Elder (eds) *The Handbook of Applied Linguistics* (pp. 82–105). London: Blackwell.

Bley-Vroman, R. (1983) The comparative fallacy in interlanguage studies: the case of systematicity. *Language Learning* 33, 1–17.

Blum-Kulka, S., House, J. and Kasper, G. (1989) *Cross-Cultural Pragmatics: Requests and Apologies*. Norwood, NJ: Ablex.

Carroll, J.M., Bever, T.G. and Pollack, C.R. (1981) The non-uniqueness of linguistic intuitions. *Language* 57, 368–382.

Cook, V.J. (1997) Monolingual bias in second language acquisition research. *Revista Canaria de Estudios Ingleses* 34, 35–29.

Coppieters, R. (1987) Competence differences between native and near-native speakers. *Language* 63, 544–573.

Cotman. C.W. (2000) Homeostatic processes in brain aging: The role of apoptosis, inflammation, and oxidative stress in regulating healthy neural circuitry in the aging brain. In P.C. Stern and L.L. Carstensen (eds) *The Aging Mind: Opportunities in Cognitive Research* (pp. 114–143). Washington, DC: National Academy Press.

Dabrowska, E. (1997) The LAD goes to school: A cautionary tale for nativists. *Linguistics* 35, 735–766.

Dörnyei, Z. and Skehan, P. (2003) Individual differences in second language learning. In C.J. Doughty and M.H. Long (eds) *The Handbook of Second Language Acquisition* (pp. 589–630). Malden, MA and Oxford, UK: Blackwell.

Doughty, C. (2003) Instructed SLA: Constraints, compensation, and enhancement. In C. Doughty and M. Long (eds) *The Handbook of Second Language Acquisition* (pp. 256–310). Oxford: Blackwell.

Dupoux, E. and Peperkamp, S. (2002) Fossil markers of language development: Phonological 'deafnesses' in adult speech processing. In J. Durand and B. Laks (eds) *Phonetics, Phonology, and Cognition* (pp. 168–190). Oxford: Oxford University Press.

Dussias, P.E. (2004) Syntactic ambiguity resolution in L2 learners: Some effects of bilinguality on L1 and L2 processing strategies. *Studies in Second Language Acquisition* 25, 529–557.

Epstein, S.D., Flynn, S. and Martohardjono, G. (1996) Second language acquisition: Theoretical and experimental issues in contemporary research. *Behavioral and Brain Sciences* 19, 677–758.

Flege, J. (2002) No perfect bilinguals. In A. James and J. Leather (eds) *New Sounds 2000: Proceedings of the Fourth International Symposium on the Acquisition of Second-Language Speech* (pp. 132–141). University of Klagenfurt.

Flege, J.E. and Hillenbrand, J. (1984) Limits on phonetic accuracy in foreign language speech production. *Journal of the Acoustical Society of America* 76, 708–721.

Frei, H. (1929). *La Grammaire des Fautes*. Paris: P. Guenther.

Gass, S. M. (1989) The reliability of second-language grammaticality judgments. In E. Tarone, S.M. Gass and A.D. Cohen (eds) *Research Methodology in Second-Language Acquisition* (pp. 303–322). Hillsdale, NJ: Erlbaum.

Grosjean, F. (1998) Studying bilinguals: Methodological and conceptual issues. *Bilingualism: Language and Cognition* 1, 131–149.

Han, Z.H. (2003) Fossilization: From simplicity to complexity. *International Journal of Bilingual Education and Bilingualism* 6, 95–128.

Harmer, L.C. (1979) *Uncertainties in French Grammar*. London: Cambridge University Press.

Hawkins, R. (1994) Accusative case assignment in French second language acquisition. *Essex Research Reports in Linguistics* 4, 37–69.

Hyltenstam, K. and Abrahamsson, N. (2003) Maturational constraints in SLA. In C.J. Doughty and M.H. Long (eds) *The Handbook of Second Language Acquisition* (pp. 539–588). Malden, MA and Oxford, UK: Blackwell.

Ioup, G., Boustagui, E., Tigi, M. and Moselle, M. (1994) Reexamining the critical period hypothesis: A case study of successful adult SLA in a naturalistic environment. *Studies in Second Language Acquisition* 16, 73–98.

Johnson, J., Shenkman, K., Newport, E. and Medin, D. (1996) Indeterminacy in the grammar of adult language learners. *Journal of Memory and Language* 35, 335–352.

Lardiere, D. (1998a) Case and tense in the "fossilized" steady state. *Second Language Research* 14, 1–26.

Lardiere, D. (1998b) Dissociating syntax from morphology in a divergent end-state grammar. *Second Language Research* 14, 359–375.

Long, M.H. (1990) Maturational constraints on language development. *Studies in Second Language Acquisition* 12, 251–285.

Long, M.H. (2003) Stabilization and fossilization in interlanguage development. In C. J. Doughty and M. H. Long (eds) *The Handbook of Second Language Acquisition* (pp. 487–535). Malden, MA and Oxford, UK: Blackwell.

Mack, M. (1997) The monolingual native speaker: Not a norm, but still a necessity. *Studies in the Linguistic Sciences* 27, 251–285.

Mack, M., Bott, S. and Boronat, C.B. (1995) Mother, I'd rather do it myself, maybe: An analysis of voice-onset time produced by early French-English bilinguals. *IDEAL* 8, 23–55.

Marinova-Todd, S.H. (2003) Comprehensive analysis of ultimate attainment in adult second language acquisition. Unpublished doctoral dissertation, Harvard University.

McClelland, J.L., Fiez, J.A. and McCandliss, B.D. (2002) Teaching the/r/-/l/-discrimination to Japanese adults: Behavioral and neural aspects. *Physiology & Behavior* 77, 657–662.

Montrul, S. and Slabakova, R. (2003) Competence similarities between native and near-native speakers: An investigation of the preterite/imperfect contrast in Spanish. *Studies in Second Language Acquisition* 25, 351–398.

Nagata, H. (1988) The relativity of linguistic intuitions: The effect of repetition on grammaticality judgments. *Journal of Psycholinguistic Research* 17, 1–17.

Papadopoulou, D. and Clahsen, H. (2004) Parsing strategies in L1 and L2 sentence processing: A study of relative clause attachment in Greek. *Studies in Second Language Acquisition* 25, 501–528.

Piller, I. (2002) Passing for a native speaker: Identity and success in second language learning. *Journal of Sociolinguistics* 6, 179–206.

Selinker, L. (1972) Interlanguage. *International Review of Applied Linguistics* 10, 209–231.

Selinker, L. and Han, Z.-H. (2001) Fossilization: Moving the concept into empirical longitudinal study. In C. Elder, A. Brown, E. Grove, K. Hill, N. Iwashita, T. Lumley, T. McNamara and K. O'Loughlin (eds) *Studies in Language Testing: Experimenting with Uncertainty* (pp. 276–291). Cambridge, UK: Cambridge University Press.

Smith, N. and Tsimpli, I.-M. (1995) *The Mind of a Savant: Language Learning and Modularity.* Oxford: Blackwell.

Sorace, A. (1993) Incomplete vs. divergent representations of unaccusativity in near-native grammars of Italian. *Second Language Research* 9, 22–47.

Sorace, A. (1996) The use of acceptability judgment in second language acquisition research. In W.C. Ritchie and T.K. Bhatia (eds) *Handbook of Second Language Acquisition* (pp. 375–409). San Diego: Academic Press.

White, L. (2003) Fossilization in steady state L2 grammars: Persistent problems with inflectional morphology. *Bilingualism: Language and Cognition* 6, 128–141.

White, L. and Genesee, F. (1996) How native is near-native? The issue of ultimate attainment in adult second language acquisition. *Second Language Research* 12, 233–265.

Chapter 10

Second Language Acquisition and the Issue of Fossilization: There Is No End, and There Is No State

DIANE LARSEN-FREEMAN

Fossilization is a term that has been with us since the inception of the modern study of second language acquisition (SLA), being introduced in an article that some would consider seminal in the launching of the field (Selinker, 1972). In addition, fossilization has been singled out as a unique property of interlanguages (Adjemian, 1976), thus distinguishing second from first language acquisition (see, e.g., Bley-Vroman's Fundamental Difference Hypothesis, 1989). Furthermore, fossilization appears to be ubiquitous. Most everyone has either experienced it or can readily accept the claim that almost all, at least older, learners fail to attain native-like competence and performance in, at least some, subsystems and aspects of a target language. Yet despite its longevity, despite its theoretical and practical significance, and despite the fact that everyone can relate to it, there are problems with the concept of fossilization: it defies easy definition, description, and explanation. Many of the authors of chapters in this volume grapple with the problems. I will begin this chapter by summarizing these. I will then suggest a way that at least some of the concerns can be ameliorated. I will conclude by pointing to the continued importance of a research agenda where work on the bounds of fossilization is balanced by studying the boundlessness of potentiality, not only for theoretical concerns, but also for its practical implications.

Problems with Defining Fossilization

To begin with, there is the definitional problem. In Chapter 9 of this volume, Birdsong notes that fossilization is a notion that has eluded ready characterization. It has been characterized as both a process and a product, an explanans and an explanandum (Long, 2003). Further, Birdsong adds that the term fossilization has been used to designate any non-nativeness, which is clearly a problem. It seems to me that the use of the term fossilization-as-product should be reserved for interlanguage features of learners who have been given every opportunity to learn, and have the will to do so, but have failed.

Nakuma, in Chapter 2 of this volume, agrees, writing that fossilization can only be used for 'involuntary' 'long-term cessation of interlanguage development' (p. 23).

Another fundamental definitional question that has been raised is whether or not stable target-like forms should also be considered fossilized. As Vigil and Oller (1976) put it long ago: 'It is not only the fossilization of so-called errors that must be explained, but also fossilization of correct forms that conform to the TL [target language] norms.' It is hard to imagine, as Long (2003) notes, a cognitive mechanism that would distinguish native from non-native forms and apply only to the latter. Most L2 researchers, however, and the authors of chapters in this volume are no exception, using the term fossilization-as-process to signify a type of 'non-learning' (Han & Odlin, this volume: chap. 1: 3).

Yet another issue concerns its scope: is fossilization global or only local? Although some authors in this volume appear to regard fossilization as a global phenomenon, saying for example, that fossilization is 'the negative impact of the passage of time on humans' ability to acquire second languages' (Tarone, this volume: chap. 8: 157), other authors, such as Lardiere, have determined that fossilization applies selectively to different subsystems of language. An analysis of the interlanguage of Patty, Lardiere's subject, demonstrated that fossilization of inflectional morpheme did not preclude development of syntax. Similarly, based on data from a grammaticality judgment task, Han (this volume: chap. 4) states that for her two subjects, part of the subsystem (i.e. unaccusatives) in the two grammars reached its end state and part of it did not. Thus, Han claims that we cannot speak of fossilization in any global sense. MacWhinney concurs, asserting that 'fossilization is not an across-the-board phenomenon. Rather, we find continual growth in some areas and relative stability of error in others' (p. 135). Lardiere offers Hawkins' (2000) term 'persistent selective fossilization' to emphasize its local scope.

A final definitional issue concerns the question of whether fossilization should apply only to invariant non-native forms or whether it can be used to refer to variable non-native forms (Han, 2003) as well. Despite Long's subject Ayako's being a candidate for a fossilization study due to the length of time of her residence in the United States, etc., the fact is that Ayako's interlanguage has not stabilized, exhibiting extensive amounts of variation, both synchronic and diachronic – 'volatility,' Long (2003: 511) calls it. At issue is whether a learner grammar that is so 'permanently unstable' (Birdsong, p. 178) can be said to have fossilized. Han believes that the term fossilization possibly applies to such a grammar, concluding her study by saying that 'variability can stabilize and possibly fossilize' (p. 74). Sorace (1996) calls it 'permanent optionality.'

Problems with Describing Fossilization

The major problem with descriptions of fossilization is their dearth. Then, too, when there are descriptions, they are not always calibrated against baseline native-speaker data, important because fossilization is an inherently target-centric concept. Furthermore, even when native speakers are studied for the sake of comparison, the data that are collected are often unpredictable or even indeterminate, much as they are for learners.

As Odlin, Alonso, and Vazquez explain in Chapter 5, not only did the Galacians have less difficulty with the English present perfect than speakers of Castillian Spanish, contrary to the researchers' predictions (at least as demonstrated by the former's attempted corrections of incorrect uses of the present perfect), but also what was even more problematic was that the native English speakers acted similarly to the Galicians in sometimes failing to correct errors with simple past where the present perfect was required.

Like Odlin, Alonso, and Vazquez, Birdsong points to the difficulty of establishing nativelikeness when there is much indeterminacy in both native and learner grammars. This is especially problematic when it comes to the use of grammaticality judgment tasks. As Han (p. 59) indicates, 'The crux of the reliability issue, then, lies in indeterminacy, which as Sorace (1988) defines it, is "the absence of a clear grammaticality status for particular linguistic constructions in the speaker's competence, and which manifests itself either in the speaker's lack of intuitions or in variability at the intuition level."'

In Chapter 6, Lakshmanan underscores this point by citing Foster-Cohen's contention that monolingual native speakers of the same dialect of a particular language may not necessarily pattern exactly alike in relation to their intuitions about grammaticality and ungrammaticality. Needless to say, it is hard to determine non-nativeness, if ascertaining nativeness is fraught with difficulty.

Lakshmanan recommends that instead of using monolingual native speaker norms, researchers need to establish criteria based on analysis of competence of people who have acquired the two languages simultaneously from birth and who have continued to maintain both languages. Also, she adds that we need descriptions of fossilization in the interlanguages of young learners. Too often it is assumed that children are successful with respect to ultimate attainment of the target language grammar, and this assumption may prove to be unfounded. Furthermore, as Long (2003) notes, if fossilization is meant to say something interesting about the inability of learners to reach full target-language competence, rather than only that there are age-constraints on SLA, determining if there is fossilization in children's interlanguage is essential.

With the few descriptions and with concerns about the reliability of those that exist, is it any wonder that Nakuma calls for treating fossilization as a hypothesis, not a phenomenon? Of course, the fact that this volume contributes empirical findings, some of them from highly desirable longitudinal studies, and the fact that Han has determined that grammaticality judgments can reliably be used in studies of fossilization, shows that the concept of fossilization does have the power to shape a robust research program, but one whose starting dictum must be 'investigate, don't assume.'

Problems with Explaining Fossilization

Despite the paucity of descriptive studies, there is no such absence of attempts to explain fossilization. As Selinker and Han (2001) noted and as Han and Odlin in this volume (Chapter 1) report, explanation and description have been 'flip-flopped.' 'What we have here is not the logically prior description before explanation, but worse: explanation without description' (p. 7).

In Chapter 7 of this volume, MacWhinney examines 12 explanations that have been advanced to account for age of arrival and fossilization patterns and then settles on one of them – one that combines L1 entrenchment and parasitic transfer (the notion that L2 develops at first as parasitic or dependent on the L1). He then appeals to two other explanations, the social stratification hypothesis and the compensatory strategies hypothesis to account for the diversity of outcomes among adult learners. The former refers to the social positioning of the older learner and the consequent type of input that this position will provide, and the latter refers to the fact that adults need to employ certain strategic mechanisms in order to overcome the effects of entrenchment and parasitism.

So, where Han (2004, Table 3.1) identifies over 50 putative causal factors and groups them into four categories of causal factors in fossilization (environmental, cognitive, neurobiological, and socio-affective), MacWhinney proposes a hierarchy among these categories by claiming that a cognitive/neural mechanism is primarily responsible for fossilization whereas the others play a secondary role in accounting for the diversity among learners in terms of their success.

Interestingly, and not surprisingly given her consistency over the years, Tarone, on the other hand, nominates the social factor as the root cause of fossilization. Acknowledging that cognitive attention or noticing is essential, she points out that it is the social relationships among speakers that can cause attentional shifts; therefore, she thinks that the social factor is primary. She also, correctly, I believe, notes that the factors that cause fossilization become increasingly interrelated and complex over time and less susceptible to isolated study.

Despite the Problems, Still the Concept of Fossilization Endures – Why?

I believe the contrast between MacWhinney's and Tarone's perspectives illustrates why the concept of fossilization endures despite its problems. The fact is that fossilization provides the stage where issues central to SLA play out. For instance, the tension around the primacy of cognitive vs. social factors has existed since the origin of the field, and those who adopt positions on either side are as passionate as ever. Another example is the fact that the twelve hypotheses that MacWhinney considers as explanations for fossilization are among those that have been proposed in the past to explain the overall process of SLA itself and its differential success, with these two foci defining the field from its genesis (see, e.g. Hatch, 1978). Third, in order to account for learning, the province of SLA, we should be able to say not only what it is, but also when and why it cannot or does not occur. So, because fossilization is a kind of non-learning (Han), it seems to be a proper object of SLA research. However, as we have yet to arrive at a satisfactory definition of learning, it is little wonder that a definition of non-learning should prove so elusive.

And then there is the matter of description. Non-nativeness of form is fairly easy to identify. And yet if we only focus on errors of form, not only do we overlook what learners get right (which Vigil and Oller say could also be fossilized), we also overlook stable patterns of non-nativeness, which do not contain errors of form, but should perhaps nonetheless be considered fossilized. Consider, for example, the linguistic performance of Bulgarians and Russians (Todeva, 1992) who overuse relative clauses at the expense of attributive infinitives as compared with native English speakers. They say things like *He is the man that you should consult* where native English speakers would use attributive infinitives (*He is the man to consult*). Because both patterns are used in English, the overuse of relative clauses might not be identified as a fossilized pattern of form, but should it not be described at least as one that is not in keeping with pragmatic norms? Indeed, because using a language requires using its elements accurately, meaningfully, and appropriately (Larsen-Freeman, 2001), surely inaccurate forms are not the only evidence of fossilization.

It seems to me that fossilization merits continued scrutiny by SLA scholars. However, the inchoate state of our knowledge does lend credence to Nakuma's admonition to consider fossilization a hypothesis rather than a phenomenon. Of course, the history of science is replete with examples of phenomena, which defy initial definition, even acknowledgment of their existence, and certainly, of their explanation. Gravity, for example, was discovered by Newton but not explained until Einstein. Although perhaps impossible to establish conclusively, suspending the study of fossilization is premature in my opinion, given its theoretical and practical importance. Its study might be facilitated, however, if we were to shift the conceptual map.

Shifting the Conceptual Map: There is No End, and There is No State

SLA researchers have written about variability, volatility, unpredictability, indeterminacy and selectivity of interlanguage performance, and they have sometimes done so as if these qualities challenge the concept of fossilization. However, they are serious problems only if one subscribes to a particular view of language – a view of monolithic, homogeneous, idealized, static end-state competence, where language acquisition is seen to be a process of conformity to uniformity.

However, what if we start from a different point? What if we acknowledge, instead, that there is no end state because, first of all, there is no end? There is no finite uniformity to conform to. When we entertain a view of language as a dynamic complex adaptive system (Larsen-Freeman, 1997,

2002, 2003, in preparation), we recognize that every use of language changes its resources, and the changed resources are then available for use in the next speech event. 'The act of playing the game has a way of changing the rules' Gleick (1987: 24) both within the individual and within the speech community. Keller (1985) observes that language change at the macrolevel results from the microlevel behaviors of individuals. As Harris points out 'We do not communicate through reference to prior fixed abstract forms, but rather ... we create language as we go, *both* as individuals and [importantly] as communities...' (in Bybee & Hopper, 2001: 19). While the concept of fossilization is inherently target-centric, researchers of it must take into account the fact that the target is not monolithic and is always moving, although, of course, different aspects of language change at different rates.

If language is a dynamic system, then variability of performance and indeterminacy of speakers' intuitions would naturally follow. For instance, indeterminacy would be expected because this view holds that there is no static standard to which all speakers subscribe. In other words, not only is there no end, there is also no state. As Klein (1998: 540–541) has put it, there is 'no structurally well-defined "external language," nor is the perfect internal representation of such a structurally well-defined and stable entity the normal case... A real language is a normative fiction.'

One explanation, therefore, for Odlin, Alonso, and Vazquez's finding that native speakers of English did not perform as predicted is that the norms governing the present perfect in English are changing (see, e.g. Celce-Murcia & Larsen-Freeman, 1999: 181, fn 14). Since the norms are in flux, it is no wonder that the researchers would find differing intuitions about grammaticality represented among their subjects. For in a dynamic system, it is not just that a system changes over time, so does the nature of the relations among the elements in subsystems that constitute it, such as happens with a developing embryo. As Cooper (1999) puts it, language is a statistical ensemble of interacting elements. After all, language is not a closed, entropic system. It does not settle down to a point of static equilibrium, unless, of course, it no longer has speakers. Instead, as with other naturally-occurring systems, language is dynamic, constantly evolving, and self-organizing. And if I may be permitted to shift to another level of scale (which should be permissible, given MacWhinney, 1999), consider this to be true not only of the evolution of language, but also of the use and development of language within an individual. An individual's language resources are ever-mutable, and their development continues, even development of the L1 (MacWhinney, this volume: chap. 7).

Stability Within Dynamic Systems

How then can the view that language is a dynamic system relate to individual learner (non)development? Specifically, how can the fluidity of language as a dynamic system be reconciled with the fixity of interlanguage highlighted by fossilization? Well, first of all, we should acknowledge, what is a given in SLA research: an interlanguage is indeed a language. As such, it is a fluid dynamic system, just as are other languages. Han hints at this possibility by asking (p. 60) 'What if indeterminacy is the norm rather than a transient feature of the interlanguage?' Indeed, Dickerson (1976) argued the case long ago for the psycholinguistic unity of language learning and language change.

It follows then that if we shift the conceptual map to conceiving of language as a dynamic system, customary ways of thinking about fossilization, reflected in phrases such as the following, which have been used in this book, may no longer serve us well: 'permanent state of not attaining a desired L2 native state,' 'the end-state,' 'ultimate attainment,' 'divergence,' 'failure to reach native-like L2 competence,' 'cessation of development/change,' 'state of incompleteness,' 'permanent cessation of learning,' 'premature stability,' 'a steady state,' where 'acquisition stops.' I suggest that these terms obfuscate more than they elucidate because they all are associated with a view of language/interlanguage that has an end state. While I would not wish to argue that there are no maturational constraints on SLA, the finiteness implied in these terms forces us into the comparative fallacy (Bley-Vroman, 1983) and a static view of finite linguistic competence, rather than looking for alternative explanations for the observed behavior. It may be the case, for instance, that definitional characteristics of fossilization, such as backsliding, can be explained in other ways. For example, it is well known that at any given time, speakers have speech repertoires that are heterochronous, practices and forms considered typical of many earlier and later stages co-exist and interact and are differentially produced in different contexts (e.g. Lemke, 2000). This is true of interlanguage as well, as evidenced, for example, in learners' 'scouting' and 'trailing' behaviors. Language development is not only uneven but proceeds at multiple rates simultaneously – hence the selectivity of putative fossilization. Also, a more superficial target-oriented analysis of interlanguage forms might obscure the significant target-like and non-target like changes that are taking place in semantic and pragmatic mappings (see, e.g. Huebner, 1985).

Second, the process of learning is nonlinear. Indeed, ongoing change may be occurring, say, at the neurobiological level, before it is manifest in performance. And even when it is manifest, perhaps it is only, or at least initially, at the individual item level (Ellis, 2002), not where it would be more obvious, say at the construction, rule, or subsystemic level. In this volume, Han, for example, discusses the item-based nature of Geng's and Fong's acquisition of unaccusatives. Without fine-grained analyses such as Han's, item-level fossilization might give interlanguage performance the appearance of volatility, when in fact, it is more consistent at the word level. Then, too, Huebner (1979) pointed out many years ago, a learner's hypotheses about the target language may be under continual revision even if his or her performance has not kept pace.

However, just because there may be a great deal of flux in the system (it is well-known that interlanguages are characterized by a great deal of synchronic and diachronic variability), this does not mean that there is no stability. For after all, language is at least partially conventionalized and must have some rigidity in order to assure efficiency of processing (Givòn, 1999). Thus, because systems are dynamic, it does not necessarily mean that *everything* is always in flux. In other words, there can be stability as well. To quote psychologist Esther Thelen at some length (Thelen, 1995: 77), in a dynamical systems approach to development, it can be seen that

> Some of the resulting self-organized patterns of action and thought are very stable because of the intrinsically preferred states of the system and the particular situation at hand. Such patterns of thought and action may be thought of as strong attractors in the behavior space . . . performance is consistent and not easily perturbed . . . Other patterns are unstable, they are easily perturbed by small changes in the conditions, and performance with the same subject is highly variable and not dependable . . . Development, then, can be envisioned as a changing landscape of preferred, but not obligatory, behavioral states with varying degrees of stability and instability, rather than as a prescribed series of structurally invariant stages leading to progressive improvement.

Appropriating such a view, I have already drawn a number of implications for SLA, suggesting, for example, that a neural commitment to the L1 can lead to the L1's becoming a strong attractor in a dynamic system (Larsen-Freeman, 1997). Of course, even a shift of conceptual map as significant as the one I am proposing does not solve the many definitional, descriptive, and explanatory problems summarized above. However, it perhaps provides a new way of thinking about them. For instance, as I stated in my 1997 article, instability and systematicity should not be seen to be incompatible. Indeed, there is persistent instability in *systems* that are complex and dynamic (Percival, 1993). The proposed shift also supports the continued importance of a research agenda where work on the bounds of fossilization is complemented by study of the boundlessness of potentiality, not only for theoretical concerns, but also for its practical implications.

An Applied Note

I would like to end on an applied note. I have suggested that a target-centric perspective is sometimes, but not always, useful in SLA research. However, in pedagogy, it would seem indispensable. Language teachers must set realistic goals about target language development. This is why teachers should know, if they do not already know from their front-row seats, about fossilization. However, setting realistic goals and the self-fulfilling prophecy are too close for comfort, so I advise teachers not to appeal to the futility of fossilization as an explanation, but rather to seek to keep learning alive. I assume that this is in part Birdsong's impulse (for his Universal Learning Hypothesis) as well, and one that resonates with me. And the quest to keep learning alive is why I have especially appreciated Tarone's suggestions for how the creative forces of language play may destabilize non-target-like performance. 'For dynamical systems to change, they must become unstable. That is the coherence of the current pattern must be somehow disrupted so that the system can seek a new configuration – when new patterns emerge' (Thelen & Corbetta, 2002: 62). I presume that L1 transfer is at least a privileged (Selinker & Lakshmanan, 1992) contributor to stable patterns and that it is disrupting these that pedagogy should, at least partly, be aimed (see the success of such an approach described in Han, 2004: 119–120).

However, in so doing, it is essential for practitioners to recognize that disrupting stable patterns will take interventions that are ongoing and consonant with the learning challenge (Larsen-Freeman, 2003) and that defining and anticipating the challenge is an important first step. Then, for maximum effectiveness, the pedagogical intervention must be designed to address the particular learning challenge, customized for the learner and the learning context. Only with optimal learning conditions will learners' full learning potential have a chance to be realized. Only then might we have the chance to distinguish fossilization-as-product from a learning plateau. Only then can we explore the line between the bounds of fossilization and the boundlessness of potentiality.

References

Adjemian, C. (1976) On the nature of interlanguage systems. *Language Learning* 26 (2), 297–332.

Bley-Vroman, R. (1983) The comparative fallacy in interlanguage studies: The case of systematicity. *Language Learning* 33 (1), 1–17.

Bley-Vroman, R. (1989) What is the logical problem of foreign language learning? In S. Gass and J. Schachter (eds) *Linguistic Perspectives on Second Language Acquisition* (pp. 41–68). Cambridge, UK: Cambridge University Press.

Bybee, J. and Hopper, P. (eds) (2001) *Frequency and the Emergence of Linguistic Structure*. Amsterdam/Philadelphia: John Benjamins Publishing Company.

Celce-Murcia, M. and Larsen-Freeman, D. (1999) *The Grammar Book: An ESL/EFL Teacher's Course* (2nd edn). Boston: Heinle & Heinle.

Cooper, D. (1999) *Linguistic Attractors: The Cognitive Dynamics of Language Acquisition and Change*. Amsterdam/Philadelphia: John Benjamins Publishing Company.

Dickerson, W. (1976) The psycholinguistic unity of language learning and language change. *Language Learning* 26 (2), 215–231.

Ellis, N. (2002) Frequency effects in language processing: A review with implications for theories of implicit and explicit language acquisition. *Studies in Second Language Acquisition* 24 (2), 143–188.

Givòn, T. (1999) Generativity and variation: The notion 'rule of grammar' revisited. In B. MacWhinney (ed.) *The Emergence of Language* (pp. 81–114). Mahwah, NJ: Lawrence Erlbaum Associates, Publishers.

Gleick, J. (1987) *Chaos: The Making of a New Science*. New York: Penguin Books.

Han, Z.-H. (2003) Fossilization: From simplicity to complexity. *International Journal of Bilingual Education and Bilingualism* 6 (2), 95–128.

Han, Z.-H. (2004) *Fossilization in Adult Second Language Acquisition* (pp. 119–120). Clevedon: Multilingual Matters.

Hatch, E. (1978) *Second Language Acquisition: A Book of Readings*. Rowley, MA: Newbury House.

Hawkins, R. (2000) Persistent selective fossilization in second language acquisition and the optimal design of the language faculty. *Essex Research Reports in Linguistics* 34, 75–90.

Huebner, T. (1979) Order-of-acquisition vs. dynamic paradigm: A comparison of method in interlanguage research. *TESOL Quarterly* 13 (1), 21–28.

Huebner, T. (1985) System and variability in interlanguage syntax. *Language Learning* 35 (2), 141–163.

Keller, R. (1985) Toward a theory of linguistic change. In T. Ballmer (ed.) *Linguistic Dynamics: Discourses, Procedures, and Evolution* (pp. 211–237). Berlin: Walter de Gruyter.

Klein, W. (1998) The contribution of second language acquisition research. *Language Learning* 48 (4), 527–550.

Larsen-Freeman, D. (1997) Chaos/complexity science and second language acquisition. *Applied Linguistics* 19 (2), 141–165.

Larsen-Freeman, D. (2001) Teaching grammar. In M. Celce-Murica (ed.) *Teaching English as a Second or Foreign Language* (pp. 251–266) (3rd edn). Boston: Heinle & Heinle.

Larsen-Freeman, D. (2002) Language acquisition and language use from a chaos/complexity theory perspective. In C. Kramsch (ed.) *Language Acquisition and Language Socialization* (pp. 33–46). London: Continuum.

Larsen-Freeman, D. (2003) *Teaching Language: From Grammar to Grammaring.* Boston: Heinle/Thomson.

Larsen-Freeman, D. (in preparation). On the need for a new metaphor of language and its development.

Lemke, J. (2000) Across time scales of time: Artifacts, activities, and meanings in ecosocial systems. Unpublished manuscript.

Long, M. (2003) Stabilization and fossilization in interlanguage development. In C. Doughty and M. Long (eds) *The Handbook of Second Language Acquisition* (pp. 487–536). Oxford: Blackwell.

MacWhinney, B. (ed.) (1999) *The Emergence of Language.* Mahwah, NJ: Lawrence Erlbaum Associates, Publishers.

Percival, I. (1993) Chaos: A science for the real world. In N. Hall (ed.) *Exploring Chaos: A Guide to the New Science of Disorder.* New York: Norton and Company.

Selinker, L. (1972) Interlanguage. *International Review of Applied Linguistics* 10 (2), 209–231.

Selinker, L. and Han, Z.-H. (2001) Fossilization: Moving the concept into empirical longitudinal study. In C. Elder, A. Brown, E. Grove, K. Hill, N. Iwashita, T. Lumpley, T. McNamara and K. O'Loughlin (eds) *Studies in Language Testing: Experimenting with Uncertainty* (pp. 276–291). Cambridge University Press.

Selinker, L. and Lakshmanan, U. (1992) Language transfer and fossilization: The multiple effects principle. In S. Gass and L. Selinker (eds) *Language Transfer in Language Learning* (pp. 197–216). Amsterdam: John Benjamins.

Sorace, A. (1988) Linguistic intuitions in interlanguage development: The problem of indeterminacy. In J. Pankhurst, M. Sharwood Smith and P. Van Buren (eds) *Learnability and Second Languages* (pp. 167–190). Dordrecht: Foris Publications.

Sorace, A. (1996) Permanent optionality as divergence in non-native grammars. Paper presented at EUROSLA 6, Nijmegen.

Thelen, E. (1995) Time-scale dynamics and the development of an embodied cognition. In R. Port and T. van Gelder (eds) *Mind as Motion* (pp. 69–100). Cambridge, MA: MIT Press.

Thelen, E. and Corbetta, D. (2002) Microdevelopment and dynamic systems: Applications to infant motor development. In N. Granott and J. Parziale (eds) *Microdevelopment: Transition Processes in Development and Learning* (pp. 59–79). Cambridge: Cambridge University Press.

Todeva, E. (1992) On fossilization in (S)LA theory. In D. Staub and C. Delk (eds) *The Proceedings of the Twelfth Second Language Research Forum* (pp. 216–254). Papers in Applied Linguistics, Michigan State University.

Vigil, N. and Oller, J. (1976) Rule fossilization: A tentative model. *Language Learning* 26 (2), 281–296.

Afterword: Fossilization 'or' Does Your Mind Mind?

LARRY SELINKER

I feel as if I've been thinking about the fossilization puzzle my whole life, because I have. 'It's a family affair' that has moved towards neurofunctional thinking, cycling back to ordinary life. This search for understanding started for me when I was about eight; I know that I had the problem pretty well-conceived when I was about 12. It involves what the English philosopher and social historian of ideas, Isaiah Berlin called 'my one big idea,' i.e. the one unifying theme to all one's work.

What I gradually realized was that no matter what we did (the 'inevitability' issue) – and we did much (the 'input/intake' issue) – my Yiddish-speaking grandmother, in the United States about 50 years (the 'length of residence' issue), could *not* be understood by her grandkids who only wanted to speak English (the 'social factors' issue). But some in that ghetto could do better than others (the 'individual differences' issue). I remember wondering: 'What's going on here?'; 'Why can't she do that?'; 'How can this be?' (the 'epistemological' issues). All these issues still intrigue and excite me.

Why do these issues endure? One reason, it is said in this volume (Chapter 10) is that fossilization has become 'the stage,' where issues of second language acquisition (SLA) are played out. It was also said several times in this volume, and this is the crux of the matter, that the phenomena are 'ubiquitous,' that everyone has felt them at one time or another; some, I would imagine many times a day! Years ago, primarily under the influence of Lenneberg's (1967) 'latent language structure,' I began to discuss (Selinker, 1972, reframed, 1992) issues of cognition, such as fossilization units, latent psychological structures, processes, strategies, and underlying mechanisms. I keep returning to these and the questions (updated) still resonate:

- What do we now know about fossilization and its units and how do we know it?
- Are we dealing with a unique type of acquisition with second LANGUAGE acquisition or should we extend this view to second DIALECT acquisition. pidgin and creole acquisition...?
- What kind of theory of mind can possibly account for these phenomena with structure dependent units?
- How would that theory relate to processes, mechanisms and strategies in cognitive neuroscience (CNS) accounts of knowledge, memory, anxiety, especially with other types of learning, looking for places where people seem to get stuck?

This is a magnificent and intelligent book which has inspired much thought and discussion in my seminars, and I thank people there. What has been addressed and stressed in the book is that we still have myriad problems associated with this central but difficult topic. We know some things though. Initially, in the 'Interlanguage paper' (Selinker, 1992), five central processes for interlanguage were set up. These have been shown to be still relevant and have all been incorporated within interlanguage fossilization frameworks along with other processes and strategies not mentioned there. How did we get here?

I recall in the 1960s being in graduate classes at Georgetown with Robert Lado, the scholar who set up the initial procedures for studying language transfer (Lado, 1957), no small feat! In Lado's classes I realized that something different was going on in the learning of an L2, something that made it different from the learning of L1 and maybe different from other types of learning. Those were classes in contrastive analysis (CA)[1] – set up as a behaviorist theory – where doing CA predicted L2 errors, for there was no SLA at the time. Though it predicted a lot of language transfer, CA generated lots of 'residue' and, as we know, CA is not a good acquisition theory.

But Lado was on the right track in pushing CA when he hypothesized (1957) that a learner 'tends to transfer,' from the native language, the forms (the linguistic units), their meanings/distributions. Importantly, from CA field methods classes (which led to current courses in 'Interlanguage Analysis') Lado sent out his students to empirically see if CA predictions were right; yes and no was the answer. He was on the wrong track when he said that the locus of the transfer he did find was 'to the foreign language.' The transfer could not possibly be to the foreign language when one clearly did not speak the L2 as a native speaker. The transfer had to go to (or constrain) the hypothesized linguistic system, the interlanguage, where, the learner 'got stuck often far from target language (TL) norms,'[2] as we used to say. This book adds to that view, while emphasizing human potential by pulling in examples from general cognition as backup to SLA arguments; if we are creating this link, as I feel we must, we must then carefully try to link our theories of a mind capable of fossilization to 'mind,' to the mind that does good and bad language learning, has good and bad memory, and minds when in fact it is bad.

From the 'Interlanguage' paper, someone once told me that they learned less about interlanguage and more about fossilization. I see that now and over the years the linguistic detail of interlanguage – as language – has been pretty well worked out with yet more linguistic detail appearing in this book. But the fossilization puzzle as initially set out remains. Note that it was clear from the beginning that if anyone could became a native speaker of the next language, it could only be a small percent, 'perhaps a mere 5%.' Here (Chapter 1) we learn that, that was an underestimate; maybe it's as high as 'over 15%,' but the upper bound of L2 native-like speakers is still small potatoes compared to L1 acquisition, where there is agreement that most, if not all acquirers, do become native speakers, even though scholars at times argue about what that means in specific detail.

One thing that is clearer because of this book (passim), is that getting stuck is not 'global' but differential in a number of ways, not only different one learner to the next, but, most importantly, within an individual interlanguage and according to some sort of 'context.' How can it be that a non-native speaker who controls the oral and written academic Englishes apparently perfectly, will in some contexts produce such fossilized interlanguage sentences as:

- It did fell down.
- I did found this program strange.
- I didn't even saw the guy from the next table.
- This could lead [led] to clashes in the long run.
- She was smart enough to came up with a person who...
- It's stucking to the paper.
- I thought it would be could be a good evidence from a researcher who...
- I hope that X would keep its previous offer to you for coming as a speaker.
- If you are the new/e/ in the game

- Those who are truly bad get yelled/e/more often in class.
- It's easy to be solved.
- That happened all over the places.
- If you do your best, she said, I will keep your name in the play.

And my favorite:

- The reason the first Bush lost was that he didn't bring the aids to Florida.

These sentences come from original diary data of native speakers of Italian and Spanish. In consultation with one of the editors of this volume, we thought it was interesting that the L1 influences could have come from either. In these examples, /e/ is technically 'empty category,' often occurring in interlanguage, sometimes in places where theoretical linguistics principles predict they 'should not' occur, but that is another story (compare with Selinker & Kaplan, 1997). The 'places' example shows interestingly that non-native speakers often improve the target language (TL) by inserting what native speakers find redundant; in this case, 'places' is what the phrase means. Note that the last two show how ambiguous a misused article can make the interlanguage sentence ambiguous or referentially opaque. For the penultimate one, the intended idiom is of course 'keep your name in play'; it is interesting that in interlanguage, if you lose the fossilized grammaticalized TL syntax, even slightly, then, the idiomatized meaning is lost and a more literal meaning comes into play. This shows the truism of linguistic anthropologist Alton Becker's edict that 'small grammatical changes make big meaning changes,' and the hypothesis is that these get easily fossilized. These examples also show that, since interlanguage data is often ambiguous, one must find out systematically what the intended interlanguage semantics is.

The neurofunctional work with Lamendella in the 1970s (summarized in Selinker & Lamendella, 1981) started talking about fossilization being constrained by domain and understanding more about the cognition of the contextual nature of when people transfer and get stuck is still essential. Note that these interlanguage sentences above involve the most basic of core English grammatical rules, ones that are taught over and over, and most important, appear impervious to correction in the contexts where they occur! Why does feedback not work here? My hypothesis is that fossilization units are 'discourse domain' constrained (compare with Selinker & Chiu, 2005) and are permeable to the 'multiple effects principle' (MEP) (developed in Selinker & Lakshmanan, 1992). The answer seems to be that transfer, either as rote, rule process or constraint, seems to be rooted in core grammar (more about core grammar and the MEP below).

Is it now then established empirically that (most) learners will not gain in L2 – no matter what they do – 'the same ultimate attainment' (if the concept is still a coherent one[3]) that native speakers possess, in all spheres, and that there will in fact be variable, subsystems of 'nativelike-ness' in the L2 co-existing alongside subsystems of 'non-nativelikeness'? I would like to see strong empirically-grounded counterarguments. We still need what we have called for elsewhere: a theory which predicts what the fossilizable units are, i.e. which structures will be fossilizable under which conditions for which sorts of learners using which strategies of learning, the key being understanding of the intersection of learning strategies with interlanguage. Our research program would then link these predictions with those from theories of memory,[4] efficient/inefficient memory struc-tures, oral/visual memory, short term/storage, procedural/declarative ... empirically testing samenesses/differences.

We also need to link better with emotional memory structure as cogni-tion (compare with, e.g. Phelps, 2002) for there are possibilities like this. A learner who creates connections between structure dependent interlan-guage units or forms with real-life ordinary 'scenes,' storing and retriev-ing them in working memory, both auditory and visual memory must then be attached to scenes and the hypothesis is that the effect is more TL-like behavior. One example, is that if your mind is trying to learn Italian and you learn the present tense for 'dare' (to give) as 'do/dai/da' and that is it, and no emotion is involved, what may happen is that you may invoke the '1:many' principle (one form, many functions) and fossilize one of these forms for all three in online domains. If you decide to attach a real scene to 'dai' – perhaps one where you have heard a hundred times on the phone 'dai, mamma, dai' ['it's enough'; the closest in English seems to be the 'give over' of Midlands English], then you attach emotion to form and differentiate the units. It is then pre-dicted that development will more easily occur and you will automatize your declarative knowledge more easily. This hypothesis of 'emotional scene to units of linguistic form' could become part of the 'counterweight' to inevitable fossilization, linking up with decision making CNS research (Rehder, 2003) seeing how purposeful procedures affect various types of learning and memory. (This hypothesis, if verified empirically, may help explain the verb raising, article problems and grammaticalized empty cat-egories in the core grammatical interlanguage examples above.)

Whenever I suggest the hypothesis of tying linguistic form explicitly to emotionally important scenes, the response is something like: 'oh, we do that in role play,' which, in my observation, does not always seem to work, even in short- to medium-term memory (i.e. beyond the test). A well-known conventional example would be if you are learning the conditional form for 'volere' (to want), input would be 'vorrei' attached to a restaurant schema where this 'I'd like' is the polite way to order something vs. the present 'voglio' ('I want') can be construed as impolite in other contexts. But in my experience, if the scene created is somehow NOT 'real' to the learner and thus NOT attached to one's emotions, this effect will not work in your mind. In this case, a real restaurant or a real case when they told you were impolite is necessary for the effect to work. It is interesting, as one of the editors pointed out, that this hypothesis may be a sort of return to Stevick's (1976) concerns of relating memory to meaning and method. It is a shame that the Stevick material never got into mainstream SLA. Lado (personal communication) had an interesting point about memory here, that in learning an L2, one of the things you learn is how to increase your 'memory span' in that L2. I haven't seen that taken up in mainstream SLA either.

A further issue is that as a result of this book, is it now established empirically that the cognition of the MEP, as described in this book (passim), is in the right ball park, and that the mechanisms underlying language transfer leads it to become a 'privileged' process when working in tandem with other processes? Certainly, the Spanish perfect case here adds weight to the argument (Chapter 5, here), as does the discussion of the Chinese speaker's continued contextual difficulties with verb inflectional morphology (Chapter 3, here) and the Hindi–Urdu word order case (Chapter 6, here). But one swallow, or two or even three, does not a summer make and the complications of what the 'target' is, do complicate the issue. There is an L1 complication here as well, for in some parts of the world, e.g. Galicia, Taiwan, it seems that input to L1 acquisition is interlanguage itself (Galician-Spanish and Taiwanized-Mandarin, apparently, Swabia too), so that we do have to extend our scope to interdialect, i.e. to second dialect acquisition[5] (Trudgill, 1986). There is an interesting caveat regarding children emphasized with the MEP here – the cognition of the MEP may apply variably to children depending on the social conditions of learning, where development not fossilization is the norm. That is, the potential for children is to go either way, with the fossilization hinted strongly at in the French immersion studies where the interlanguage hypothesis was first extended to children. Creating CNS theories acknowledging that sometimes SLA children look like adults/sometimes like L1 acquirers makes the MEP more central since the effects in each may very well be different.

I predict that the MEP, plus a revisiting of the latent psychological structure postulated as underlying interlanguage mechanism, will be around for some time.

As this book emphasizes, fossilization researchers are agreed that only longitudinal studies provide the relevant data for fossilization (passim, this volume). The study of 'error' is fraught with difficulty and, again, we need to know when feedback does not work here by linking with CNS theories which cover cases where they do work (Marcus, 2004). A complicating example might be the situation a restaurant where the Chinese speaker gets up from the table and the native speaker says: 'It's really late,' the interlanguage mind answering: 'If we don't have to work tomorrow, we can sit here and chat all night' (simple/open conditional); the native speaker looks confused. The interlanguage speaker makes the meta-comment: 'I can't believe I didn't use hypothetical condition,' i.e. 'If we didn't have to work tomorrow, we could sit here and chat all night,' clearly the interlanguage intention being that they do have to work the next day. The Chinese speaker is asked about this later and says: 'Again this shows that my L1 Chinese can very easily throw my English off,' clearly showing an imperviousness to feedback in core grammar and where transfer-induced sentence structure can get you in trouble. The fossilization prediction of MEP is most probably working in this case, as well.[6]

What strategies exist for understanding a balance more towards learning potential and away from fossilization? That is, I want to know if the 'unfossilizable learner' is possible. We know that conscious attention to form can lead to an inability to use that form, from which we get learning strategies where attention is on communication and expressing meaning. We also know that attention away from form towards meaning may sometimes lead to automatizing that form. Here is another hypothesis we might explore empirically: attention diverted from core to non-core, peripheral form[7] can lead to automatizing core form. Take the four subjunctives in Italian subordinate clauses; subjunctive is redundant (therefore non-core grammar), being signaled by the setup in the main clause,. These forms are not used by many Italians in their ordinary conversation nor in their non-academic writing. This seems to be true for Spanish as well, with new norms developing in some domains in many dialects. In non-native Italian, it seems that these tenses and their pragmatic nuances are rarely mastered. But in learning Italian, much time is spent on practicing these structures, and in my observation of undergraduate Italian L2 learners, these structures are not really being learned while, paradoxically, learners are getting more fluent; something is being learned in this practice. One wonders what is learned when attention is on non-core structures and units? It seems to me that when attention is on practicing non-core structures and units, it is core linguistic form (tense-aspect, agreement...) that is in fact being consolidated in memory, 'memory consolidation' being a neglected area for us (compare with e.g. Rehder, 2003, in press). Thus, the hypothesis here is that 'attention to non-core forms' can automatize grammaticized core form and either delay or avoid possible fossilization. We can call this the 'attention to other form' hypothesis, with attention to non-core, peripheral structures being privileged. This hypothesis, if verified empirically, may help explain the verb raising, article problems and grammaticalized empty categories in the core grammatical interlanguage examples above.

Not only do we have to understand, when it happens, how L2 native-like interlanguage pieces occur allowing transfer-of-training units to enter the system because of feedback. We also have to understand how these co-exist with L2 non-nativelike units (the 'co-existing' issue) where transfer-of-training clearly is blocked. We must realize again that *second* language acquisition is many times a misnomer since most people seem to have snippets of multiple languages and dialects in their heads. We have to admit we can come to no conclusions about transfer and fossilization without admitting that interlanguage and interdialect transfer in is real. We have to understand better, how knowledge units of the native language are suppressed, allowing IL1 units to go through to IL2...ILn. A personal example of continued problems for me is when I am in 'talk foreign mode' (discussed in detail elsewhere) and hear at the beginning of a sentence the phonetic segment [lo-], I cannot help thinking that someone is going to begin a negative sentence because my strongest L2 is Hebrew and that is the negative particle. But, some nanoseconds later, I realize that the Italian person cannot be doing this but they are producing either full object pronoun, 'lo' and/or that plus perfect auxiliary as in: 'l'ho gia visto...' 'I already saw it.' It is again the curse of the interlanguage transfer constraint! And my mind does in fact mind!

You can be sure that your mind minds when it produces fossilized structures. Frustration and anxiety often occur when one cannot adjust to how prior linguistic knowledge and skills make current performance not very target-like, especially when you are told over and over things like the Italian pronoun cannot come between the modal and the infinitive ('...transferring again from your French...your minor in French coming back to haunt you...'), but you seem to be unable to stop doing it. We have now come full circle where the situated mind, even after years of practice, still seems to know that transfer is rooted in core grammar, that we get stuck with the most basic things in the most ordinary of experiences and that our earlier knowledge, for good or ill, may never leave us.

Notes

1. This approach to CA led directly to pattern practice as essential to language learning, but this point has been misunderstood and 'Lado-Fries' has been set up as a trope, as in 'Lado-Fries pattern practice method' (Selinker *et al.*, 1984 for detailed discussion). Lado was a behaviorist in that he openly believed (and told us in class) in the habit-formation theory, strength of stimulus-response, dominant in behavioristic linguistics of the time as interpreted by Bloomfield (1933) from behaviorist psychology. Fries, on the other hand, believed deeply in semantics and never seemed to be a believer in the dominant theory of stimulus-response learning. Fries had his 'oral approach' only as a 'first stage' to language learning and the rest was in no way 'behaviorist.' These points are most clearly seen in the volume Fries and Fries (1985) in the extensive discussion of 'meaning,' its place in structural linguistics and the various learning concerns invoked. This history has to be explained today since we are so far from what Jakobson is supposed to have said: 'Linguistics without meaning is meaningless.'
2. In fact, I remember saying elsewhere, that without fossilization, there would have been no SLA. It was in reading Weinreich (1953) and his student Nemser (1971) – both from Columbia – that I realized the depth of what was 'different' in this getting stuck in the third 'approximative system.' Both these sources should be revisited for predictive detail.
3. One corollary that I liked about this book is that the discussion has forced us to abandon some previous problems that we worried about a lot, such as 'fossilized learner/user' (Chapter 1) for there can be no such thing if no 'global fossilization' is possible. This also means that unusable terms such as 'ultimate attainment' and 'near-native speaker,' if not abandoned, should be clearly operationally defined with each empirical use.
4. We should also be focusing on 'theories of forgetting' where we would be concerned with either 'storage' issues, specifically the loss of information, vs. 'access' issues, i.e. apparent loss of access to stored information which later might be retrievable with certain stimuli. This latter seems to happen often with what is traditionally labeled 'backsliding' and this backsliding process is why there might be a confusion in the discussion between development and stabilization leading to possible fossilization. The difficulties in teasing out storage vs. access in memory are well-researched in CNS work. (There is a nice summary of theories of forgetting in Ecke, 2004.)
5. I do not recall in the L1 acquisition literature, studies where the effects of *interlanguage input to L1* is a major factor; this is important since the MEP might only be functioning in L2 acquisition and not in L1. The cases discussed here involves parental economic and social motivation, the belief being that learning the local dialect will keep the child down.
6. This was also shown earlier in an unpublished paper by Pauline David at NYU where middle school Chinese learners regularly wrote the open conditional when they intended the remote, hypothetical one, seemingly affecting their

learning of cases where hypothesis creation is essential, such as the learning of history.
7. The inability to always distinguish core from non-core peripheral structures should not deter us from the hypothesis which might delay the onset of fossilization or avoid it altogether. We can deal with this prototypically where we know some clear cases of each.

References

Bloomfield, L. (1933) *Language*. Chicago: University of Chicago Press.

Ecke, P. (2004) Language attrition and theories of forgetting. *The International Journal of Bilingualism. Special Issue on Language Attrition* 8.3.

Fries, P.H. and Fries, N.M. (eds) (1985). *Toward an Understanding of Language: Charles C. Fries in Perspective, Current Issues in Linguistic Theory 40*. Amsterdam: John Benjamins.

Lado, R. (1957) *Linguistics Across Cultures*. University of Michigan Press.

Lenneberg, E.H. (1967) *Biological Foundations of Language*. New York: John Wiley and Sons.

Marcus, G. (2004) *The Birth of the Mind: How a Tiny Number of Genes Creates the Complexities of Human Thought*. New York: Basic Books.

Nemser, W. (1971) *An Experimental Study of Phonological Interference in the English of Hungarians*. The Hague: Mouton.

Phelps, E.A. (2002) The cognitive neuroscience of emotion. In M.S. Gazzaniga, R.B. Ivry and G.R. Mangun (eds) *Cognitive Neuroscience: The Biology of Mind* (2nd edn). New York: Norton.

Rehder, R. (in press) When similarity and causality collide in category-based property induction. *Memory & Cognition*.

Rehder, R. (2003) Categorization as causal reasoning. *Cognitive Science* 27, 709–748.

Selinker, L. (1972) Interlanguage. *International Review of Applied Linguistics* 10, 209–231.

Selinker, L. (1992) *Rediscovering Interlanguage*. London: Longman.

Selinker, L. and Chiu, H.-C.P. (2005) 20 years of the discourse domains hypothesis in interlanguage. *Acquisition of Japanese as a Second Language: Special Contribution* 12.7.

Selinker, L. and Lakshmanan, U. (1992) Language transfer and fossilization: The 'multiple effects principle'. In S. Gass and L. Selinker (eds) *Language Transfer in Language Learning* (revised edn). Amsterdam: John Benjamins.

Selinker, L. and Lamendella, J.T. (1981) Updating the interlanguage hypothesis: A neurofunctional perspective. *Studies in Second Language Acquisition* 3.2, 201–220.

Selinker, L., Morley, J., Robinett, B.W. and Woods, D. (1984) ESL theory and the Fries legacy. *JALT Journal* 6, 171–207.

Selinker, L. and Kaplan, T. (1997) Empty, null, deleted, missing, omitted, absent . . . items in interlanguage. Review article: Klein, Elaine C. 1993: *Toward Second Language Acquisition: A Study of Null-Prep*. Dordrecht: Kluwer Academic Publishers, 289 pp. *Second Language Research* 13 (2), 170–186.

Stevick, E. (1976) *Memory Meaning & Method: Some Psychological Perspectives on Language And Learning*. Rowley, MA: Newbury House.

Trudgill, P. (1986) *Dialects in Contact*. Cambridge: Blackwell.

Weinreich, U. (1953) *Languages in Contact* (No 1). Publication of the Linguistic Circle of New York.

Index